TOWARD CONSTITUTIONAL COMPETENCE

A Casebook for Public Administrators

DAVID H. ROSENBLOOM
Syracuse University

JAMES D. CARROLL
The Brookings Institution

PRENTICE HALL, Englewood Cliffs, New Jersey 07632

AJE 2965- 8/1

Library of Congress Cataloging-in-Publication Data

Rosenbloom, David H.
   Toward constitutional competence.

  1. Administrative law—United States—Cases.
2. United States—Constitutional law—Cases.
3. Civil rights—United States—Cases. I. Carroll,
James D. II. Title.
KF5402.A4R67 1989   342.73′066   89–22934
ISBN 0–13–926122–2   347.30266

Editorial/production supervision
and interior design: *Mary Kathryn Leclercq*
Cover design: *Wanda Lubelska*
Manufacturing buyer: *Robert Anderson*

Prentice-Hall International (UK) Limited, *London*
Prentice-Hall of Australia Pty. Limited, *Sydney*
Prentice-Hall Canada Inc., *Toronto*
Prentice-Hall Hispanoamericana, S.A., *Mexico*
Prentice-Hall of India Private Limited, *New Delhi*
Prentice-Hall of Japan, Inc., *Toyko*
Simon & Schuster Asia Pte. Ltd., *Singapore*
Editora Prentice-Hall do Brasil, Ltda., *Rio de Janeiro*

To Mark, Matthew, James, Jon,
and
the Abellas

It may seem contrary to common sense to assert that a municipality will actually have a policy of not taking reasonable steps to train its employees. But it may happen that in light of the duties assigned to specific officers or employees the need for more or different training is so obvious, and the inadequacy so likely to result in the violation of constitutional rights, that the policymakers of the city can reasonably be said to have been deliberately indifferent to the need. In that event, the failure to provide proper training may fairly be said to represent a policy for which the city is responsible, and for which the city may be held liable if it actually causes injury.

The U.S. Supreme Court in *City of Canton, Ohio* v. *Harris,* 103 L.Ed. 2d 412, 427-428 (1989).

CONTENTS

3

DECISION-MAKING   53

4

ADMINISTRATIVE EFFECTIVENESS   74

5

EFFICIENCY   95

6

ADMINISTRATIVE STANDARDIZATION   127

7

ECONOMY   148

8

INTEGRATING PUBLIC ADMINISTRATION AND THE CONSTITUTION   169

PREFACE

Toward Constitutional Competence: A Casebook for Public Administrators fills a very important educative need. Its theme is taken from the United States Supreme Court's declaration, in 1982, that "a reasonably competent public official should know the law governing his conduct" and the related fact that most public administrators can be held legally liable for conduct that violates "clearly established . . . constitutional rights of which a reasonable person would have known."[1] This book's purpose is to assist students and practitioners in gaining a reasonable, working knowledge of the basic constitutional values and concepts that currently govern American public administration. In nontechnical, plain language, the book explains how standard public administrative values, such as efficiency and economy, are often in tension with constitutional requirements.

The book particularly seeks to impart an administratively useful understanding of the structure of individuals' substantive, procedural, and equal protection rights under the Constitution. Our method is to address these constitutional concerns squarely from a public administrative perspective. Each chapter begins with a brief essay analyzing a central administrative topic and then introduces legal cases, mostly at the Supreme Court level, that set forth competing constitutional values. For the most part, the cases involve administrative behavior that is proper on its own terms, but nevertheless violates the Constitution. Because the cases involve efforts to achieve administrative values, they are intrinsically interesting to those concerned with public administration. The decisions are clearly written, and they can be readily understood by readers

[1]*Harlow* v. *Fitzgerald*, 457 U.S. 800, 818 (1982).

who have only the most rudimentary background in constitutional law. They have been excerpted to enhance their readability and to eliminate technical and secondary issues, such as concerns with justiciability. Taken as a whole, the cases convey a very broad range of the knowledge of constitutional law that public administrators should reasonably have. The commentary preceding the cases identifies their main issues. Each case is followed by a series of incisive discussion questions that will consolidate the reader's understanding of the constitutional values and concepts presented and lead to further consideration of the Constitution's role in public administration. Some readers may find it beneficial to look over these questions prior to reading the cases.

Ultimately, *Toward Constitutional Competence* is a book about public administration within the framework of the United States Constitution. It is not a book on constitutional or administrative law per se. It intends to provide students and practitioners with reasonable awareness and knowledge of how the Constitution applies to the practice of public administration. Constitutional competence is an important step toward a broader public administrative education which will, in the words of Constance Horner, former Director of the federal Office of Personnel Management, promote "constitutional literacy." In her view, such literacy is highly desirable because

> we may often disagree about what our shared commitment to constitutional values requires—what liberty or equality or justice demands in any given instance. But discourse about those principles should be the unique, common language of the Federal executive. Literacy in these concepts and ideas—constitutional literacy—can help unify and vivify the Federal executive corps. From many professions, it can make one vocation.[2]

Horner's focus was on the federal service, but state and local public administrators equally need constitutional competence, and they can benefit from constitutional literacy just as much.

Toward Constitutional Competence is a book for all public administrators in each of the nation's 83,000 governments. The material it presents has been developed over several years in a course on Public Administration and Democracy taught at Syracuse University's Maxwell School of Citizenship and Public Affairs. It has worked very successfully with students at all levels, from those just considering careers in public administration to those who are getting ready to enter the federal government's Senior Executive Service. The book is appropriate as either a core text or supplement in courses on public administration, public management, bureaucratic politics, and public administration and law.

Toward Constitutional Competence has been written and edited with a sense of mission. We believe that it can help improve public administrative education in the United States considerably by making clear how central the Constitution has become—and must be—to contemporary administrative practices. We view the book as a potentially important new step toward harmonizing our constitutional

---

[2]Constance Horner, "Remarks on FEI's [Federal Executive Institute's] 20th Anniversary Dinner." Charlottesville, Virginia, October 14, 1988, p. 14.

and administrative states. It is up to constitutionally competent public administrators to take the next steps. We hope this book will help to guide them on that journey.

ACKNOWLEDGMENTS

The central idea for *Toward Constitutional Competence: A Casebook for Public Administrators* began to develop eight years ago at the Maxwell School of Citizenship and Public Affairs, Syracuse University. Maxwell provided a highly supportive environment for its incubation and growth. We have benefited greatly from an intellectual give-and-take with the several hundred students who found their presence required in a course on Public Administration and Democracy, from which the book evolved. We have also learned much from the recent outpouring of scholarship dealing broadly with public administration and law. To name all those whose ideas and work have contributed to our thinking in this book would take pages. However, a few individuals who made specific contributions should be thanked personally. John A. Rohr, Virginia Polytechnic Institute, provided very helpful ideas for the book's organization and for improving the manuscript. Patricia Ingraham used sections of an earlier draft in her courses and provided us with insightful and encouraging feedback. Robert Roberts, David Sadofsky, and Rosemary O'Leary, each of whom already held law degrees while completing their Ph.D.s in public administration at Maxwell, provided invaluable help with the development of the book's organizing concept and some of its specifics. Dennis Wittmer and James Ferreira provided thoughtful critiques of the manuscript. We also thank the reviewers of the text: Ernest Collins, Ohio University; Lana Stein, University of Missouri–St. Louis; and Douglas H. Shumavon, Miami University. Of course, we take full responsibility for the book's contents.

David H. Rosenbloom
James D. Carroll

FOREWORD

During the past few years, the public administration community has contributed substantially to the impressive literature that has marked the observance of the bicentennial of the Constitution of the United States. A generous array of books, articles, monographs, and symposia has enriched the field and made us all aware of the constitutional foundations of our work. As a result of this scholarship, we are witnessing the gradual reintegration of constitutionalism and public administration. I say *re*integration because of the obvious connection between public administration and constitutionalism in *The Federalist Papers*.* So integral was administration to the intent of the framers that the authors of *The Federalist Papers* made more frequent use of the word *administration* and its cognates than they did of the words *Congress, President,* or *Supreme Court.*

Scholars and practitioners concerned with constitutionalism and public administration can only applaud this reintegration. And yet there is an undercurrent of concern about its permanence. Is it merely a flower of a day? Will public administrators forget about constitutionalism after the nation concludes its bicentennial remembrances by commemorating the two-hundredth anniversary of the Bill of Rights in 1991? I do not believe this will be the case.

The reason for my optimism is threefold. First, for all federal employees and for the vast majority of state employees, the oath of office is an oath to

---

The Federalist Papers were written by Alexander Hamilton, James Madison, and John Jay, under the pen name of "Publius," in support of ratification of the Constitution. They originally appeared in New York newspapers in 1787-1788. For a compilation, see Clinton Rossiter, ed., *The Federalist Papers* (New York: The New American Library, 1961).

uphold the Constitution of the United States. If this oath is administered in a meaningful way, it will serve as a powerful symbol of the moral foundation of public service in the United States. We can hope that alert personnel officers will see to it that the oath is not squeezed into a brief lull between the lecture on retirement benefits and the instruction on how to fill out a W-2 form.

Secondly, there is the leadership that is currently being exercised by the United States Office of Personnel Management (OPM) in proclaiming constitutional literacy in the federal work force as one of the goals of its training program. This effort follows up on Constance Horner's thoughtful remarks in an address at the Federal Executive Institute shortly before she concluded her service as director of OPM. Horner's remarks and the subsequent OPM follow-through augur well for institutionalizing the current interest in the Constitution.

The third reason for my optimism is this superb book, which I have the honor of introducing in this foreword. David Rosenbloom and James Carroll have rendered signal service to the public administration community by providing us with an eminently readable book that integrates public administration into the American constitutional tradition. In their preface, they promise to "address . . . constitutional concerns squarely from a public administrative perspective," and throughout the book they redeem this pledge. The constitutional themes are organized around such garden-variety administrative matters as efficiency, effectiveness, economy, and decision-making. One need not be a specialist in constitutional law to learn the lessons this book teaches so well.

It is my earnest hope that this fine book will be used in introductory public administration courses throughout the United States. It will provide a new generation of public administration students with a thoughtful and reflective appreciation of the fundamental political order they are sworn to uphold.

John A. Rohr

1

PUBLIC ADMINISTRATION AND CONSTITUTIONAL COMPETENCE: AN INTRODUCTION

THE NEED FOR CONSTITUTIONAL COMPETENCE

Seeking to budget more rationally and to reduce fraud and error, Connecticut, Pennsylvania, and the District of Columbia establish a one-year residency requirement as part of their eligibility standards for receiving welfare benefits. In Texas, a constable fires an employee who, after hearing of an attempted assassination of President Ronald Reagan, remarks, "Shoot, if they go for him again, I hope they get him." Over a period of years, a small Mississippi town concentrates its economic development and new infrastructure in its business district and an adjacent neighborhood. In Delaware, a patrolman, for no particular reason other than that it is part of his job, makes a routine stop of a car to check the driver's license and registration. In a city in Georgia, several patrolmen are dismissed for removing the American flags from their uniforms as part of a public protest against racism on the police force. In Cleveland, a school district security guard is removed for failing to report that he had once been convicted of a felony. Well into the 1970s, Chicago and surrounding Cook County continue to practice the historic arts of firing members of the opposition party from the public service. On the federal level, Congress delegates its legislative authority to an executive branch agency and subsequently attempts to control its use through a legislative veto. The Gramm-Rudman-Hollings Budget Deficit Reduction Act of 1985 vests budget-cutting authority in the Comptroller

General, who heads the General Accounting Office.[1] What do all these cases have in common? In each, the action taken by public administrators or with regard to them was found to be unconstitutional by the courts.

Today, as these examples suggest, whole areas of public administration have become permeated by constitutional law. This is true of personnel administration, the management of prisons, public mental health facilities, public schools, "street-level" administration,[2] and some aspects of decision-making, organization, and budgeting. Even routine, day-to-day administrative activities are now frequently regulated directly by constitutional concerns. Consequently, simply to do their jobs properly, public administrators need to understand the nation's constitutional framework, as well as the substance and structure of individuals' constitutional rights as never before. We call this body of necessary knowledge *constitutional competence*. Public administrators who lack it may not only fail to perform correctly, but may also become the targets of successful lawsuits seeking financial compensation. The costs of inadequate constitutional competence can be substantial to private individuals and public administrators alike. (Public administrators' potential liability is the subject of Chapter 2.)

The purpose of this book is to aid students and practitioners of public administration to gain constitutional competence. It focuses on conflicts between public administrative and constitutional values. It discusses the content of constitutional rights within the framework of public administration and how judicial thinking about these rights is organized. The book is accessible to students and practitioners of public administration because it is arranged according to standard administrative values. It uses actual legal cases in which the administrative action taken was more or less sensible on its own terms as a springboard for consideration of countervailing or otherwise relevant constitutional concerns. The discussion questions following each case are an integral part of the book's method. They are intended to provoke deeper thinking about how to integrate public administrative and constitutional values to a greater extent and in a practical way. These questions should be wrestled with at some length.

Constitutional competence does not require that public administrators become constitutional lawyers any more than statistical or economic competence requires them to be statisticians or economists. Just as public administrators need to know how to interpret statistical regression and cost-benefit analyses, they must often have knowledge of the constitutional rights of their subordinates and the individuals on whom their official actions bear directly. The purpose of this book is to provide students and practitioners of public administration with the basic knowledge of constitutional rights that will enable

---

[1]The cases from which these facts are drawn are: *Shapiro* v. *Thompson*, 394 U.S. 618 (1969); *Rankin* v. *McPherson*, 97 L.Ed. 2d 315 (1987); *Hawkins* v. *Town of Shaw*, 437 F.2d 1286 (1971), 461 F.2d 1171 (1972); *Delaware* v. *Prouse*, 440 U.S. 648 (1979); *Leonard* v. *City of Columbus*, 705 F.2d 1299 (1983); *Cleveland Board of Education* v. *Loudermill*, 470 U.S. 532 (1985); *Elrod* v. *Burns*, 427 U.S. 347 (1976); *Immigration and Naturalization Service* v. *Chadha*, 462 U.S. 919 (1983); *Bowsher* v. *Synar*, 92 L.Ed. 2d 583 (1986).

[2]Michael Lipsky, *Street-Level Bureaucracy* (New York: Russell Sage Foundation, 1980).

them to become constitutionally competent. We begin with a discussion of the broad tensions between public administration and constitutional democracy in the United States. The cases toward the end of this chapter focus on the broad concern with maintaining the Constitution's integrity, on the one hand, and fully utilizing the nation's administrative capacity to promote the public interest, on the other.

THE CONSTITUTION AND PUBLIC ADMINISTRATION:
AN UNEASY PARTNERSHIP

In the United States, the relationship between public administration and the constitutional order is complex and uneasy. There is no doubt that public administration is necessary to fulfill the broad objectives set forth in the Constitution's Preamble:

> We the People of the United States, in Order to form a more perfect Union, establish Justice, insure domestic Tranquility, provide for the common defence, promote the general Welfare, and secure the Blessings of Liberty to ourselves and our Posterity, do ordain and establish this Constitution for the United States of America.

As Alexander Hamilton argued in *Federalist* Number 68, "we may safely pronounce that the true test of a good government is its aptitude and tendency to produce a good administration."[3] Conversely, in *Federalist* Number 70, he noted that "a government ill executed, whatever it may be in theory, must be, in practice, a bad government."[4] Good constitutional democracy without good public administration is inconceivable.

But while the Constitution depends on public administration for its success, it predated the rise of large-scale administration by at least a century. The Framers could not possibly have anticipated or foreseen the need to incorporate anything like the modern administrative state into the government they chartered. Indeed, there are almost as many federal civil servants today as there were citizens in the colonies when the American Revolution began! The Framers' provisions for public administration were rudimentary. Moreover, fundamental aspects of the constitutional scheme, including the separation of powers, federalism, and broad individual rights, complicate public administration immensely. The Supreme Court has even gone so far as to say that "[t]he choices we discern as having been made in the Constitutional Convention impose burdens on governmental processes that often seem clumsy, inefficient, even unworkable. . . ."[5] It has fallen to subsequent generations to "retrofit" public administration into the constitutional system, without violating constitutional

[3]Alexander Hamilton, James Madison, and John Jay, *The Federalist Papers*, ed. by Clinton Rossiter (New York: The New American Library, 1961), p. 414.
[4]Ibid., p. 423.
[5]*Immigration and Naturalization Service* v. *Chadha*, 462 U.S. 919, 959 (1983).

integrity. But the task has not been easy. In fact, Dwight Waldo, preeminent public administrative theorist for more than a generation, concluded in 1984 that "all we can hope for is piecemeal solutions, temporary agreements."[6] The impediments to a fully harmonious relationship between the Constitution and contemporary public administration are several.

Structural Tensions

The Constitution creates a threefold separation of powers that does not easily accomodate public administration. The Constitution separates power over public administration. The president is granted the "executive power" and charged with responsibility to "take Care that the Laws be faithfully executed." He is commander-in-chief, and with the advice and consent of the Senate can appoint ambassadors and department heads. Congress can grant the president authority to make such other appointments as it sees fit. But the legislature's powers regarding public administration are also substantial. All administrative offices and appropriations must be based on congressional enactment. This requirement has given Congress a very substantial role in the core administrative functions of organization (will an agency be independent, a regulatory commission, or a department?), personnel (the merit system, equal opportunity/ affirmative action, and collective bargaining), and budgeting. Additionally, agencies' legal authority, missions, and much of their procedure is determined by law. The judiciary also has role in public administration—one that has increased dramatically during the past three decades.[7] It adjudicates the legality and constitutionality of administrative actions. Judges also use their power to fashion equitable remedies in ways that may cut deeply into the management of public schools, public mental health facilities, prisons, public housing, public personnel, and other administrative affairs. Effective public administration often requires that these three constitutional branches of goverment act in a coordinated fashion. But the constitutional system of checks and balances militates against such coordination. The president and Congress have different terms of office, and "we the people" to whom they are accountable and presumed to represent form separate constituencies for each. The same is true with regard to the House and Senate, and therefore bicameralism can make coordination within Congress itself difficult. The judiciary is unelected, independent, and holds office indefinitely during the judges' "good behavior."

Historically, the separation of powers over public administration has led to anomalies and crisis. For instance, in 1935 the Supreme Court concluded that the head of the Federal Trade Commission, an independent regulatory commission, "occupies no place in the executive department";[8] during the

---

[6]Dwight Waldo, *The Administrative State*, 2nd ed. (New York: Holmes and Meier, 1984), p. xviii.
[7]See David H. Rosenbloom, *Public Administration and Law* (New York: Marcel Dekker, 1983); Phillip Cooper, *Public Law and Public Administration*, 2nd ed. (Englewood Cliffs, N.J.: Prentice Hall, 1987); Kenneth Warren, *Administrative Law* (St. Paul, Minn.: West, 1982).
[8]*Humphrey's Executor* v. *United States*, 295 U.S. 602, 628 (1935).

India-Pakistan War of 1971, the U.S. Departments of State and Defense supported opposite sides;[9] and competing views of proper scope of administrative power provoked a major constitutional confrontation between the president and the Supreme Court in the 1930s.[10] In 1952, Supreme Court Justice Robert Jackson emphasized how much the growth of public administrative agencies challenges the constitutional framework: "They have become a veritable fourth branch of the Government, which has deranged our three-branch legal theories much as the concept of a fourth dimension unsettles our three dimensional thinking."[11]

The separation of powers also frowns on the combination of executive, legislative, and judicial authority in the same hands. As James Madison expressed this view in *Federalist* Number 47, "The accumulation of all powers, legislative, executive, and judiciary in the same hands, whether of one, a few, or many, and whether hereditary, self-appointed, or elective, may justly be pronounced the very definition of tyranny."[12] But ironically, public administration necessarily bridges and reduces the separation of powers by enabling executive, legislative, and judical functions to be combined in single governmental units. Kenneth Culp Davis, "dean" of American administrative law scholars, notes that "The volume of [the] legislative output [administrative rule-making] of federal agencies far exceeds the volume of [the] legislative output of Congress,"[13] while Peter Woll, an expert on public administration and constitutional structure, writes that "In terms of the day-to-day activities of the citizenry administrative adjudication is probably more ubiquitous than that carried out by the courts of law, with the exception of criminal actions."[14] In essence, the separation of powers collapses into public administration. This makes it easier—perhaps even possible—for the government to take action, but as Supreme Court Justice Byron White pointed out, "There is no doubt that the development of the administrative agency in response to modern legislative and administrative need has placed severe strain on the separation-of-powers principle in its pristine formulation."[15]

In practice, the separation of powers requires public administrators to be responsive and accountable to three masters: the elected executive and his or her appointees, the legislature, and, at times, the courts. This arrangement may go far toward achieving the goal of efficiently preventing the concentration of political power, but it does not well serve the nation's contemporary interests in administrative efficiency. This is precisely the point illustrated in Case 1.3

[9]Peter Woll and Rochelle Jones, "Bureaucratic Defense in Depth" in Ronald Pynn, ed., *Watergate and the American Political Process* (New York: Praeger, 1975), pp. 216–17.

[10]See Robert H. Jackson, *The Struggle for Judicial Supremacy* (New York: Knopf, 1941), especially Chapter 4.

[11]*Federal Trade Commission* v. *Ruberoid Co.*, 343 U.S. 470, 487 (1952).

[12]Rossiter, ed., *The Federalist Papers*, p. 301.

[13]Kenneth Culp Davis, *Administrative Law and Government*, 2nd ed. (St. Paul, Minn.: West, 1975), p. 8.

[14]Peter Woll, *American Bureaucracy* (New York: Norton, 1963), p. 10

[15]*Buckley* v. *Valeo*, 424 U.S. 1, 280–81 (1976).

(*American Federation of Government Employees* v. *Phillips* [1973]) presented later in this chapter.

Popular Sovereignty

The Constitution's announcement that "We the people" ordain and establish that document as the supreme law of the land represents one of the most significant events in the political history of the world. Constitutional government in the United States rests on the consent of the governed and is exercised for them by their representatives. Constitutional processes seek to assure that these representatives are chosen by the public and are accountable to them, directly or indirectly, through elections. The judiciary is shielded from the public's will in order to enhance its ability to protect the constitutional order and the rule of law from misguided or short-term popular whims and passions. But in order to assure representativeness, a degree of responsiveness, and accountability in general, the Constitution favors election as the basis for legitimizing the exercise of political authority. It favors citizen participation in the selection of government officials. The relatively short terms of office for the president and members of the House of Representatives offer a public accounting at frequent intervals. They also suggest that the Constitution favors the principle of rotation in office, which has been formalized in the Twenty-Second Amendment (limiting to two the number of terms a president can serve). Additionally, for elections and popular participation to work well, the constitutional scheme favors free and open discussion of governmental affairs as well as the development and expression of competing points of view.

The contemporary administrative state challenges these constitutional outlooks in three major ways. First, historically, public administrative theory, often matched by practice, has tended to favor opposing values. It has sought to remove public administrators from politics by insulating them from partisan elections—the merit system and Hatch Acts[16] are examples.[17] Traditional public administration premises the legitimacy of the public service on its politically neutral expertise, rather than on its direct representativeness or responsiveness to the public. Such expertise is enhanced by seniority, rather than by rotation in office. Orthodox or classical public administration primarily favors accountability to the people that is mediated through administrative hierarchies, legislative oversight, and the efforts of political appointees. Additionally, for at least the past half-century, public administrative theory has generally favored unity of command rather than pluralistic centers of influence and power. It has often relied on secrecy and has not encouraged free and open debate by career administrators. One of the sharper juxtapositions between the constitutional

---

[16]The Hatch Acts prevent most federal and many state and local public employees from engaging in partisan political activities, such as campaigning for candidates in partisan elections.

[17]See David H. Rosenbloom, *Federal Service and the Constitution* (Ithaca, N.Y.: Cornell University Press, 1971).

political order and the administrative system is that whereas it is a civic virtue of private citizens to become active in partisan political campaigns, it is often illegal for public administrators to do so. The fear that public administrative values might come to dominate the polity was once expressed by Justice William O. Douglas as follows: "The sovereign of this Nation is the people, not the bureaucracy. The statement of accounts of public expenditures goes to the heart of the problem of sovereignty [Article I, § 9]. If taxpayers may not ask that rudimentary question, their sovereignty becomes an empty symbol and a secret bureaucracy is allowed to run our affairs."[18]

Second, the growth of public administration has been accompanied by a very pronounced devolution of political power and authority to the hands of unelected government officials and employees. It is not just public administrators who are more numerous today. There are also more staff in the Congress and in the Executive Office of the President as well as more political executives in the executive branch generally. Although this is highly pronounced in the federal government, similar patterns hold in many of the states. When coupled with the overall power and centrality of federal public administration, the impact of the unelected component of government on popular sovereignty can be quite severe. Former Supreme Court Justice Lewis Powell, generally regarded as a moderate, described the problem in stark terms:

> Federal legislation is drafted primarily by the staffs of the congressional committees. In view of the hundreds of bills introduced at each session of Congress and the complexity of many of them, it is virtually impossible for even the most conscientious legislators to be truly familiar with many of the statutes enacted. Federal departments and agencies customarily are authorized to write regulations. Often these are more important than the text of the statutes. As is true of the original legislation, these are drafted largely by staff personnel. The administration and enforcement of federal laws and regulations necessarily are largely in the hands of staff and civil service employees. These employees may have little or no knowledge of the States and localities that will be affected by the statutes and regulations for which they are responsible. . . .[19]

Powell emphasized that the challenges posed to democracy by the administrative state are exacerbated by the large role that the federal government now plays in regulating states and localities:

> My point is simply that members of the immense federal bureaucracy are not elected, know less about the services traditionally rendered by States and localities, and are inevitably less responsive to recipients of such services, than are state legislatures, city councils, boards of supervisors, and state and local commissions, boards, and agencies. It is at these state and local levels—not in Washington. . .— that "democratic self-government" is best exemplified.[20]

Third, as the public becomes increasingly dependent on the administrative state, its members tend to be transformed from citizens to subjects. Politically,

[18]*United States* v. *Richardson*, 418 U.S. 166, 201 (1974).
[19]*Garcia* v. *San Antonio Metropolitan Transit Authority*, 469 U.S. 528, 576–77 (1985).
[20]Ibid., p. 577.

the administrative state is too complex and active to allow an individual to influence, or even follow, more than a tiny portion of what it does. In Emmette Redford's words:

> The first characteristic of the great body of men subject to the administrative state is that they are dormant regarding most of the decisions being made with respect to them. Their participation cannot in any manner equal their subjection. Subjection comes from too many directions for a man's span of attention, much less his active participation, to extend to all that affects him. Any effort of the subject to participate in all that affects him would engulf him in confusion, dissipate his activity, and destroy the unity of his personality.[21]

Economically, the administrative state tends to promote the public's dependence on government largess, which partly replaces private property and reduces individual autonomy. Charles Reich explains:

> One of the most important developments in the United States during the past decade [1950s] has been the emergence of government as a major source of wealth. Government is a gigantic syphon. It draws in revenue and power, and pours forth wealth: money, benefits, services, contracts, franchises, and licenses. Government has always had this function. But while in early times it was minor, today's distribution of largess is on a vast, imperial scale.
>   The valuables dispensed by government take many forms, but they all share one characteristic. They are steadily taking the place of traditional forms of wealth—forms which are held as private property. Social insurance substitutes for savings; a government contract replaces a businessman's customers and goodwill. The wealth of more and more Americans depends upon a relationship to government. Increasingly, Americans live on government largess. . . .[22]

As Reich notes, administrative processes can enlarge or diminish such economic dependency: because "when government—national, state, or local—hands out something of value, whether a relief check or a television license, government's power grows forthwith; it automatically gains such power as is necessary and proper to supervise its largess. It obtains new rights to investigate, to regulate, and to punish."[23] Especially important is whether individuals' interests regarding largess, which Reich calls "the new property," can be protected much in the way that their rights to due process have traditionally protected private property. This brings us to the question of individual rights in the administrative state.

Individual Rights

In 1789, the Constitution looked toward government as a limited actor in the society and economy. Over the years, through political and economic development, judicial interpretation, and constitutional amendment (Thirteen through Sixteen), government's role has expanded tremendously. The potential

---

[21]Emmette Redford, *Democracy in the Administrative State* (New York: Oxford University Press, 1969), p. 66.
[22]Charles Reich, "The New Property," *Yale Law Journal*, 73 (1964), 733-87.
[23]Ibid., p. 746.

for a single force, government, to combine control of polity with dominance of the economy and society has led some scholars to fear that the United States has embarked on the *Road to Serfdom*[24] or totalitarianism.[25] Though such views may exaggerate the dangers, the tensions between individual rights and the administrative state are real and have been noted many times. For instance, Justice Douglas, a strong advocate of civil rights and liberties, argued in Supreme Court cases that "the bureaucracy of modern government is not only slow, lumbering, and oppressive; it is omnipresent" and "today's mounting bureaucracy, both at the state and federal levels, promises to be suffocating and repressive unless it is put into the harness of procedural due process."[26] Administrative interests in efficiency, standardization, economy, and effectiveness can interfere with individuals' substantive rights, such as free exercise of religion, their procedural rights to fair processes when their liberty or property interests are being infringed on, and their equal protection rights under the Constitution. Although in recent years the judiciary has done much to protect these rights against such encroachment, if the tension is resolvable at all, active administrative efforts to reduce it will be required. That is exactly what this book is about.

DEVELOPING CONSTITUTIONAL COMPETENCE

Our emphasis on the tensions between the Constitution and the administrative state should not be taken as a criticism of public administration or administrators. Public administration is overwhelmingly constitutional, and few public administrators actually violate individuals' constitutional rights. By worldwide standards, the United States has an outstandingly honest and competent public service. Clearly, despite so much of the "bureaucrat bashing" found in recent political rhetoric, the constitutional order and the society gain immensely from public administration. But during the past three decades it has become increasingly evident that public administration needs to incorporate constitutional concerns into its doctrines and actions to a far greater extent than in the past. In part, this is because the size and scope of contemporary public administration intensify its impact on the constitutional scheme. Additionally, fundamental changes in a variety of judicial doctrines have articulated new constitutional rights for individuals as they come into contact with public administration and have required that public administrators know and respect these rights. In the Supreme Court's words, "a reasonably competent public official should know the law governing his conduct."[27]

Developing constitutional competence is not as daunting as it may sound. It does not require that public administrators become constitutional lawyers or even gain a deep understanding of the development of constitutional doctrines. Rather, first and foremost, it requires familiarity with constitutional values. Second, it is necessary to gain a general, nontechnical, working knowledge of the

[24]Friedrich A. Hayek, *The Road to Serfdom* (Chicago: University of Chicago Press, 1944).
[25]Elton Mayo, *Human Problems of an Industrial Civilization* (New York: Viking Press, 1933).
[26]*Wyman* v. *James*, 400 U.S. 309, 335 (1971); *Spady* v. *Mount Vernon*, 419 U.S. 985 (1974).
[27]*Harlow* v. *Fitzgerald*, 457 U.S. 800, 819 (1982).

scope of constitutional rights and the ways in which the judiciary thinks about issues pertaining to these rights. For instance, one needs to know how the rights to equal protection of the laws, procedural due process, and privacy are structured: What are the first questions that should be asked when it appears that an administrative regulation or activity may infringe on such rights? What considerations follow? What conclusions seem appropriate? Thus, in order to think sensibly about equal protection, it is necessary to understand the concept of a *suspect classification*; understanding privacy rights requires knowledge of the importance of an individual's reasonable expectation of privacy. Third, and most difficult, constitutionally competent public administrators are able to integrate their knowledge of constitutional values and rights into administrative practice. Given the broad variety of administrative settings and concerns, there can be no simple prescriptions for this third demand. However, the materials in this book are intended to advance all three elements of constitutional competence by presenting discussions of administrative and constitutional values, cases that consider these values and the nature of constitutional rights clearly and in plain English; and by raising questions that should encourage the reader to think about constitutional concerns in ways that are relevant to administrative practice.

The following cases address the impact of constitutional structure, especially the separation of powers, on public administration. Case 1.1, *Bowsher* v. *Synar* (1986), concerns Congress's attempt, in the Gramm–Rudman–Hollings Act, to vest budget-cutting functions in the Comptroller General, who heads the General Accounting Office, which is in the legislative branch. In finding this aspect of the act unconstitutional, the Supreme Court engages in an enlightening discussion of the separation of powers. In reading the case, it will be useful to consider the Court's understanding of the value of the separation of powers as well as how, in practice, the separation of powers can interfere with administrative processes favored by Congress. Case 1.2, *Immigration and Naturalization Service* v. *Chadha* (1983), involves a process called the *legislative veto*. Congress relied on this device as a means of blocking particular exercises of the legislative authority it routinely delegates to executive branch agencies. In finding the legislative veto at issue in Chadha unconstitutional, the Supreme Court emphasizes the importance of maintaining the integrity of constitutional processes and requirements. Finally, Case 1.3, *American Federation of Government Employees* v. *Phillips* (1973), demonstrates how the separation of powers can place public administrators under more than one master—here the president and Congress. It also suggests how this situation can hamper administrative action and make it more expensive. In considering the Phillips case, it will be helpful to imagine yourself in his predicament.

ADDITIONAL READING

ROHR, JOHN. *To Run A Constitution*. Lawrence, Kans.: University Press of Kansas, 1986.

WOLL, PETER. *American Bureaucracy*, 2nd ed. New York: Norton, 1977.

CASE 1.1
THE SEPARATION OF FUNCTIONS

CHARLES A. BOWSHER,
Comptroller General of the United
States, Appellant

v

MIKE SYNAR, Member of
Congress, et al. (No. 85-1377)
478 US 714, 92 L Ed 2d
583, 106 S Ct 3181
(Nos. 85-1377, 85-1378, and
85-1379)
Argued April 23, 1986. Decided
July 7, 1986.

Decision: Gramm–Rudman Act pro-vision, assigning Comptroller General duty of reporting to President what spending reductions are needed to reduce deficit to target amount held to violate separation-of-powers doctrine.

Summary

The Balanced Budget and Emergency Deficit Control Act of 1985 (2 USCS §§ 901 et seq.), popularly known as the Gramm–Rudman–Hollings Act, set a maximum deficit amount for federal spending for each of fiscal years 1986 through 1991. If in any fiscal year the federal budget deficit were to exceed the maximum deficit amount by more than a specified sum, the Act required across-the-board cuts in federal spending to reach the targeted deficit level. These "automatic" reductions were to be accomplished through the provisions of § 251 of the Act (2 USCS § 901), under which the Comptroller General of the United States was assigned the responsibility of preparing and submitting to the President a report containing detailed estimates of projected federal revenues and expenditures and specifying the reduc-

tions, if any, needed to reduce the deficit to the target for the appropriate fiscal year. The President in turn was to issue an order manadating the spending reductions specified by the Comptroller General (§ 252 of the Act (9 USCS § 902)). The Act also contained a "fallback" provision, to take effect in the event that any of the reporting procedures described in § 251 were to be invalidated, under which deficit reduction proposals would be submitted to the President in a joint resolution of both Houses of Congress rather than in a report by the Comptroller General (§ 274(f) of the Act (2 USCS § 922(f)). After the Act was signed into law, 12 members of Congress filed complaints in the United States District Court for the District of Columbia challenging the constitutionality of the Act and seeking declaratory relief. These actions were consolidated with a virtually identical lawsuit filed by the National Treasury Employees Union, which alleged that its members were injured by the Act's automatic spending reduction provisions, under which certain cost-of-living benefit increases they were scheduled to receive were suspended. In the United States District Court for the District of Columbia, three-judge court, appointed pursuant to the Act (2 USCS § 922(a)(5)), invalidated the reporting provisions, holding that (1) the plaintiffs had standing to challenge the Act, (2) the Act did not involve an unconstitutional delegation of legislative powers, and (3) the role of the Comptroller General in the deficit reduction process violated the constitutionally imposed separation of powers (626 F Supp 1374).

On direct appeal, the United States Supreme Court affirmed. In an opinion by BURGER, Ch. J., joined by BRENNAN, POWELL, REHNQUIST, and O'CONNOR, JJ., it was held that (1) individual members of the Treasury Employees Union had standing to challenge the Act because it was shown that they had suffered injury, so the standing of the union and the members of Congress did not have to be considered, (2) the Comptroller General is subservient to Congress because he is removable only at the initiative of Congress, (3) the powers assigned to the Comptroller General under § 251 of the Act were executive in nature, (4) by placing the responsibility for execution of the Act in the hands of an officer who is subject to removal only by itself, Congress in effect retained control over such execution, (5) § 251 was therefore invalid as violating the doctrine of separation of powers, and (6) the proper remedy was to permit the fallback deficit reduction provisions of § 274(f) to come into play, rather than to nullify the statutory provisions that authorized Congress to remove the Comptroller General; accordingly, judgment was stayed for a period not to exceed 60 days to permit Congress to implement the fallback provisions.

Opinion

Chief Justice **Burger** delivered the opinion of the Court.

The question presented by these appeals is whether the assignment by Congress to the Comptroller General of the United States of certain functions under the Balanced Budget and Emergency Deficit Control Act of 1985 violates the doctrine of separation of powers.

I

A

On December 12, 1985, the President signed into law the Balanced Budget and Emergency Deficit Control Act of 1985, Pub L 99-177, 99 Stat 1038, 2 USCA § 901 et seq. (Supp 1986). . . popularly known as the "Gramm–Rudman–Hollings Act." The purpose of the Act is to eliminate the federal budget deficit. To that end, the Act sets a "maximum deficit amount" for federal spending for each of fiscal years 1986 through 1991. The size of that maximum deficit amount progressively reduces to zero in fiscal year 1991. If in any fiscal year the federal budget deficit exceeds the maximum deficit amount by more than a specified sum, the Act requires across-the-board cuts in federal spending to reach the targeted deficit level, with half of the cuts made to defense programs and the other half made to non-defense programs. The Act exempts certain priority programs from these cuts. § 255.

These "automatic" reductions are accomplished through a rather complicated procedure, spelled out in § 251, the so-called "reporting provisions" of the Act. Each year, the Directors of the Office of Management and Budget (OMB) and the Congressional Budget Office (CBO) independently estimate the amount of the federal budget deficit for the upcoming fiscal year. If that deficit exceeds the maximum targeted deficit amount for that fiscal year by more than a specified amount, the Directors of OMB and CBO independently calculate, on a program-by-program basis, the budget reductions necessary to ensure that the deficit does not exceed the maximum deficit amount. The Act then requires the Directors to report jointly their deficit estimates and budget reduction calculations to the Comptroller General.

The Comptroller General, after reviewing the Directors' reports, then reports his conclusions to the President. § 251(b). The President in turn must issue a "sequestration" order mandating the spending reductions specified by the Comptroller General. § 252. There follows a period during which Congress may by legislation reduce spending to obviate, in whole or in part, the need for the sequestration order. If such reductions are not enacted, the sequestration order becomes effective and the spending reductions included in that order are made.

Anticipating constitutional challenge to these procedures, the Act also contains a "fallback" deficit reduction process to take effect "[i]n the event that any of the reporting procedures described in section 251 are invalidated." § 274(f). Under these provisions, the report prepared by the Directors of OMB and the CBO is submitted directly to a specially-created Temporary Joint Committee on Deficit Reduction, which must report in five days to both Houses a joint resolution setting forth the content of the Directors' report. Congress then must vote on the resolution under special rules, which render amendments out of order. If the resolution is passed and signed by the President, it then serves as the basis for a Presidential sequestration order.

* * *

III

We noted recently that "[t]he Constitution sought to divide the delegated powers of the new Federal Government into three defined categories, Legislative,

Executive, and Judicial." . . . The declared purpose of separating and dividing the powers of government, of course, was to "diffus[e] power the better to secure liberty." . . . Justice Jackson's words echo the famous warning of Montesquieu, quoted by James Madison in The Federalist No. 47, that " 'there can be no liberty where the legislative and executive powers are united in the same person, or body of magistrates'. . . ."

Even a cursory examination of the Constitution reveals the influence of Montesquieu's thesis that checks and balances were the foundation of a structure of government that would protect liberty. The Framers provided a vigorous legislative branch and a separate and wholly independent executive branch, with each branch responsible ultimately to the people. The Framers also provided for a judicial branch equally independent with "[t]he judicial Power . . . extend[ing] to all Cases, in Law and Equity, arising under this Constitution, and the Laws of the United States." Art III, § 2.

Other, more subtle, examples of separated powers are evident as well. Unlike parliamentary systems such as that of Great Britain, no person who is an officer of the United States may serve as a Member of the Congress. Art I, § 6. Moreover, unlike parliamentary systems, the President, under Article II, is responsible not to the Congress but to the people, subject only to impeachment proceedings which are exercised by the two Houses as representatives of the people. Art II, § 4. And even in the impeachment of a President the presiding officer of the ultimate tribunal is not a member of the legislative branch, but the Chief Justice of the United States. Art I, § 3.

That this system of division and separation of powers produces conflicts, confusion, and discordance at times is inherent, but it was deliberately so structured to assure full, vigorous and open debate on the great issues affecting the people and to provide avenues for the operation of checks on the exercise of governmental power.

The Constitution does not contemplate an active role for Congress in the supervision of officers charged with the execution of the laws it enacts. The President appoints "Officers of the United States" with the "Advice and Consent of the Senate. . ." Article II, § 2. Once the appointment has been made and confirmed, however, the Constitution explicitly provides for removal of Officers of the United States by Congress only upon impeachment by the House of Representatives and conviction by the Senate. An impeachment by the House and trial by the Senate can rest only on "Treason, Bribery or other high Crimes and Misdemeanors." Article II, § 4. A direct congressional role in the removal of officers charged with the execution of the laws beyond this limited one is inconsistent with separation of powers.

*   *   *

[W]e conclude that Congress cannot reserve for itself the power of removal of an officer charged with the execution of the laws except by impeachment. To permit the execution of the laws to be vested in an officer answerable only to Congress would, in practical terms, reserve in Congress control over the execution of the laws. As the District Court observed, "Once an officer is appointed, it is only the authority that can remove him, and not the authority that appointed him, that he must fear and, in the performance of his functions, obey.". . . The structure of the Constitution does not permit Congress to execute the laws; it follows that Congress

cannot grant to an officer under its control what it does not possess.

*   *   *

The dangers of congressional usurpation of Executive Branch functions have long been recognized. "[T]he debates of the Constitutional Convention, and the Federalist Papers, are replete with expressions of fear that the Legislative Branch of the National Government will aggrandize itself at the expense of the other two branches.". . . Indeed, we also have observed only recently that "[t]he hydraulic pressure inherent within each of the separate Branches to exceed the outer limits of its power, even to accomplish desirable objectives, must be resisted.". . . With these principles in mind, we turn to consideration of whether the Comptroller General is controlled by Congress.

IV

Appellants urge that the Comptroller General performs his duties independently and is not subservient to Congress. We agree with the District Court that this contention does not bear close scrutiny.

The critical factor lies in the provisions of the statute defining the Comptroller General's office relating to removability. Although the Comptroller General is nominated by the President from a list of three individuals recommended by the Speaker of the House of Representatives and the President pro tempore of the Senate, . . . and confirmed by the Senate, he is removable only at the initiative of Congress. He may be removed not only by impeachment but also by Joint Resolution of Congress "at any time" resting on any one of the following bases:

"(i) permanent disability;
"(ii) inefficiency;

"(iii) neglect of duty;

"(iv) malfeasance; or

"(v) a felony or conduct involving moral turpitude.". . .

This provision was included, as one Congressman explained in urging passage of the Act, because Congress "felt that [the Comptroller General] should be brought under the sole control of Congress, so that Congress at the moment when it found he was inefficient and was not carrying on the duties of his office as he should and as the Congress expected, could remove him without the long, tedious process of a trial by impeachment." . . .

* * *

[W]e see no escape from the conclusion that, because Congress had retained removal authority over the Comptroller General, he may not be entrusted with executive powers. The remaining question is whether the Comptroller General has been assigned such powers in the Balanced Budget and Emergency Deficit Control Act of 1985.

V

The primary responsibility of the Comptroller General under the instant Act is the preparation of a "report." This report must contain detailed estimates of projected federal revenues and expenditures. The report must also specify the reductions, if any, necessary to reduce the deficit to the target for the appropriate fiscal year. The reductions must be set forth on a program-by-program basis.

In preparing the report, the Comptroller General is to have "due regard" for the estimates and reductions set forth in a joint report submitted to him by the Director of CBO and the Director of OMB, the President's fiscal and budgetary advisor. However, the Act plainly contemplates that the Comptroller General will exercise his independent judgment and evaluation with respect to those estimates. The Act also provides that the Comptroller General's report "shall explain fully any differences between the contents of such report and the report of the Directors." . . .

Appellants suggest that the duties assigned to the Comptroller General in the Act are essentially ministerial and mechanical so that their performance does not constitute "execution of the law" in a meaningful sense. On the contrary, we view these functions as plainly entailing execution of the law in constitutional terms. Interpreting a law enacted by Congress to implement the legislative mandate is the very essence of "execution" of the law. Under § 251, the Comptroller General must exercise judgment concerning facts that affect the application of the Act. He must also interpret the provisions of the Act to determine precisely what budgetary calculations are required. Decisions of that kind are typically made by officers charged with executing a statute.

The executive nature of the Comptroller General's functions under the Act is revealed in § 252(a)(3) which gives the Comptroller General the ultimate authority to determine the budget cuts to be made. Indeed, the Comptroller General commands the President himself to carry out, without the slightest variation (with exceptions not relevant to the constitutional issues presented), the directive of the Comptroller General as to the budget reductions:

"The [Presidential] order *must provide* for reductions in the manner specified in section 251(a)(3), *must incorporate* the provisions of the [Comptroller General's] report submitted under section 251(b), and *must be consistent with such report in all respects.* The President *may not modify or recalculate any of the estimates, determinations, specifications, bases, amounts, or percentages* set forth in the report submitted under section 251(b) in determining the reductions to be specified in the order with respect to programs, projects, and activities, or with respect to budget activities, within an account. . . ."

Congress of course initially determined the content of the Balanced Budget and Emergency Deficit Control Act; and undoubtedly the content of the Act determines the nature of the executive duty. However, . . . once Congress makes its choice in enacting legislation, its participation ends. Congress can thereafter control the execution of its enactment only indirectly—by passing new legislation. . . .

By placing the responsibility for execution of the Balanced Budget and Emergency Deficit Control Act in the hands of an officer who is subject to removal only by itself, Congress in effect has retained control over the execution of the Act and has intruded into the executive function. The Constitution does not permit such intrusion.

VI

We now turn to the final issue of remedy. Appellants urge that rather than striking down § 251 and invalidating the significant power Congress vested in the Comptroller General to meet a national fiscal emergency, we should take the lesser course of nullifying the statutory provisions of the 1921 Act that authorizes Congress to remove the Comptroller General. At oral argument, counsel for the Comptroller General suggested that this might make the Comptroller General removable by the President. All appellants urge that Congress would prefer invalidation of the removal provisions rather than invalidation of § 251 of the Balanced Budget and Emergency Deficit Control Act.

Severance at this late date of the removal provisions enacted 65 years ago would significantly alter the Comptroller General's office, possibly by making him subservient to the Executive Branch. Recasting the Comptroller General as an officer of the Executive Branch would accordingly alter the balance that Congress had in mind in drafting the Budget and Accounting Act of 1921 and the Balanced Budget and Emergency Deficit Control Act, to say nothing of the wide array of other tasks and duties Congress has assigned the Comptroller General in other statutes. . . .

Fortunately this is a thicket we need not enter. The language of the Balanced Budget and Emergency Deficit Control Act itself settles the issue. In § 274(f), Congress has explicitly provided "fallback" provisions in the Act that take effect "[i]n the event . . . *any* of the reporting procedures described in section 251 are invalidated." . . .

*   *   *

VII

No one can doubt that Congress and the President are confronted with fiscal and economic problems of unprecedented magnitude, but "the fact that a given law or procedure is efficient, convenient, and useful in facilitating functions of government, standing alone, will not save it if it is contrary to the Constitution. Convenience and efficiency are not the primary objectives—or the hallmarks—of democratic government. . . ."

Justice **Stevens,** with whom Justice **Marshall** joins, concurring in the judgment.

When this Court is asked to invalidate a statutory provision that has been approved by both Houses of the Congress and signed by the President, particularly an Act of Congress that confronts a deeply vexing national problem, it should only do so for the most compelling constitutional reasons. I agree with the Court that the "Gramm–Rudman–Hollings" Act contains a constitutional infirmity so severe that the flawed provision may not stand. I disagree with the Court, however, on the reasons why the Constitution prohibits the Comptroller General from exercising the powers assigned to him by § 251(b) and § 251(c) (2) of the Act. It is not the dormant, carefully circumscribed congressional removal power that represents the primary constitutional evil. Nor do I agree with the conclusion of both the majority and the dissent that the analysis depends on a labeling of the functions assigned to the Comptroller General as "executive powers." . . . Rather, I am convinced that the Comptroller General must be characterized as an agent of Congress because of his longstanding statutory responsibilities; that the powers assigned to him under the Gramm–Rudman–Hollings Act require him to make policy that will bind the Nation; and that, when Congress, or a component or an agent of Congress, seeks to make policy that will bind the Nation, it must follow the procedures mandated by Article I of the Constitution—through passage by both Houses and presentment to the President. In short, Congress may not exercise its fundamental power to formulate national policy by delegating that power to one of its two Houses, to a legislative committee, or to an individual agent of the Congress such as The Speaker of the House of Representatives, the Sergeant at Arms of the Senate, or the Director of the Congressional Budget Office. . . . That principle, I believe, is applicable to the Comptroller General. . . .

*　　*　　*

If Congress were free to delegate its policymaking authority to one of its components, or to one of its agents, it would be able to evade "the carefully crafted restraints spelled out in the Constitution." . . . That danger—congressional action that evades constitutional restraints—is not present when Congress delegates lawmaking power to the executive or to an independent agency.

DISCUSSION QUESTIONS

1. In his dissent, Justice White noted that "The Court, acting in the name of separation of powers, takes upon itself to strike down the Gramm–Rudman–Hollings Act, one of the most novel and far-reaching legislative responses to a national crisis since the New Deal. The basis of the Court's action is a solitary provision of another statute that was passed over sixty years ago and has lain dormant since that time." White went on to accuse the majority of the Court of having a "distressingly formalistic view of separation of powers." In considering the possibility that the Court is being *too* formalistic in its effort to protect constitutional integrity, what concerns or issues should be addressed? For instance, how much weight should be given to the Framers' views? How flexibly should the Constitution be treated in attempts to deal with contemporary political and governmental matters?

2. The Court reasoned that the separation of powers "produces conflicts, confusion, and discordance at times. . . ." Can you think of examples involving public administration? For instance, would the Iran–Contra affair of

1986–1987 be an example? Are you aware of instances in your state in which the governor and legislature disagreed over important aspects of administration? How might the conflict, confusion, and discordance that accompanies the separation of powers be reduced? Do political parties and elections have any bearing on the matter?

3. How does the Court define execution of the law? How satisfactory is its definition?

4. Justice Stevens's concurring opinion argues that Congress cannot delegate its fundamental power to, or exercise it through, one of its subunits, such as a standing committee or the Comptroller General. Consider the full implications of this position for the operation of legislative agencies, such as the General Accounting Office and the Congressional Budget Office. Could the same idea be applied to the executive; that is, could the president be prohibited from allowing other executive branch officials (such as cabinet members) from exercising his fundamental executive power?

CASE 1.2:
CONSTITUTIONAL INTEGRITY

IMMMIGRATION AND
NATURALIZATION SERVICE,
Appellant

v

JAGDISH RAI CHADHA et al.
(No. 80-1832)
462 US 919
Argued February 22, 1982—
Reargued December 7, 1982—
Decided June 23, 1983.

Summary

An immigration judge suspended an alien's deportation pursuant to § 244(c)(1) of the Immigration and Nationality Act (8 USCS § 1254(c)(1)). The United States House of Representatives passed a resolution vetoing the suspension pursuant to § 244(c)(2) of the Act (8 USCS § 1254(c)(2)), which authorizes one House of Congress to invalidate the decision of the executive branch to allow a particular deportable alien to remain in the United States. The immigration judge reopened the deportation proceedings to implement the House order, and the alien was ordered deported. The Board of Immigration Appeals dismissed the alien's appeal, holding that it had no power to declare unconstitutional an act of Congress. The United States Court of Appeals for the Ninth Circuit held the House was without constitutional authority to order the alien's deportation and that § 244(c)(2) violated the constitutional doctrine of separation of powers (634 F2d 408).

On appeal, the United States Supreme Court affirmed. In an opinion by BURGER, Ch. J., joined by BRENNAN, MARSHALL, BLACKMUN, STEVENS, and O'CONNOR,

JJ., it was held that the legislative veto provision in § 244(c)(2) was unconstitutional since the one-house veto was legislative in purpose and effect and subject to the procedures set out in Article I of the Constitution requiring passage by a majority of both Houses and presentment to the President.

Opinion

Chief Justice **Burger** delivered the opinion of the Court.

* * *

I

Chadha is an East Indian who was born in Kenya and holds a British passport. He was lawfully admitted to the United States in 1966 on a nonimmigrant student visa. His visa expired on June 30, 1972. On October 11, 1973, the District Director of the Immigration and Naturalization Service ordered Chadha to show cause why he should not be deported for having "remained in the United States for a longer time than permitted." . . . Pursuant to § 242(b) of the Immigration and Nationality Act (Act), 8 USC § 1252(b), . . . a deportation hearing was held before an Immigration Judge on January 11, 1974. Chadha conceded that he was deportable for overstaying his visa and the hearing was adjourned to enable him to file an application for suspension of deportation. . . .

After Chadha submitted his application for suspension of deportation, the deportation hearing was resumed on February 7, 1974. On the basis of evidence adduced at the hearing, affidavits submitted with the application, and the results of a character investigation conducted by the INS, the Immigration Judge, on June 25, 1974, ordered that Chadha's deportation be suspended. The Immigration Judge found that Chadha met the requirements of § 244(a)(1): he had resided continuously in the United States for over seven years, was of good moral character, and would suffer "extreme hardship" if deported.

Pursuant to § 244(c)(1) of the Act, 8 USC § 1254(c)(1), . . . the Immigration Judge suspended Chadha's deportation and a report of the suspension was transmitted to Congress. . . [in the form of a recommendation by the Attorney General that Chadha's deportation be suspended].

Once the Attorney General's recommendation for suspension of Chadha's deportation was conveyed to Congress, Congress had the power under § 244(c)(2) of the Act, 8 USC § 1254(c)(2), . . . to veto the Attorney General's determination that Chadha should not be deported. Section 244(c)(2) provides:

"if during the session of the Congress at which a case is reported, or prior to the close of the session of the Congress next following the session at which a case is reported, either the Senate or the House of Representatives passes a resolution stating in substance that it does not favor the suspension of such deportation, the Attorney General shall thereupon deport such alien or authorize the alien's voluntary departure at his own expense under the order of deportation in the manner provided by law. If, within the time above specified, neither the Senate nor the House of Representatives shall pass such a resolution, the Attorney General shall cancel deportation proceedings."

The June 25, 1974, order of the Immigration Judge suspending Chadha's deportation remained outstanding as a valid order for a year and a half. For reasons not disclosed by the record, Congress did not exercise the veto authority reserved to it under § 244(c)(2) until the first session of the 94th Congress.

* * *

After the House veto of the Attorney General's decision to allow Chadha to remain in the United States, the Immigration Judge reopened the deportation proceedings to implement the House order deporting Chadha. Chadha moved to terminate the proceedings on the ground that § 244(c)(2) is unconstitutional. The Immigration Judge held that he had no authority to rule on the constitutional validity of § 244(c)(2). On November 8, 1976, Chadha was ordered deported pursuant to the House action.

Chadha appealed the deportation order to the Board of Immigration Appeals, again contending that § 244(c)(2) is unconstitutional. The Board held that it had "no power to declare unconstitutional an act of Congress" and Chadha's appeal was dismissed. . . .

Pursuant to § 106(a) of the Act, 8 USC § 1105a(a), . . . Chadha filed a petition for review of the deportation order in the United States Court of Appeals for the Ninth Circuit. The Immigration and Naturalization Service agreed with Chadha's position before the Court of Appeals and joined him in arguing that § 244(c)(2) is unconstitutional. In light of the importance of the question, the Court of Appeals invited both the Senate and the House of Representatives to file briefs amici curiae.

After full briefing and oral argument, the Court of Appeals held that the House was without constitutional authority to order Chadha's deportation; accordingly it directed the Attorney General "to cease and desist from taking any steps to deport this alien based upon the resolution enacted by the House of Representatives." . . . The essence of its holding was that § 244(c)(2) violates the constitutional doctrine of separation of powers.

We granted certiorari. . . .

* * *

III

A

We turn now to the question whether action of one House of Congress under § 244(c)(2) violates strictures of the Constitution. We begin, of course, with the presumption that the challenged statute is valid. Its wisdom is not the concern of the courts; if a challenged action does not violate the Constitution, it must be sustained. . . .

By the same token, the fact that a given law or procedure is efficient, convenient, and useful in facilitating functions of government, standing alone, will not save it if it is contrary to the Constitution. Convenience and efficiency are not the primary objectives—or the hallmarks—of democratic government and our inquiry is sharpened rather than blunted by the fact that congressional veto provisions are appearing with increasing frequency in statutes which delegate authority to executive and independent agencies:

"Since 1932, when the first veto provision was enacted into law, 295 congressional veto-type procedures have been inserted in 196 different statutes as follows: from 1932 to 1939, five statutes were affected; from 1940–49, nineteen statutes; between 1950–59, thirty-four statutes; and from 1960–69, forty-nine. From the year 1970 through 1975, at least one hundred sixty-three such provisions were included in eighty-nine laws." . . .

Justice White undertakes to make a case for the proposition that the one-House veto is a useful "political invention," . . . [dissent] and we need not challenge that assertion. We can even concede this utilitarian argument although the long-range political wisdom of this "invention" is arguable. . . . But policy arguments supporting even useful "political inventions" are subject to the demands of the Constitution which defines powers and, with respect to this subject, sets out just how those powers are to be exercised.

Explicit and unambiguous provisions of the Constitution prescribe and define the respective functions of the Congress and of the Executive in the legislative process. Since the precise terms of those familiar provisions are critical to the resolution of this case, we set them out verbatim. Article I provides:

"All legislative Powers herein granted shall be vested in a Congress of the United States, which shall consist of a Senate *and* House of Representatives." Art I, § 1. (Emphasis added.)

"Every Bill which shall have passed the House of Representatives *and* the Senate, *shall*, before it becomes a Law, be presented to the President of the United States. . . ." Art I, § 7, cl 2. (Emphasis added.)

"*Every* Order, Resolution, or Vote to which the Concurrence of the Senate and House of Representatives may be necessary (except on a question of Adjournment) *shall be* presented to the President of the United States; and before the Same shall take Effect, *shall be* approved by him, or being disapproved by him, *shall be* repassed by two thirds of the Senate and House of Representatives, according to the Rules and Limitations prescribed in the Case of a Bill." Art I, § 7, cl 3. (Emphasis added.)

These provisions of Art I are integral parts of the constitutional design for the separation of powers. We have recently noted that "[t]he principle of separation of powers was not simply an abstract generalization in the minds of the Framers: it was woven into the document that they drafted in Philadelphia in the summer of 1787." . . .

Just as we relied on the textual provision of Art II, § 2, cl 2, to vindicate the principle of separation of powers in Buck-ley [v Valeo, 1976] we see that the purposes underlying the Presentment Clauses, Art I, § 7, cls 2, 3, and the bicameral requirement of Art I, § 1, and § 7, cl 2, guide our resolution of the important question presented in these cases. The very structure of the articles delegating and separating powers under Arts I, II, and III exemplifies the concept of separation of powers, and we now turn to Art I.

B

The Presentment Clauses

The records of the Constitutional Convention reveal that the requirement that all legislation be presented to the President before becoming law was uniformly accepted by the Framers. Presentment to the President and the Presidential veto were considered so imperative that the draftsmen took special pains to assure that these requirements could not be circumvented. During the final debate on Art I, § 7, cl 2, James Madison expressed concern that it might easily be evaded by the simple expedient of calling a proposed law a "resolution" or "vote" rather than a "bill." . . .

As a consequence, Art I, § 7, cl 3 . . . was added. . . .

The decision to provide the President with a limited and qualified power to nullify proposed legislation by veto was based on the profound conviction of the Framers that the powers conferred on Congress were the powers to be most carefully circumscribed. It is beyond doubt that lawmaking was a power to be shared by both Houses and the President. In The Federalist No. 73, . . . Hamilton focused on the President's role in making laws:

"If even no propensity had ever discovered itself in the legislative body to invade the rights of the Executive, the rules of just reasoning and theoretic propriety would of themselves teach us that the one ought not to be left to the mercy of the other, but ought to possess a constitutional and effectual power of self-defence. . . .

The President's role in the law-making process also reflects the Framers' careful efforts to check whatever propensity a particular Congress might have to enact oppressive, improvident, or ill-considered measures. The President's veto role in the legislative process was described later during public debate on ratification:

"It establishes a salutary check upon the legislative body, calculated to guard the community against the effects of faction, precipitancy, or of any impulse unfriendly to the public good, which may happen to influence a majority of that body.

". . . The primary inducement to conferring the power in question upon the Executive is, to enable him to defend himself; the secondary one is to increase the chances in favor of the community against the passing of bad laws, through haste, inadvertence, or design." [Quoting Federalist No. 73]. . .

The Court also has observed that the Presentment Clauses serve the important purpose of assuring that a "national" perspective is grafted on the legislative process:

"The President is a representative of the people just as the members of the Senate and of the House are, and it may be, at some times, on some subjects, that the President elected by all the people is rather more representative of them all than are the members of either body of the Legislature whose constituencies are local and not countrywide. . . ." Myers v United States, [1926]. . . .

C

Bicameralism

The bicameral requirement of Art I, §§ 1, 7, was of scarcely less concern to the Framers than was the Presidential veto and indeed the two concepts are interdependent. By providing that no law could take effect without the concurrence of the prescribed majority of the Members of both Houses, the Framers reemphasized their belief, already remarked upon in connection with the Presentment Clauses, that legislation should not be enacted unless it has been carefully and fully considered by the Nation's elected officials. In the Constitutional Convention debates on the need for a bicameral legislature, James Wilson, later to become a Justice of this Court, commented:

"Despotism comes on mankind in different shapes. Sometimes in an Executive, sometimes in a military, one. Is there danger of a Legislative despotism? Theory & practice both proclaim it. If the Legislative authority be not restrained, there can be neither liberty nor stability; and it can only be restrained by dividing it within itself, into distinct and independent branches. In a single house there is no check, but the inadequate one, of the virtue & good sense of those who compose it.". . .

Hamilton argued that a Congress comprised of a single House was antithetical to the very purpose of the Constitution. Were the Nation to adopt a Constitution providing for only one legislative organ, he warned:

"[W]e shall finally accumulate, in a single body, all the most important prerogatives of sovereignty, and thus entail upon our posterity one of the most execrable forms of government that human infatuation ever contrived. Thus we should create in reality that very tyranny which the adversaries of the new Constitution either are, or affect to be, solicitous to avert." The Federalist No. 22. . . .

This view was rooted in a general skepticism regarding the fallibility of human nature later commented on by Joseph Story:

"Public bodies, like private persons, are occasionally under the dominion of strong passions and excitements; impatient, irritable, and impetuous. . . . If [a legislature] feels no check but its own will, it rarely has the firmness to insist upon holding a question long enough under its own view, to see and mark it in all its bearings and relations on society.". . .

These observations are consistent with what many of the Framers expressed, none more cogently than Madison in pointing up the need to divide and disperse power in order to protect liberty:

"In republican government, the legislative authority necessarily predominates. The remedy for this inconveniency is to divide the legislature into different branches; and to render them, by different modes of election and different principles of action, as little connected with each other as the nature of their common functions and their common dependence on the society will admit." The Federalist No. 51. . . .

However familiar, it is useful to recall that apart from their fear that special interests could be favored at the expense of public needs, the Framers were also concerned, although not of one mind, over the apprehensions of the smaller states. Those states feared a commonality of interest among the larger states would work to their disadvantage; representatives of the larger states, on the other hand, were skeptical of a legislature that could pass laws favoring a minority of the people. . . . It need hardly be repeated here that the Great Compromise, under which one House was viewed as representing the people and the other the states, allayed the fears of both the large and small states.

We see therefore that the Framers were acutely conscious that the bicameral requirement and the Presentment Clauses would serve essential constitutional functions. The President's participation in the legislative process was to protect the Executive Branch from Congress and to protect the whole people from improvident laws. The division of Congress into two distinctive bodies assures that the legislative power would be exercised only after opportunity for full study and debate in separate settings. The President's unilateral veto power, in turn, was limited by the power of two-thirds of both Houses of Congress to overrule a veto thereby precluding final arbitrary action of one person. . . . It emerges clearly that the prescription for legislative action in Art I, §§ 1, 7, represents the Framers' decision that the legislative power of the Federal Government be exercised in accord with a single, finely wrought and exhaustively considered, procedure.

IV

The Constitution sought to divide the delegated powers of the new Federal Government into three defined categories, Legislative, Executive, and Judicial, to assure, as nearly as possible, that each branch of government would confine itself to its assigned responsibility. The hydraulic pressure inherent within each of the separate Branches to exceed the outer limits of its power, even to accomplish desirable objectives, must be resisted.

*   *   *

Since it is clear that the action by the House under § 244(c)(2) was not within any of the express constitutional exceptions authorizing one House to act alone, and equally clear that it was an exercise of legislative power, that action was subject to the standards prescribed in Art I. The bicameral requirement, the Presentment Clauses, the President's veto, and Congress' power to override a veto were intended to erect enduring checks on each Branch and to protect the people from the improvident exercise of power by mandating certain prescribed steps. To preserve those checks, and maintain the separation of powers, the carefully defined limits on the power of each Branch must not be eroded. To accomplish what has been attempted by one House of Congress in this case requires action in conformity with the express procedures of the Constitution's prescription for legislative action: passage by a majority of both Houses and presentment to the President.

The veto authorized by § 244(c)(2) doubtless has been in many respects a convenient shortcut; the "sharing" with the Executive by Congress of its authority over aliens in this manner is, on its face, an appealing compromise. In purely practical terms, it is obviously easier for action to be taken by one House without submission to the President; but it is crystal clear from the records of the Convention, contemporaneous writings and debates, that the Framers ranked other values higher than efficiency. The records of the Convention and debates in the States preceding ratification under-

score the common desire to define and limit the exercise of the newly created federal powers affecting the states and the people. There is unmistakable expression of a determination that legislation by the national Congress be a step-by-step, deliberate and deliberative process.

The choices we discern as having been made in the Constitutional Convention impose burdens on governmental processes that often seem clumsy, inefficient, even unworkable, but those hard choices were consciously made by men who had lived under a form of government that permitted arbitrary governmental acts to go unchecked. There is no support in the Constitution or decisions of this Court for the proposition that the cumbersomeness and delays often encountered in complying with explicit constitutional standards may be avoided, either by the Congress or by the President. . . . With all the obvious flaws of delay, untidiness, and potential for abuse, we have not yet found a better way to preserve freedom than by making the exercise of power subject to the carefully crafted restraints spelled out in the Constitution.

DISCUSSION QUESTIONS

1. In dissent, Justice White wrote: "Without the legislative veto, Congress is faced with a Hobson's choice: either to refrain from delegating the necessary authority, leaving itself with a hopeless task of writing laws with the requisite specificity to cover endless special circumstances across the entire policy landscape, or in the alternative, to abdicate its lawmaking function to the Executive Branch and independent agencies. To choose the former leaves major national problems unresolved; to opt for the latter risks unaccountable policy-making by those not elected to fill that role." Do you think White has properly framed the issue? Are there intermediate courses Congress might take? If so, what are they and what are their advantages and disadvantages?

2. The Court writes that governmental processes based on the Constitution "often seem clumsy, inefficient, even unworkable." Can you think of clear instances in which U.S. government has been "unworkable"? In your view, does the demise of the legislative veto make government more workable or less workable?

3. Administrative doctrine often frowns on duplication and overlap between agencies. Does the bicameralism of Congress differ significantly from such

overlaps as are found among agencies such as Interior (national parks) and Agriculture (national forests), the Bureau of Reclamation, the Soil Conservation Service, and the Army Corps of Engineers, or the Equal Employment Opportunity Commission and the Department of Labor's Office of Federal Contract Compliance? If so, how? If not, can we expect to derive benefits from agency overlaps that are similar to those that the Court believes we derive from bicameralism? What would those benefits be?

CASE 1.3:
CAUGHT BETWEEN THE SEPARATION OF POWERS

LOCAL 2677, the AMERICAN FEDERATION OF GOVERNMENT EMPLOYEES, et al., Plaintiffs,

v.

Howard J. PHILLIPS, both Individually and in his capacity as Acting Director, Office of Economic Opportunity, Defendant.
Civ. A. Nos. 371-73, 375-73 and 379-73.
United States District Court, District of Columbia.
April 11, 1973.
358 F. Supp. 60

Summary

Consolidated actions by representatives of employees of Office of Economic Opportunity and Community Action Agency against acting director of Office of Economic Opportunity to declare unlawful and enjoin what they alleged to be unlawful dismantlement of Office of Economic Opportunity by defendant. . . . [T]he District Court, William B. Jones, J., held, inter alia, that until Congress chooses to terminate Community Action Agency program before its authorization has expired, either indirectly by failing to supply funds through a continuing resolution or appropriation, or by explicitly forbidding further use of funds for the programs, acting director is obligated to continue to operate the programs as was intended by Congress, and not terminate them. . . .

Opinion

WILLIAM B. JONES, District Judge.
These three consolidated actions have been brought to declare unlawful and enjoin what the plaintiffs alleged to be the unlawful dismantlement of the Office of Economic Opportunity (OEO) by the defendant, Howard J. Phillips, Acting Director of OEO. The plaintiffs in Local 2677, American Federation of Government Employees, et al. v. Phillips, Civil Action No. 371–73 (hereinafter *Local 2677*), by an amended complaint, are the labor orga-

nization-bargaining agent for the Washington, D. C. headquaters employees of OEO, and two individual OEO headquarters employees. Suit is brought on behalf of all OEO employees throughout the country who have been or are about to be adversely affected by the alleged unlawful acts of the defendant.

* * *

On January 29, 1973, President Nixon submitted his 1974 Budget Message to Congress. That budget message set forth the administration's plan to transfer responsibility for certain OEO functions to other agencies. The message specifically notes that

No funds are requested for . . . [OEO] for 1974. Effective July 1, 1973, new funding for . . . [CAAs] will be at the discretion of local communities. . . . With Community Action concepts now incorporated into ongoing programs and local agencies [if the budget proposals are approved], the continued existence of OEO as a separate Federal agency is no longer necessary. . . .

On January 29, 1973, the defendant issued a memorandum to all OEO regional offices . . . regarding the "termination of section 221 [CAA] funding." That memorandum, at page two, further noted that the cessation of funding would rescind individual designations as CAAs. OEO Instruction 6730–3, issued March 15, 1973, at page two, repeats the same instruction of the defendant that CAA funding will cease and further warns that use of funds by a CAA for any purpose except phasing out its activity or the failure of a CAA to submit an "acceptable" phase-out plan 120 days prior to the termination of section 221 funding will result in summary suspension of OEO funds. The same Instruction 6730–3 sets out 21 pages of guidelines

for CAAs to follow in shutting down their section 221 operations, with various deadlines to be met throughout that process.

Thus, . . . all program evaluations and processing of CAA applications for purposes other than phasing out CAA activities have stopped. CAAs have been instructed to stop purchasing or repairing essential equipment. The day-to-day business operations of CAAs have been hindered if not halted by the unwillingness of third parties to deal with CAAs because of the announcement by the defendant of the termination of funding. The orderly continuation of CAA functions . . . has been halted or severely disrupted by the requirements imposed by OEO regarding termination. Finally, CAA employees are leaving their jobs in anticipation of the cessation of funding in compliance with OEO directives.

* * *

The defendant contends that because the budget message of the President, as the latest assessment of national needs and priorities, requests no funds for OEO to operate after June 30, 1973, the fiscally responsible course for the defendant to undertake is to phase out the CAA program that will be out of existence on July 1, 1973. In support of this theory, the defendant cites the general proposition of the law with which the plaintiffs are in total agreement—that the defendant cannot be forced to spend any funds which have not yet been appropriated. The defendant, however, goes on to argue that once the President has submitted his budget to the Congress, a program administrator must look to that message. If no funds are proposed for his agency, it is his duty to terminate that agency's functions to effect the least "waste" of funds. Because the Court can find no support for this position in the budget act, the OEO act, the history of OEO appropriations, or the Constitution itself, the Court finds for the plaintiffs on this count.

*   *   *

. . . Assuming, as the defendant argues, that a fiscally responsible administrator must terminate programs under his supervision in the absence, as here, of either an appropriation or a budget request for funds, any program from OEO to agricultural crop subsidies could be terminated by the Executive by not requesting any funds in the budget to continue its operation. That construction would in effect give the President a veto power through the use of his budget message, a veto power not granted him by Article I, section 7, of the Constitution.

*   *   *

In effect the defendant argues that by use of the budget message the Executive can force the Congress to legislate to keep an authorized program from terminating. The defendant contends further that he can use the funds appropriated by Congress to run section 221 programs to terminate them and force the Congress to act before the time that it has set for itself (June 30, 1973) to act on appropriating the funds as allowed by the authorization. Thus the Executive would effectively legislate the termination of section 221 programs before Congress has declared that they shall end. Article I, section 1, of the Constitution vests "[a]ll legislative powers" in the Congress. No budget message of the President can alter that power and force the Congress to act to preserve legislative programs from extinction prior to the time Congress has declared that they shall terminate, either by its action or inaction.

*   *   *

An authorization does not necessarily mean that a program will continue. Congress, of course, may itself decide to terminate a program before its authorization has expired, either indirectly by failing to supply funds throught a continuing resolution or appropriation, or by explicitly forbidding the further use of funds for the programs . . . . But Congress has not chosen either of these courses, although it may in the future. Until that time, historical precedent, logic, and the text of the Constitution itself obligate the defendant to continue to operate the section 221 programs as was inteded by the Congress, and not terminate them.

*   *   *

In the present case, the Congress has not directed that funds be granted to any particular CAA. The OEO Director has been granted discretion in the disbursing of funds so as to effectuate the goals of the program. . . . But discretion in the implementation of a program is not the freedom to ignore the standards for its implementation. . . . An administrator's responsibility to carry out the Congressional objectives of a program does not give him the power to discontinue that program, especially in the face of a Congressional mandate that it shall go on.

*   *   *

Congress has told the Director of OEO through its authorization that it intends that section 221 programs continue. Until Congress changes that command, the defendant is bound to honor it.

Counsel for the defendant urged at oral argument that unless the defendant ignored that Congressional command and terminated section 221 programs, financial chaos would result on July 1, 1973, if the Congress failed to include OEO in a continuing resolution or pass an appropriation bill. This Court will not presume that Congress will act in such an irresponsible manner, any more than it assumes that the defendant is acting in bad faith in his assertion of the duty to terminate section 221 funding. But Congress has shown how the problem posed by counsel for the defendant would be solved in its past action terminating funding for the SST program . . . Funds were appropriated "[f]or expenses, not otherwise provided for, necessary for the termination of development of the civil supersonic aircraft and to refund the contractors' cost shares, $97,300,000, to remain available until expended." Pub.L. No. 92–18, 85 Stat. 40. Thus when Congress orders that a program go forth and later changes its mind, it is for the Congress in the responsible exercise of its legislative power to make provisions for termination. Until those provisions are made, the function of the Executive is to administer the program in accord with the legislated purposes.

DISCUSSION QUESTIONS

1. The defendant, Phillips, appears to have been caught dead-center between the separation of powers. Should he have kept spending funds in routine fashion, including for equipment repairs and new projects, even though there was a substantial possibility that the OEO's Community Action Programs would come to a screeching halt at the end of the fiscal year? If you were in Phillips's position, what might you have done? Would Phillips have been more successful simply to use his discretion to deny additional expenditures on a case-by-case basis as opposed to issuing his across-the-board directives for dismantling the CAA's? If so, does such "fudging" raise additional constitutional issues? Ethical issues?

2. The Court's opinion certainly bespeaks of a great deal of congressional direction of executive branch agencies. Does it suggest that in constitutional theory, Congress has the bulk of authority over administration? Consider all of Congress's powers over executive branch agencies.

3. How can the separation of legislative and executive powers over public administration be coordinated? For instance, can political parties be useful in this context? Can the heads of bureaus in the federal bureaucracy develop political relationships with the members of congressional subcommittees, interest groups, and with presidential appointees and others that could facilitate coordination? What might such relationships look like?

2

AT YOUR OWN RISK!
PUBLIC ADMINISTRATORS'
LIABILITY FOR LACKING
CONSTITUTIONAL COMPETENCE

The previous chapter emphasized how public administration must be adapted to the nation's constitutional framework. Often of more immediate concern to many public administrators is that the Constitution is directly relevant to their day-to-day activities. In order to do their jobs properly, public administrators must be constitutionally competent in the sense of knowing how the Constitution constrains the administrative practices in which they personally engage. Many of those who lack such constitutional competence run a substantial risk of being sued personally by individuals whose constitutional rights they may have unknowingly injured. This chapter discusses the expansion of individual constitutional rights vis-à-vis public administrative action and the character of public administrators' liability for breaches of those rights. The cases presented in this chapter explain the logic and scope of administrators' liabilities for violating individuals' constitutional rights. *Harley* v. *Schuylkill County* (1979), the final case, connects this type of liability to a fledgling right of public administrators to disobey unconstitutional directives.

OVERVIEW

In recent decades, the Supreme Court has fundamentally redefined the relationship between the practice of public administration and the United States

Constitution. A century ago, Woodrow Wilson could write in his classic essay "The Study of Administration" that "The field of administration is a field of business. It is removed from the hurry and strife of politics; it at most points stands apart even from the debatable ground of constitutional study."[1] The effort to secure public administration in the field of business or management was further developed by Leonard D. White, whose influential *Introduction to the Study of Public Administration* (1926)[2] was the first American textbook on the subject. White argued that "the study of administration should start from the base of management rather than the foundation of law, and is therefore more absorbed in the affairs of the American Management Association than in the decisions of the courts." Whatever the merits of the classical or orthodox tradition to which Wilson and White contributed so substantially, at present, as federal Judge David Bazelon notes, "As the Constitutional right to due process of law expands more and more, administrators will find themselves locked into involuntary partnerships with the courts."[3] Today, knowledge of constitutional law is considered a matter of basic *job competence* for public administrators. Those who lack what the courts—or as Bazelon might put it, the "senior partners"—deem to be "reasonable" knowledge of the constitutional rights of their clients, their patients and inmates, their subordinates, and individuals that they encounter in other ways may be held *personally* liable in civil suits for money damages. In other words, the public administrator who knew or reasonably should have known that he or she was violating someone's constitutional rights may have to pay substantial sums to the injured party out of his or her own pocketbook. In a related development, the courts have held that municipalities whose administrative actions violate individuals' constitutional rights also face liabilities.

Suits against public administrators and municipalities are now common. For instance, between 1977 and 1983, approximately 3,000 suits against government officials and governmental entities appear to have been litigated in the federal courts.[4] The majority of these were brought by private individuals (37%), public employees (26%), and prisoners (21%), with businesses (7%), interest groups (5%), and recipients of public assistance (4%) making up the remainder.[5] According to one estimate, in 1985 the average amount of damages sought per

[1] Woodrow Wilson, "The Study of Administration," *Political Science Quarterly*, 56 (December 1941): 481–506, at pp. 493–94. Originally published in 1887.

[2] Leonard D. White, *Introduction to the Study of Public Administration* (New York: Macmillan, 1926), see pp. vii–viii.

[3] David Bazelon, "The Impact of the Courts on Public Administration," *Indiana Law Journal*, 52 (1976): 101–10, at p. 105.

[4] Yong S. Lee, "Civil Liability of State and Local Governments: Myth and Reality," *Public Administration Review*, 47 (March/April 1987): 160–70, especially p. 162. Lee identified approximately 1,700 cases in the *odd* years from 1977 to 1983, for an average of about 425 cases per year. We have assumed that the even years during the period would witness the same number of cases. Our estimate, like Lee's, is confined to *reported* cases. The number of unpublished decisions involving public administrators' liability is presumably large, though apparently unknown.

[5] Ibid., p. 163, Table 2.

suit was between $100 million and $200 million.[6] While some law firms have made a staple out of such suits, some cities have had to sell bonds to pay the damages assessed, and the costs of insurance have skyrocketed. Although their pockets are not nearly so deep, individual public administrators have also been forced to pay damages and legal costs. Many of these suits involve police misconduct and conditions of confinement in prisons and public mental health facilities, but even more concern public employment practices and alleged violations of the constitutional right to due process.[7] For the individual public administrator, the best way to avoid such suits is to understand individuals' constitutional rights and to avoid encroaching on them. How has the Constitution become so relevant to the practice of pubic administration?

THE EXPANSION OF INDIVIDUALS' CONSTITUTIONAL RIGHTS

Article VI of the Constitution requires that "The Senators and Representatives . . . and the Members of the several State Legislatures, and all executive and judicial Officers, both of the United States and of the several States, shall be bound by Oath or Affirmation, to support this Constitution. . . ." However, it has only been since the 1950s that the courts have ruled that individuals have wide-ranging constitutional rights vis-à-vis public administrative action. The declaration of new constitutional rights for individuals as they encounter the administrative state is one of the most dramatic and important developments in American public administrative history.[8] Since the 1960s, clients of administrative agencies, such as welfare recipients, have been afforded far greater substantive, equal protection, and procedural due process constitutional rights. Government benefits that were once defined as a privilege to which one had no constitutional right were redefined as a form of "new property," in which one does have a constitutionally cognizable interest. The constitutional rights of public employees to freedom of speech and association, procedural due process, and equal protection have also been vastly expanded. Individuals involuntarily confined to public mental health facilities have been granted a constitutional right to treatment or training, and some of their ordinary rights as members of the polity have also been vastly expanded. The Eighth Amendment rights of prisoners against cruel and unusual punishment and their right to equal protection of the laws have also been dramatically strengthened through marked departures from earlier legal doctrines. Additionally, some constitutional protections have been developed for individuals engaged in "street-level" encounters with public administrators. Taken together, these constitutional developments constitute a kind of "Bill of Rights" for individuals in the contemporary

[6]Andrew Blum, "Lawsuits Put Strain on City Budgets," *National Law Journal*, 10 (May 16, 1988), pp. 1ff.
[7]Lee, "Civil Liability of State and Local Governments," p. 163, Table 2.
[8]See David H. Rosenbloom, *Public Administration and Law* (New York: Marcel Dekker, 1983) for an extended discussion.

American administrative state that places new constraints on public administrative activity in many areas of public policy.

Protecting individuals' current constitutional rights can deeply affect public administrative operations, budgets, routines, and authority. For instance, the constitutional right to treatment for those involuntarily confined to public mental health facilities translates operationally into a humane environment in which there is a temperature range of 68 degrees F to 83 degrees F, sufficient staff to provide treatment and safety, and no overcrowding (see case 7.3, *Wyatt* v. *Stickney* [1971]). Declaring that public employees have a property interest in their jobs requires that they be afforded fair hearings, at some stage, in dismissal procedures. Depriving clients of governmental benefits or licenses may also require an elaborate procedure. Even short suspensions from public schools require a modicum of due process. Police behavior, in particular, has been modified by new constitutional protections for individuals in stop-and-frisk, arrests, or other encounters. A majority of the states have had to reform at least one prison, if not virtually their entire penal systems, in order to comply with today's constitutional standards. Similarly, many public school systems have been drastically redesigned—sometimes by judges—in order to desegregate them as required by the Fourteenth Amendment's provision that no person be deprived of equal protection of the laws. In Boston, in 1981, the "partnership" between judges and public administrators encompassed 48% of the city's budgetary appropriations, which were "presided" over by federal and state judges.[9] In short, public organizational arrangements, personnel administration, budgets, and decision-making processes have sometimes been changed substantially in response to judicial decisions involving individuals' constitutional rights. Moreover, as noted earlier, public administrators now have a very personal stake in assuring that they do not violate these rights.

FROM ABSOLUTE TO QUALIFIED IMMUNITY

During the 1970s, the federal judiciary broadly revised legal doctrines that presumed that public administrators had an *absolute* immunity from civil suits seeking damages for the violation of individuals' constitutional or federally protected statutory rights. The Supreme Court resurrected what had been regarded as a moribund provision of the Civil Rights Act of 1871, generally referred to as 42 U.S. Code 1983, which reads in part that "every person who," while acting under color of state authority, causes another individual within that state to be subjected "to the deprivation of any rights, privileges, or immunities secured by the Constitution and laws, shall be liable to the party injured in an action at law, suit in equity, or other proper proceeding for redress."[10]

[9]Robert Turner, "Governing From the Bench," *Boston Globe Magazine,* November 8, 1981, pp. 12 ff.
[10]For the classic discussion, see "Section 1983 and Federalism," *Harvard Law Review,* 90 (1977): 1133–1361.

Historically, the federal judiciary was reluctant to apply this provision literally to public administrators because they did not think that Congress, in drafting the words, "every person who," intended to override a long-standing common law doctrine making public officials immune to the kind of civil suits authorized by the statute. By 1975, as part of the broader effort to protect individuals' constitutional rights from administrative encroachment, the Supreme Court was well on the way to holding that most public administrators exercising nonjudicial functions have only a *qualified* immunity from such suits. Municipalities are treated as "persons" under the act, and they may be liable if their policies cause a violation of federally protected rights. Federal administrators with nonjudicial functions, including presidential aides, but not the president, may be held liable directly under the Constitution as a means of enforcing its requirements. Compensatory and punitive damages can be assessed against individual public administrators personally, but municipalities face only compensatory liability. Judges and legislators generally enjoy a broader immunity than executive branch officials.

The cases that follow explain the rationale for public administrators' qualified immunity, or put the other way around, their liability, and its offshoot, their incipient constitutional right to disobey unconstitutional directives. In Case 2.1, *Harlow* v. *Fitzgerald* (1982), the Supreme Court developed the current standard for administrators' liability: "government officials performing discretionary functions generally are shielded from liability for civil damages insofar as their conduct does not violate clearly established statutory or constitutional rights of which a reasonable person would have known." Case 2.2, *Smith* v. *Wade* (1983), discusses the purpose of punitive damages and the appropriate standard for assessing them against the public administrator who has violated an individual's constitutional rights. Case 2.3, *Pembaur* v. *Cincinnati* (1986), presents a fascinating discussion of the theory of municipal liability and an interesting example of how it can apply. Case 2.4, *Harley* v. *Schuylkill County* (1979), explains the logic of public administrators' constitutional right to disobey. Each case is followed by key questions for discussion. The chapter ends with a brief note on how public administrators might best think about constitutional rights and values.

ADDITIONAL READING

OLSON, WALTER. *New Directions in Liability Law.* New York: Academy of Political Science, 1988.

ROSENBLOOM, DAVID H. *Public Administration and Law.* New York: Marcel Dekker, 1983.

SCHUCK, PETER. *Suing Government: Citizen Remedies for Official Wrongs.* New Haven, Conn.: Yale University Press, 1982.

CASE 2.1:
QUALIFIED IMMUNITY

BRYCE N. HARLOW and
ALEXANDER P. BUTTERFIELD,
Petitioners

v

A. ERNEST FITZGERALD
457 US 800
[No. 80-945]
Argued November 30, 1981.
Decided June 24, 1982.

Decision: Senior aides and advisers of President of United States, held entitled to qualified immunity from civil damages suits insofar as their conduct does not violate rights of which reasonable person would have known.

Summary

A civilian employee of the Department of the Air Force was terminated from his position. He instituted a suit for civil damages in the United States District Court for the District of Columbia against two senior aides and advisers of the President of the United States, alleging that they participated in a conspiracy to violate his constitutional and statutory rights, and entered the conspiracy in their official capacities, to effect his unlawful discharge. [T]he District Court . . . ruled that the aides were not entitled to absolute immunity. The aides appealed the denial of their immunity defense to the United States Court of Appeals for the District of Columbia which dismissed the appeal.

Opinion

Justice **Powell** delivered the opinion of the Court.

The issue in this case is the scope of the immunity available to the senior aides and advisers of the President of the United States in a suit for damages based upon their official acts.

I

In this suit for civil damages petitioners Bryce Harlow and Alexander Butterfield are alleged to have participated in a conspiracy to violate the constitutional and statutory rights of the respondent A. Ernest Fitzgerald. . . .

*   *   *

. . . As evidence of Harlow's conspiratorial activity respondent relies heavily on a series of conversations in which Harlow discussed Fitzgerald's dismissal with Air Force Secretary Robert Seamans. The other evidence most supportive of Fitzgerald's claims consists of a recorded conversation in which the President later voiced a tentative recollection that Harlow was "all for canning" Fitzgerald.

*   *   *

Petitioner Butterfield also is alleged to have entered the conspiracy not later than May 1969. Employed as Deputy Assistant to the President and Deputy Chief of Staff to H. R. Haldeman, Butterfield circulated a White House memorandum in that month in which he claimed to have learned that Fitzgerald planned to "blow the whistle" on some "shoddy purchasing practices" by exposing these practices to public view. Fitzgerald characterizes this memorandum as evidence that Butterfield had commenced efforts to secure Fitzgerald's retaliatory dismissal.

. . . [O]ur decisions consistently have held that Government officials are entitled to some form of immunity from suits for damages. As recognized at common law, public officers require this protection to shield them from undue interference with their duties and from potentially disabling threats of liability.

Our decisions have recognized immunity defenses of two kinds. For officials whose special functions or constitutional status requires complete protection from suit, we have recognized the defense of "absolute immunity." The absolute immunity of legislators, in their legislative functions. . . and of judges, in their judicial functions, . . . now is well settled. Our decisions also have extended absolute immunity to certain officials of the Executive Branch. These include prosecutors and similar officials, . . . executive officers engaged in adjudicative functions . . . and the President of the United States. . . .

For executive officials in general, however, our cases make plain that qualified immunity represents the norm. In Scheuer v Rhodes [1974] . . . we acknowledged that high officials require greater protection than those with less complex discretionary responsibilities. Nonetheless, we held that a governor and his aides could receive the requisite protection from qualified or good-faith immunity. . . .

In Butz v Economou [1978] we extended the approach of Scheuer to high federal officials of the Executive Branch. Discussing in detail the considerations that also had underlain our decision in Scheuer, we explained that the recognition of a qualified immunity defense for high executives reflected an attempt to balance competing values: not only the importance of a damages remedy to protect the rights of citizens, . . . but also "the need to protect officials who are required to exercise their discretion and the related public interest in encouraging the vigorous exercise of official authority."

Butz continued to acknowledge that the special functions of some officials might require absolute immunity. But the Court held that "federal officials who seek absolute exemption from personal liability for unconstitutional conduct must bear the burden of showing that public policy requires an exemption of that scope."

*   *   *

. . . In order to establish entitlement to absolute immunity a Presidential aide first must show that the responsibilities of his office embraced a function so sensitive as to require a total shield from liability. He then must demonstrate that he was discharging the protected function when performing the act for which liability is asserted.

Applying these standards to the claims advanced by petitioners Harlow and Butterfield, we cannot conclude on the record before us that either has shown that "public policy requires [for any of the functions of his office] an exemption of [absolute] scope." . . . Nor, assuming that petitioners did have functions for which absolute immunity would be warranted, could we now conclude that the acts charged in this lawsuit—if taken at all— would lie within the protected area.

Even if they cannot establish that their official functions require absolute immunity, petitioners assert that public policy at least mandates an application of the qualified immunity standard that would permit the defeat of insubstantial claims without resort to trial. We agree.

The resolution of immunity questions inherently requires a balance between the evils inevitable in any available alternative. In situations of abuse of office, an action for damages may offer the only realistic avenue for vindication of constitutional guarantees. . . .

It is this recognition that has required the denial of absolute immunity to most public officers. At the same time, however, it cannot be disputed seriously that claims frequently run against the innocent as well as the guilty—at a cost not only to the defendant officials, but to the society as a whole. These social costs include the expenses of litigation, the diversion of official energy from pressing public issues, and the deterrence of able citizens from acceptance of public office. Finally, there is the danger that fear of being sued will "dampen the ardor of all but the most resolute, or the most irresponsible [public officials], in the unflinching discharge of their duties."

In identifying qualified immunity as the best attainable accommodation of competing values, in Butz, . . . as in Scheuer . . . we relied on the assumption that this standard would permit "[i]nsubstantial lawsuits [to] be quickly terminated."

* * *

Consistently with the balance at which we aimed in Butz, we conclude today that bare allegations of malice should not suffice to subject government officials either to the costs of trial or to the burdens of broad-reaching discovery. We

therefore hold that government officials performing discretionary functions generally are shielded from liability for civil damages insofar as their conduct does not violate clearly established statutory or constitutional rights of which a reasonable person would have known. . . .

Reliance on the objective reasonableness of an official's conduct, as measured by reference to clearly established law, should avoid excessive disruption of government and permit the resolution of many insubstantial claims on summary judgment. On summary judgment, the judge appropriately may determine, not only the currently applicable law, but whether that law was clearly established at the time an action occurred. If the law at that time was not clearly established, an official could not reasonably be expected to anticipate subsequent legal developments, nor could he fairly be said to "know" that the law forbade conduct not previously identified as unlawful. Until this threshold immunity question is resolved, discovery should not be allowed. If the law was clearly established, the immunity defense ordinarily should fail, since a reasonably competent public official should know the law governing his conduct. Nevertheless, if the official pleading the defense claims extraordinary circumstances and can prove that he neither knew nor should have known of the relevant legal standard, the defense should be sustained. But again, the defense would turn primarily on objective factors.

By defining the limits of qualified immunity essentially in objective terms, we provide no license to lawless conduct. The public interest in deterrence of unlawful conduct and in compensation of victims remains protected by a test that focuses on the objective legal reasonableness of an official's acts. Where an official could be expected to know that certain conduct would violate statutory or constitutional rights, he should be made to hesitate; and a person who suffers injury caused by such conduct may have a cause of action. But where an official's duties legitimately re-quire action in which clearly established rights are not implicated, the public inter-est may be better served by action taken "with independence and without fear of consequences." . . .

DISCUSSION QUESTIONS

1. In Harlow, the Court tries to establish a balance that will protect public administrators from frivolous suits or harassment by litigation and at the same time enable individuals whose constitutional rights have been abridged to recover. What problems, if any, do you see with the balance the Court strikes? Can you think of other ways of essentially achieving the same purposes?

2. Most public administrators are not shielded from liability if their conduct violates clearly established constitutional rights of which a reasonable person would have known. One can fairly infer that the "reasonable person" to which the Court refers would be assessed in the context of the particular public administrative job he or she holds. For instance, a "reasonable" police officer would be expected to know more about the constitutional rights of those involved in arrests or stops-and-frisks than would a budget analyst in the State Department. Does this mean that the "reasonable person" standard is really one of administrative competence, as assessed by judges? How can an administrator develop reasonable knowledge of the constitutional rights that bear on his or her job? How can a judge determine what "reasonable" knowledge of this kind an administrator should have? Do you think that judges are likely to understand public administration well enough to make sound decisions in this regard?

CASE 2.2:
DAMAGES: COMPENSATORY
AND PUNITIVE

SMITH v. WADE
461 US 30
CERTIORARI TO THE UNITED
STATES COURT OF APPEALS
FOR THE EIGHTH CIRCUIT
No. 81-1196.
Argued November 10, 1982—
Decided April 20, 1983

Summary

Respondent, while an inmate in a Missouri reformatory for youthful first offenders, was harassed, beaten, and sex-ually assaulted by his cellmates. He brought suit under 42 U. S. C. § 1983 in Federal District Court against petitioner, a guard at the reformatory, and others, alleging that his Eighth Amendment rights had been violated. Because of petitioner's qualified immunity, as a prison guard, from § 1983 liability, the trial judge instructed the jury that respondent could recover only if petitioner was guilty of "gross negligence" or "egregious failure to protect" respondent. The judge also charged the jury that it could award punitive damages in addition to actual damages if petitioner's conduct was shown to be "a reckless or callous disregard of, or indifference to, the rights or safety of others." The District Court entered judgment on a verdict finding petitioner liable and awarding both compensatory and punitive damages. The Court of Appeals affirmed.

Held: 1. Punitive damages are available in a proper case under § 1983. While there is little in the legislative history of § 1 of the Civil Rights Act of 1871 (from which § 1983 is derived) concerning the damages recoverable for the tort liability created by the statute, the availability of punitive damages was accepted as settled law by nearly all state and federal courts at the time of enactment. Moreover, this Court has rested decisions on related issues on the premise that punitive damages are available under § 1983. . . .

2. A jury may be permitted to assess punitive damages in a § 1983 action when the defendant's conduct involves reckless or callous indifference to the plaintiff's federally protected rights, as well as when it is motivated by evil motive or intent. The common law, both in 1871 and now, allows recovery of punitive damages in tort cases not only for actual malicious intent, but also for reckless indifference to the rights of others. Neither the policies nor the purposes of § 1983 require a departure from the common-law rule. Petitioner's contention that an actual-intent standard is preferable to a recklessness standard because it is less vague, and would more readily serve the purpose of deterrence of future egregious conduct, is unpersuasive. . . .

3. The threshold standard for allowing punitive damages for reckless or callous indifference applies even in a case, such as here, where the underlying standard of liability for compensatory damages is also one of recklessness. . . .

*   *   *

Opinion

JUSTICE BRENNAN delivered the opinion of the Court.

We granted certiorari in this case . . . to decide whether the District Court for the Western District of Missouri applied the correct legal standard in instructing the jury that it might award punitive damages under 42 U. S. C. § 1983. . . . The Court of Appeals for the Eighth Circuit sustained the award of punitive damages. . . . We affirm.

The petitioner, William H. Smith, is a guard at Algoa Reformatory, a unit of the Missouri Division of Corrections for youthful first offenders. The respondent, Daniel R. Wade, was assigned to Algoa as an inmate in 1976. In the summer of 1976 Wade voluntarily checked into Algoa's protective custody unit. Because of disciplinary violations during his stay in protective custody, Wade was given a short term in punitive segregation and then transferred to administrative segregation. On the evening of Wade's first day in administrative segregation, he was placed in a cell with another inmate. Later, when Smith came on duty in Wade's dormitory, he placed a third inmate in Wade's cell. According to Wade's testimony, his cellmates harassed, beat, and sexually assaulted him.

Wade brought suit under 42 U. S. C. § 1983 against Smith and four other guards and correctional officials, alleging that his Eighth Amendment rights had been violated. At trial his evidence showed that he had placed himself in protective custody because of prior incidents of violence against him by other inmates. The third prisoner whom Smith added to the cell had been placed in administrative segregation for fighting. Smith had made no effort to find out whether another cell was available; in fact there was another cell in the same dormitory with only one occupant. Further, only a few weeks earlier, another inmate had been beaten to death in the same dormitory during the same shift, while Smith had been on duty. Wade asserted that Smith and the other defendants knew or should have known that an assault against him was likely under the circumstances.

During trial, the District Judge entered a directed verdict for two of the defendants. He instructed the jury that Wade could make out an Eighth Amendment violation only by showing "physical abuse of such base, inhumane and barbaric proportions as to shock the sensibilities.". . . Further, because of Smith's qualified immunity as a prison guard, . . . the judge instructed the jury that Wade could recover only if the defendants were guilty of "gross negligence" (defined as "a callous indifference or a thoughtless disregard for the consequences of one's act or failure to act") or "[e]gregious failure to protect" (defined as "a flagrant or remarkably bad failure to protect") Wade. . . . He reiterated that Wade could not recover on a showing of simple negligence. . . .

The District Judge also charged the jury that it could award punitive damages on a proper showing:

"In addition to actual damages, the law permits the jury, under certain circumstances, to award the injured person punitive and exemplary damages, in order to punish the wrongdoer for

some extraordinary misconduct, and to serve as an example or warning to others not to engage in such conduct.

"If you find the issues in favor of the plaintiff, and if the conduct of one or more of the defendants is shown to be *a reckless or callous disregard of, or indifference to, the rights or safety of others,* then you may assess punitive or exemplary damages in addition to any award of actual damages.

". . . The amount of punitive or exemplary damages assessed against any defendant may be such sum as you believe will serve to punish that defendant and to deter him and others from like conduct.". . .

The jury returned verdicts for two of the three remaining defendants. It found Smith liable, however, and awarded $25,000 in compensatory damages and $5,000 in punitive damages. The District Court entered judgment on the verdict, and the Court of Appeals affirmed. . . .

In this Court, Smith attacks only the award of punitive damages. He does not challenge the correctness of the instructions on liability or qualified immunity, nor does he question the adequacy of the evidence to support the verdict of liability for compensatory damages.

Section 1983 is derived from § 1 of the Civil Rights Act of 1871, 17 Stat. 13. It was intended to create "a species of tort liability" in favor of persons deprived of federally secured rights.

*   *   *

Smith correctly concedes that "punitive damages are available in a 'proper' § 1983 action. . . ." . . . Although there was debate about the theoretical correctness of the punitive damages doctrine in the latter part of the last century, the doctrine was accepted as settled law by nearly all state and federal courts, including this Court. It was likewise generally established that individual public officers were liable for punitive damages for their misconduct on the same basis as other individual defendants.

Further, although the precise issue of the availability of punitive damages under § 1983 has never come squarely before us, we have had occasion more than once to make clear our view that they are available; indeed, we have rested decisions on related questions on the premise of such availability.

Smith argues, nonetheless, that this was not a "proper" case in which to award punitive damages. More particularly, he attacks the instruction that punitive damages could be awarded on a finding of reckless or callous disregard of or indifference to Wade's rights or safety. Instead, he contends that the proper test is one of actual malicious intent—"ill will, spite, or intent to injure." . . .

*   *   *

. . . Most cases under state common law, although varying in their precise terminology, have adopted more or less the . . . rule, recognizing that punitive damages in tort cases may be awarded not only for actual intent to injure or evil motive, but also for recklessness, serious indifference to or disregard for the rights of others, or even gross negligence.

The remaining question is whether the policies and purposes of § 1983 itself require a departure from the rules of tort common law. As a general matter, we discern no reason why a person whose federally guaranteed rights have been violated should be granted a more restrictive remedy than a person asserting an ordinary tort cause of action. Smith offers us no persuasive reason to the contrary.

Smith's argument, which he offers in several forms, is that an actual-intent standard is preferable to a recklessness standard because it is less vague. He points out that punitive damages, by their very nature, are not awarded to compensate the injured party. . . .

He concedes, of course, that deterrence of future egregious conduct is a primary purpose of both § 1983 . . . and of punitive damages. . . . But deterrence, he contends, cannot be achieved unless the standard of conduct sought to be deterred is stated with sufficient clarity to enable potential defendants to conform to the law and to avoid the proposed sanction. Recklessness or callous indifference, he argues, is too uncertain a standard to achieve deterrence rationally and fairly. A prison guard, for example, can be expected to know whether he is acting with actual ill will or intent to injure, but not whether he is being reckless or callously indifferent.

Smith's argument, if valid, would apply to ordinary tort cases as easily as to § 1983 suits; hence, it hardly presents an argument for adopting a different rule under § 1983. In any event, the argument is unpersuasive. While, *arguendo*, an intent standard may be easier to understand and apply to particular situations than a recklessness standard, we are not persuaded that a recklessness standard is too vague to be fair or useful. . . .

More fundamentally, Smith's argument for certainty in the interest of deterrence overlooks the distinction between a standard for punitive damages and a standard of liability in the first instance. Smith seems to assume that prison guards and other state officials look mainly to the standard for punitive damages in shaping their conduct. We question the premise; we assume, and hope, that most officials are guided primarily by the underlying standards of federal substantive law—both out of devotion to duty, and in the interest of avoiding liability for compensatory damages. At any rate, the conscientious officer who desires clear guidance on how to do his job and avoid lawsuits can and should look to the standard for actionability in the first instance. The need for exceptional clarity in the standard for punitive damages arises only if one assumes that there are substantial numbers of officers who will not be deterred by compensatory damages; only such officers will seek to guide their conduct by the punitive damages standard. The presence of such officers constitutes a powerful argument *against* raising the threshold for punitive damages.

* * *

Smith contends that even if § 1983 does not ordinarily require a showing of actual malicious intent for an award of punitive damages, such a showing should be required in this case. He argues that the deterrent and punitive purposes of punitive damages are served only if the threshold for punitive damages is higher in every case than the underlying standard for liability in the first instance. In this case, while the District Judge did not use the same precise terms to explain the standards of liability for compensatory and punitive damages, the parties agree that there is no substantial difference between the showings required by the two instructions; both apply a standard of reckless or callous indifference to Wade's rights. Hence, Smith argues, the District Judge erred in not requiring a higher standard for punitive damages, namely, actual malicious intent.

This argument incorrectly assumes that, simply because the instructions specified the same *threshold* of liability for pu-

nitive and compensatory damages, the two forms of damages were equally available to the plaintiff. The argument overlooks a key feature of punitive damages—that they are never awarded as of right, no matter how egregious the defendant's conduct. "If the plaintiff proves sufficiently serious misconduct on the defendant's part, the question whether to award punitive damages is left to the jury, which may or may not make such an award." . . .

Compensatory damages, by contrast, are mandatory; once liability is found, the jury is required to award compensatory damages in an amount appropriate to compensate the plaintiff for his loss. Hence, it is not entirely accurate to say that punitive and compensatory damages were awarded in this case on the same standard. To make its punitive award, the jury was required to find not only that Smith's conduct met the recklessness threshold (a question of ultimate fact), but *also* that his conduct merited a punitive award of $5,000 in addition to the compensatory award (a discretionary moral judgment).

* * *

We hold that a jury may be permitted to assess punitive damages in an action under § 1983 when the defendant's conduct is shown to be motivated by evil motive or intent, or when it involves reckless or callous indifference to the federally protected rights of others. We further hold that this threshold applies even when the underlying standard of liability for compensatory damages is one of recklessness. . . . The judgment of the Court of Appeals is affirmed.

DISCUSSION QUESTIONS

1. Justice Rehnquist dissented in *Smith* v. *Wade* partly on the basis that: "After the Court's decision, governmental officials will be subjected to the possibility of damages awards unlimited by any harm they may have caused or the fact that they acted with unquestioned good faith: when swift action is demanded, their thoughts likely will be on personal financial consequences that may result from their conduct—but whose limits they cannot predict—and not upon their official duties." Do you think Rehnquist accurately predicts administrative behavior? Why or why not?

2. The foregoing statement by Rehnquist suggests that if punitive damages are to be allowable at all, they ought to be related to (a) the harm caused, and/or (b) whether the administrator acted in good faith. Do you think either or both of these elements ought to be taken into account in assessing punitive damages? What would be the consequences to injured individuals and administrators? In practice, do you think juries are likely to award the same punitive damages in instances of minor injury as compared to cases of severe harm?

3. Do you think public administrators ought to be indemnified (that is, reimbursed by their public employers) for (a) compensatory damages assessed against them, (b) punitive damages, or (c) neither? Explain. Should indemnification be a standard procedure, or should it depend on how an employer assesses the administrator's behavior? Should the government pay the legal fees of public administrators who successfully defend § 1983 suits? Unsuccessfully defend them?

CASE 2.3:
MUNICIPAL LIABILITY

BERTOLD J. PEMBAUR,
Petitioner

v

CITY OF CINCINNATI et al.
475 US 469
[No. 84-1160]
Argued December 2, 1985. Decided
March 25, 1986.

Decision: County prosecutor's instructions to deputy sheriffs to force entry into medical clinic to serve process on grand-jury witnesses held to subject county to liability under 42 USCS § 1983.

Summary

A physician who operated a medical clinic was indicted by a grand jury for fraudulently accepting welfare payments.

When two of his employees were subpoenaed as witnesses, but failed to appear before the grand jury, capiases* were obtained to compel the appearance of the subpoenaed witnesses, and county deputy sheriffs attempted to serve the capiases at

---

*A capias is a writ of attachment commanding a county official to bring a subpoenaed witness who has failed to appear before the court to testify and to answer for civil contempt.

the physician's clinic. The physician refused to let the deputies enter, and after being informed of the situation by the deputies, an assistant county prosecutor conferred with the county prosecutor, who told the assistant prosecutor to instruct the deputy sheriffs "to go in and get" the witnesses. The assistant prosector passed these instructions along to the deputies, who entered the clinic after city police officers, who had also been advised of these instructions, chopped down the door with an axe. The physician filed a civil rights action for damages against the county and other defendants, under 42 USCS § 1983, in the United States District Court for the Southern District of Ohio, alleging violations of his rights under the Fourth and Fourteenth Amendments of the Federal Constitution. The District Court dismissed the complaint. On appeal, the United States Court of Appeals for the Sixth Circuit upheld the dismissal of the claims against the county (746 F 2d 337).

On certiorari, the United States Supreme Court reversed and remanded the case. In an opinion by BRENNAN, J., joined by WHITE, MARSHALL, BLACKMUN, STEVENS, and O'CONNOR, JJ., it was held that the county was subject to liability under 42 USCS § 1983, on the grounds that: (1) the county prosecutor's instruction to the deputy sheriffs to "go in and get" the witnesses was a decision to take an action by an official authorized to establish county policy, although the action was taken only once, and (2) municipal liability may be imposed for a single decision by municipal policymakers under appropriate circumstances; also, in an opinion by BRENNAN, J., joined by WHITE, MARSHALL, BLACKMUN, and STEVENS, JJ., it was held that the county was subject to liability under 42 USCS § 1983, on the additional ground that, in so instructing the deputies, the county prosecu-

tor was acting as the final decisionmaker for the county.

Opinion

Justice **Brennan** delivered the opinion of the Court, except as to Part II-B.

In Monell v New York City Dept. of Social Services. . . (1978), the Court concluded that municipal liability under 42 USC § 1983 [42 USCS § 1983] is limited to deprivations of federally protected rights caused by action taken "pursuant to official municipal policy of some nature. . . ." . . .

The question presented is whether, and in what circumstances, a decision by municipal policymakers on a single occasion may satisfy this requirement.

I

Bertold Pembaur is a licensed Ohio physician and the sole proprietor of the Rockdale Medical Center, located in the city of Cincinnati in Hamilton County. Most of Pembaur's patients are welfare recipients who rely on government assistance to pay for medical care. During the spring of 1977, Simon Leis, the Hamilton County Prosecutor, began investigating charges that Pembaur fraudulently had accepted payments from state welfare agencies for services not actually provided to patients. A grand jury was convened, and the case was assigned to Assistant Prosecutor William Whalen. In April, the grand jury charged Pembaur in a six-count indictment.

During the investigation, the grand jury issued subpoenas for the appearance of two of Pembaur's employees. When these employees failed to appear as directed, the Prosecutor obtained capiases for their arrest and detention from the

Court of Common Pleas of Hamilton County.

On May 19, 1977, two Hamilton County Deputy Sheriffs attempted to serve the capiases at Pembaur's clinic. Although the reception area is open to the public, the rest of the clinic may be entered only through a door next to the receptionist's window. Upon arriving, the Deputy Sheriffs identified themselves to the receptionist and sought to pass through this door, which was apparently open. The receptionist blocked their way and asked them to wait for the doctor. When Pembaur appeared a moment later, he and the receptionist closed the door, which automatically locked from the inside, and wedged a piece of wood between it and the wall. Returning to the receptionist's window, the Deputy Sheriffs identified themselves to Pembaur, showed him the capiases and explained why they were there. Pembaur refused to let them enter, claiming that the police had no legal authority to be there and requesting that they leave. He told them that he had called the Cincinnati police, the local media, and his lawyer. The Deputy Sheriffs decided not to take further action until the Cincinnati police arrived.

Shortly thereafter, several Cincinnati police officers appeared. The Deputy Sheriffs explained the situation to them and asked that they speak to Pembaur. The Cincinnati police told Pembaur that the papers were lawful and that he should allow the Deputy Sheriffs to enter. When Pembaur refused, the Cincinnati police called for a superior officer. When he too failed to persuade Pembaur to open the door, the Deputy Sheriffs decided to call their supervisor for further instructions. Their supervisor told them to call Assistant Prosecutor Whalen and to follow his instructions. The Deputy Sheriffs then tele-

phoned Whalen and informed him of the situation. Whalen conferred with County Prosecutor Leis, who told Whalen to instruct the Deputy Sheriffs to "go in and get [the witnesses]." Whalen in turn passed these instructions along to the Deputy Sheriffs.

After a final attempt to persuade Pembaur voluntarily to allow them to enter, the Deputy Sheriffs tried unsuccessfully to force the door. City police officers, who had been advised of the County Prosecutor's instructions to "go in and get" the witnesses, obtained an axe and chopped down the door. The Deputy Sheriffs then entered and searched the clinic. Two individuals who fit descriptions of the witnesses sought were detained, but turned out not to be the right persons.

*   *   *

On April 20, 1981, Pembaur filed the present action in the United States District Court for the Southern District of Ohio against the city of Cincinnati, the county of Hamilton, the Cincinnati Police Chief, the Hamilton County Sheriff, the members of the Hamilton Board of County Commissioners (in their official capacities only), Assistant Prosecutor Whalen, and nine city and county police officers. Pembaur sought damages under 42 USC § 1983 [42 USCS § 1983], alleging that the county and city police had violated his rights under the Fourth and Fourteenth Amendments. His theory was that, absent exigent circumstances, the Fourth Amendment prohibits police from searching an individual's home or business without a search warrant even to execute an arrest warrant for a third person. We agreed with that proposition in Steagald v United States . . . (1981), decided the day after Pembaur filed this lawsuit. Pembaur sought $10 million in actual and $10 million in punitive damages, plus costs and attorney's fees.

* * *

II

A

Our analysis must begin with the proposition that "Congress did not intend municipalities to be held liable unless action pursuant to official municipal policy of some nature caused a constitutional tort." . . . As we read its opinion, the Court of Appeals held that a single decision to take particular action, although made by municipal policymakers, cannot establish the kind of "official policy" required by Monell as a predicate to municipal liability under § 1983. The Court of Appeals reached this conclusion without referring to Monell—indeed, without any explanation at all. However, examination of the opinion in Monell clearly demonstrates that the Court of Appeals misinterpreted its holding.

Monell is a case about responsibility. In the first part of the opinion, we held that local government units could be made liable under § 1983 for deprivations of federal rights. . . . In the second part of the opinion, we recognized a limitation on this liability and concluded that a municipality cannot be made liable by application of the doctrine of *respondeat superior*. . . .

The conclusion that tortious conduct, to be the basis for municipal liability under § 1983, must be pursuant to a municipality's "official policy" is contained in this discussion. The "official policy" requirement was intended to distinguish acts of the *municipality* from acts of *employees* of the municipality, and thereby make clear that municipal liability is limited to action for which the municipality is actually responsible.

Monell reasoned that recovery from a municipality is limited to acts that are, properly speaking, acts "of the municipality"—that is, acts which the municipality has officially sanctioned or ordered.

With this understanding, it is plain that municipal liability may be imposed for a single decision by municipal policymakers under appropriate circumstances. No one has ever doubted, for instance, that a municipality may be liable under § 1983 for a single decision by its properly constituted legislative body—whether or not that body had taken similar action in the past or intended to do so in the future—because even a single decision by such a body unquestionably constitutes an act of official government policy. . . .

But the power to establish policy is no more the exclusive province of the legislature at the local level than at the state or national level. Monell's language makes clear that it expressly envisioned other officials "whose acts or edicts may fairly be said to represent official policy,". . . and whose decisions therefore may give rise to municipal liability under § 1983.

Indeed, any other conclusion would be inconsistent with the principles underlying § 1983. To be sure, "official policy" often refers to formal rules or understandings—often but not always committed to writing—that are intended to, and do, establish fixed plans of action to be followed under similar circumstances consistently and over time. That was the case in Monell itself, which involved a written rule requiring pregnant employees to take unpaid leaves of absence before such leaves were medically necessary. However, . . . a government frequently chooses a course of action tailored to a particular situation and not intended to control decisions in later situations. If the decision to adopt that particular course of action is properly made by that government's authorized decisionmakers, it surely represents an act of official goverment "policy" as that term is commonly understood. More importantly, where action is directed by those who establish governmental policy, the municipality is equally responsible whether that action is to be taken only once or to be taken repeatedly. To deny compensation to the victim would therefore be contrary to the fundamental purpose of § 1983.

B

Having said this much, we hasten to emphasize that not every decision by municipal officers automatically subjects the municipality to § 1983 liability. Municipal liability attaches only where the decisionmaker possesses final authority to establish municipal policy with respect to the action ordered. The fact that a particular official —even a policymaking official—has discretion in the exercise of particular functions does not, without more, give rise to municipal liability based on an exercise of that discretion. . . . The official must also be responsible for establishing final government policy respecting such activity before the municipality can be held liable. Authority to make municipal policy may be granted directly by a legislative enactment or may be delegated by an official who possesses such authority, and of course, whether an official had final policymaking authority is a question of state law. However, like other governmental entities, municipalities often spread policymaking authitity among various officers and official bodies. As a result, particular officers may have authority to establish binding county policy respecting particular matters and to adjust

that policy for the county in changing circumstances. To hold a municipality liable for actions ordered by such officers exercising their policymaking authority is no more an application of the theory of *respondeat superior* than [is] holding the municipalities liable for the decisions of the City Councils. . . . In each case municipal liability attached to a single decision to take unlawful action made by municipal policymakers. We hold that municipal liability under § 1983 attaches where—and only where—a deliberate choice to follow a course of action is made from among various alternatives by the official responsible for establishing final policy with respect to the subject matter in question. . . .

C

Applying this standard to the case before us, we have little difficulty concluding that the Court of Appeals erred in dismissing petitioner's claim against the county. The Deputy Sheriffs who attempted to serve the capiases at petitioner's clinic found themselves in a difficult situation. Unsure of the proper course of action to follow, they sought instructions from their supervisors. The instructions they received were to follow the orders of the County Prosecutor. The Prosecutor made a considered decision based on his understanding of the law and commanded the officers forcibly to enter petitioner's clinic. That decision directly caused the violation of petitioner's Fourth Amendment rights.

Respondent argues that the County Prosecutor lacked authority to establish municipal policy respecting law enforcement practices because only the County Sheriff may establish policy respecting such practices. Respondent suggests that the County Prosecutor was merely rendering "legal advice" when he ordered the Deputy Sheriffs to "go in and get" the witnesses. Consequently, the argument concludes, the action of the individual Deputy Sheriffs in following this advice and forcibly entering petitioner's clinic was not pursuant to a properly established municipal policy.

We might be inclined to agree with respondent if we thought that the Prosecutor had only rendered "legal advice." However, the Court of Appeals concluded, based upon its examination of Ohio law, that both the County Sheriff and the County Prosecutor could establish county policy under appropriate circumstances, a conclusion that we do not question here. . . .

Pursuant to standard office proce-

dure, the Sheriff's office referred this matter to the Prosecutor and then followed his instructions. The Sheriff testified that his Department followed this practice under appropriate circumstances and that it was "the proper thing to do" in this case. We decline to accept respondent's invitation to overlook this delegation of authority by disingenuously labeling the Prosecutor's clear command mere "legal advice." In ordering the Deputy Sheriffs to enter petitioner's clinic, the County Prosecutor was acting as the final decisionmaker for the county, and the county may therefore be held liable under § 1983.

The decision of the Court of Appeals is reversed, and the case is remanded for further proceedings consistent with this opinion.

DISCUSSION QUESTIONS

1. What are the implications of treating the statement by the prosecutor, "to go in and get" the witnesses, as official governmental policy? Do you think the prosecutor foresaw that it would lead the police to chop down Pembaur's door? Would a reasonable administrator foresee such a consequence?

2. In a concurring opinion, Justice White emphasized that, at the time it occurred, "the forcible entry made in this case was not . . . illegal under federal, state, or local law." But later, in *Steagald* v. *U.S.*, 451 U.S. 204 (1981), such an entry was found unconstitutional. Justice Stevens's concurring opinon stated, "In my view, it is not at all surprising that [Cincinnati] . . . 'conceded' the retroactivity of Steagald. For Steagald plainly presented its holding as compelled by and presaged in, well-established precedent." Thus, Pembaur points to a very fundamental question: If a type of administrative action has never been directly challenged in court as unconstitutional, can a reasonable public administrator know, nevertheless, that the action is in fact unconstitutional? If so, what kind of knowledge of constitutional law and values must an administrator have? (See the conclusion of this chapter for more on this topic).

3. In *Canton* v. *Harris*, 103 L. Ed. 2d 412 (1989), the Supreme Court held that a municipality could be liable for indifference to training its employees when it could be foreseen that the lack of such training would likely result in violations of individuals' constitutional rights. Can you think of a situation in which failing to train public employees with regard to constitutional rights would probably lead to infringements of those rights? Are there many such situations?

CASE 2.4:
PUBLIC ADMINISTRATORS'
CONSTITUTIONAL RIGHT TO
DISOBEY

John R. HARLEY
v.
SCHUYLKILL COUNTY et al.
Civ. A. No. 78-861.
United States District Court,
E. D. Pennsylvania.
Aug. 23, 1979.
476 F. Supp. 191

Summary

Discharged prison guard filed civil rights suit against county and warden, alleging that his discharge was wrongful in that it was a deprivation of his liberty interest without according him due process, constituted a violation of his First Amendment rights, was based on his refusal to perform an unconstitutional act, and constituted a violation of rights secured under the Pennsylvania Constitution. On a defense motion to dismiss, the District Court, Huyett, J., held that: (1) the right to refuse to perform an unconstitutional act is a right "secured by the Constitution" within the meaning of the Civil Rights Act of 1871; accordingly, in the instant case, prison guard had the right to refrain from performing an act, ordered by the warden, which would have deprived prisoner of his constitutional rights, and (2) a county is liable for acts of its employees which violate Article 1, Section 1 of the Pennsylvania Constitution, where those employees are acting within the scope of their official duties.

Motion denied.

Opinion

HUYETT, District Judge.
Plaintiff John R. Harley has brought this civil rights action, raising a variety of theories in support of his request for relief. . . .

There now remain[s] before us . . . [the] issue [ ] for decision: . . . whether the right to refuse to perform an unconstitutional act is a "right, privilege, or immunity secured by the Constitution and laws" within the meaning of 42 U.S.C. § 1983; . . .

I.

As this is a motion to dismiss, we must take plaintiff's factual allegations as true and construe them in a light most favorable to plaintiff. . . . The complaint alleges that plaintiff John Harley was employed by the Schuylkill County Prison as a prison guard. On February 28, 1976, plaintiff reported to work on the second shift and was informed by the Acting Deputy of the First Shift that defendant Joseph Dooley, at that time the Acting Warden of Schuylkill County Prison, had left orders that inmate Kenneth Hennessey was to "stand check" in front of his cell, even if he had to be dragged from his cell. . . . Upon examining Hennessey, plaintiff discovered that the inmate had previously been beaten and, in fact, Hennessey informed plaintiff that he had been dragged from his cell and beaten because he refused to stand check. . . .

Hennessey further informed plaintiff that he had refused to stand check because of his religious beliefs. . . .

Plaintiff determined that Hennessey intended to refuse to stand check again, and that at that time, under the circumstances, the only way that the "check could be effectuated would have been to use unwarranted force, which would aggravate Hennessey's injuries.". . . Plaintiff then proceeded, at the time of the first check, to secure Hennessey's cell and file a conduct report instead of forcing Hennessey to stand check. . . .

Later that evening, plaintiff informed Dooley of these events and stated that in plaintiff's opinion further physical abuse of Hennessey would be illegal and improper under the circumstances. . . . Dooley stated that he wanted Hennessey to stand check no matter what the circumstances and insisted that Hennessey be dragged from his cell. . . . Plaintiff continued to refuse to obey this order because he felt that it was immoral and illegal. The complaint further alleged that the orders given by Dooley were unconstitutional, and that "their effectuation deprived Hennessey of his Fourth, Eighth, and Fourteenth Amendment Rights under the Constitution of the United States, and such orders, if carried out by plaintiff, would have subjected plaintiff to liability for such unconstitutional acts." . . .

Subsequently, plaintiff and other guards met with the Schuylkill County Commissioners to discuss this incident. The meeting ended without resolution of the issues; however, the Commissioners stated that they would investigate the incident and notify plaintiff and the other guards of the results of the investigation. . . .

Plaintiff alleges that at no time during this meeting was he given notice of any charge for which he might be dismissed, nor was he given the opportunity to address any such charge. . . . Later, plaintiff was informed that he was discharged, but given no reasons for his discharge.

However, the Commissioners' reasons for discharging plaintiff were widely reported in area newspaper articles. According to those reports, plaintiff was discharged for causing dissension between Dooley and the guards in the second shift. . . . One of the defendants also appeared on a radio talk show and stated that plaintiff was dismissed for insubordination. . . .

Plaintiff alleges that the reasons given for his discharge were false. Finally, plaintiff alleges that, as a result of his discharge and the resultant injury to his good name and reputation, he was unable to find employment for approximately one year. . . . Additionally, plaintiff alleges that his political affiliation was a substantial factor in his discharge. . . .

II.

Plaintiff seeks relief pursuant to 42 U.S.C. § 1983 on the grounds that he was discharged for refusing to perform an unconstitutional act. In connection with this claim, it is important to note that plaintiff is *not* seeking to vindicate prisoner Hennessey's constitutional rights. Rather, plaintiff is asserting a right personal to him; the right to refuse an order which would result in the violation of another's constitutional rights. The question presented here is whether this "right" is a "right[s], privilege[s], or immunit[y] secured by the Constitution and laws" as required by 42 U.S.C. § 1983.

At first blush, this question would appear to be one for which there is a simple answer, buttressed by a plethora of authority. In fact, there are surprisingly few authorities on this issue, and we could locate no case which discusses the matter in any great depth. *See, e. g., Parrish v. Civil Service Commission of County of Alameda, . . .* 425 P.2d 223 (1967) (holds that there is a right to refuse to obey an unconstitutional order; however, it is not clear from this case whether this right is secured by the United States Constitution); . . . Despite the absence of authority, however, we are confident that the right to refuse to violate another's federal constitutional rights is a right secured by the constitution.

*   *   *

Under the facts as alleged in the complaint, plaintiff would have been liable for a deprivation of Hennessey's constitutional rights if he had proceeded to obey the order given to him. . . . To put the matter another way, plaintiff had a clear duty under the constitution to refrain from acting in a manner that would deprive Hennessey of his constitutional rights. If plaintiff is under a *duty* to refrain from performing an act, then we believe that he has the concurrent *right* to so act. To hold otherwise would create an unconscionable burden upon one charged with the duty to uphold another's constitutional rights.

The issue remaining is whether that right is one "secured by the Constitution." The *duty* to refrain from acting in a manner which would deprive another of constitutional rights is a duty created and imposed by the constitution itself. It is logical to believe that the concurrent *right* is also one which is created and secured by the constitution. Therefore, we hold that the right to refuse to perform an unconstitutional act is a right "secured by the Constitution" within the meaning of § 1983.

We believe that our conclusion is supported by strong policy considerations. Parties such as plaintiff, who are acting in the capacities of prison administrators, policemen and the like, may daily be faced with situations where they are required to act in a manner which is consonant with the constitutional rights of others who are subject to their authority. The potential for abuse in these situations scarcely needs to be mentioned. If such persons are to be *encouraged* to respect the constitutional rights of others, they must at least have the minimal assurance that their actions are also protected by the constitution in those cases where they are confronted with the difficult choice of obeying an official order or violating another's constitutional rights.

DISCUSSION QUESTIONS

1. How might public adminstrators' right to disobey unconstitutional orders affect hierarchical control and accountability in public agencies?
2. Assuming that the right to disobey is constitutionally protected, how would you deal with a subordinate who (a) correctly asserted that one of your orders was unconstitutional, and (b) incorrectly so asserted and refused to obey?
3. Suppose you were a police officer in the Pembaur case (Case 2.3) and were ordered to chop down the door. Suppose, in addition, that you knew such an action in those circumstances would be an unconstitutional breach of the Fourth Amendment, even though it had never actually been declared so by a court. What would you do?

CONCLUSION

The cases in this section clearly indicate that under current judicial doctrines public administrators are expected to know the constitutional law that is relevant to their jobs. Such knowledge is now a matter of basic job competence. The public administrator who lacks reasonable knowledge of the constitutional rights of those individuals on whom he or she acts may face stiff liabilities, including punitive damages, as in *Smith* v. *Wade*. However, as suggested by *Pembaur* v. *Cincinnati*, the Constitution is more than the sum of specific past decisions. As the courts are called on to apply constitutional principles to new situations and circumstances, they may articulate rights that have never been declared before. Yet, in constitutional theory, these are not really "new" rights. They are considered to have always existed even though they were not explicitly declared by the courts. Sometimes, the judiciary will reverse its doctrines. But here too, it is apt to avoid the image of creating new constitutional rights (or doing away with existing ones). Rather, it is likely to indicate that previously the proper application of constitutional principles to the circumstances involved was misunderstood or that social, political, and/or economic changes in American life compel a different interpretation of those principles. For instance, in 1976 and again in 1980, the Supreme Court declared unconstitutional a common administrative practice that has been used throughout the history of the United States at all levels of government—that of partisan firings from the public service (*Elrod* v. *Burns*, 427 U.S. 347 [1976], Case 4.2; *Branti* v. *Finkel*, 445 U.S. 507 [1980]).

Consequently, the public administrator who would have constitutional competence must be aware not only of specific judicial decisions, but also of general constitutional principles and broad judicial tendencies in interpreting them. Of course, the administrator who harbors doubts about the constitutionality of an action should consult with his or her agency's attorney. This book is intended to convey basic knowledge of constitutional law that is generally essential to public administrators. Although this is accomplished in the remaining chapters, a few basic frames of reference are mentioned here.

First, the judiciary values a robust scope of individual rights. Constitutional rights are not absolute, but the courts do not accept lightly their infringement. Generally, governments are required to have compelling interests in order to impinge permissibly on individuals' constitutional rights. Mere administrative convenience is not likely to be a sufficient basis for abridging such rights.

Second, where it is deemed necessary that rights be curtailed, the courts generally favor adopting the alternative approach that is least restrictive of their exercise. Regulations that are overly broad, in the sense of prohibiting more than they need to, are likely to be ruled unconstitutional. The same is true of those that are so vague that it is impossible for individuals to know what kinds of activity they prohibit. Additionally, a regulation may be unconstitutional because it has a chilling effect on the exercise of constitutionally protected rights. For instance, a regulation requiring public employees to divulge all the organizations to which they belong might "chill" their freedom of association (see *Shelton* v.

Tucker, 364 U.S. 479 [1960]). Finally, in terms of equal protection, remedies for past unconstitutional discrimination that create differential treatment based on race (and presumably ethnicity, sex, and religion as well) must be "narrowly tailored" so that they do not place unnecessary burdens on individuals who were not parties to the discrimination involved (*U.S.* v. *Paradise*, 94 L.Ed. 2d 203 [1987], Case 4.3). The application of these general concerns to public administration will be considered in more detail in the remainder of this book.

3

DECISION-MAKING

Decision-making is a central administrative activity. It has been the focus of study at least since the 1940s, when Herbert Simon wrote, in his classic work *Administrative Behavior*, that "The task of 'deciding' pervades the entire administrative organization. . . ."[1] It is difficult to think of public administrative activities that do not require decision-making of some sort. Certainly budgeting, personnel administration, and organizing administrative structures and work processes are completely infused with the need to make decisions. At a broader level, public administrators must make decisions regarding the interpretation of statutes and court rulings. Many agencies are charged with rule-making and adjudication, both of which are decision-making processes. The implementation of agency missions also requires a great deal of decision-making: How should broad legal mandates or objectives be applied to specific cases? How strictly should a regulation be enforced? Where should a field office or a military base be located? To whom should a contract be let? When should the agency pursue its objectives through litigation? When should it settle out of court? Which of the multitude of private organizations subject to agency jurisdiction should be inspected or audited? More problematically, if the agency lacks the resources to enforce its regulations universally, on what basis should selective enforcement and selective nonenforcement occur? These are some of the kinds of decisions administrators face daily.

[1]Herbert Simon, *Administrative Behavior: A Study of Decision-Making Process in Administrative Organization*, 2nd ed. (New York: Free Press, 1957), p.1. Originally copyrighted in 1945.

Because public administration requires decision-making, administrators *must* exercise considerable discretion, whether in formulating public policies, developing the means to achieve their objectives, or in implementing them. However, the exercise of administrative discretion is in general tension with the Constitution's firm commitment to the rule of law. In fact, as the fledgling American administrative state grew during the early part of the twentieth century, a very influential legal scholar, Roscoe Pound, thought that administrative adjudication was "one of those reversions to justice *without* law."[2]

This chapter discusses three major types of administrative decision-making and how the dynamic of each is constrained by constitutional requirements. Its purpose is to foster constitutional competence by showing the pitfalls of standard decision-making processes. It is important to emphasize that the chapter is concerned with the decision-making models themselves, and their congruity with contemporary constitutional law, rather than the specific content of particular administrative decisions and the actions following from them. As we will see throughout this book, specific administrative actions in pursuit of standard administrative values can violate the Constitution in a number of ways and for a variety of reasons.

MODEL I: INTUITION

Intuition can be defined as the "direct perception of truth or fact, independent of any reasoning process" or "a keen and quick insight."[3] Everyone relies on intuition on occasion, especially when dealing with other people. We often reach quick judgments or feel as though we "just know" something, even though we cannot explain how in rational or logical terms. Of course, sometimes intuitive judgments are wrong, just as may be the most formally reasoned deductive or inductive conclusions. Although public administrators in a wide variety of settings may use intuition from time to time, those who are engaged in "street-level bureaucracy" must rely on it constantly in order to do their jobs properly.

In *Terry* v. *Ohio* (1968), Chief Justice Earl Warren considered "the role of the Fourth Amendment in the confrontation on the street between the citizen and the policeman . . . ."[4] Later, in 1980, Michael Lipsky's *Street-Level Bureaucracy* formalized the concept and brought it to the forefront of public administrative study. Lipsky defines street-level bureaucrats in the following terms:

> public service workers who interact directly with citizens in the course of their jobs, and who have substantial discretion in the execution of their work. . . . Typical street-level bureaucrats are teachers, police officers and other law enforcement personnel, social workers, [trial] judges, public lawyers and other court officers,

[2]Roscoe Pound, "Justice According to Law," *Columbia Law Review*, 14 (1914), 1–26, at p. 18.
[3]*Random House Dictionary* (New York: Random House, 1980).
[4]*Terry* v. *Ohio*, 392 U.S. 1, 4 (1968).

health workers, and many other public employees who grant access to government programs and provide services within them.[5]

He notes that

> . . .when taken together the individual decisions of these workers become, or add up to, agency policy. Whether government policy is to deliver 'goods'—such as welfare or public housing—or to confer status—such as 'criminal' or 'mentally ill'—the discretionary actions of public employees are the benefits and sanctions of government programs or determine access to government rights and benefits.[6]

Among the major characteristics of street-level bureaucrats' jobs are that they: (a) constantly interact with members of the public in face-to-face encounters; (b) have considerable independence, because they often work in the absence of direct visual or close proximate supervision and because a great deal of information about their conduct is supplied by the street-level bureaucrats themselves; (c) are in a position to have a great impact on the individuals on whom they act, or chose not to act; (d) tend to interact with "clients" who would prefer not to have to go through the encounter, even though they might want a benefit, such as public housing, that might result from it; (e) work with heavy caseloads in an environment of scarce resources and, sometimes, one in which physical and psychological threats are common; (f) have limited control over their "involuntary" clients, who may not be well socialized to accept administrative authority and to deal effectively with bureaucratic processes; and (g) face difficulties in adequately measuring their performance.

Street-level bureaucrats often adopt a posture toward their "clients" or target populations that has a very substantial impact on how these people are treated. For instance, officials in the U.S. Immigration and Naturalization Sevice (INS) call an illegal border crossing route near El Paso, Texas, the "Ho Chi Minh Trail" and consider those who use it to be an enemy.[7] Accordingly, illegal aliens, and even American citizens who fit a general profile, are treated in demeaning and dehumanizing ways. Such a posture helps individual street-level bureaucrats to form intuitive judgments about people.

Even in the absence of such a posture, however, street-level administrators often rely almost entirely on intuition in exercising discretion. The following illustration is from the testimony in court of a police officer who stopped a car at a roadblock because he thought it was being used to transport marihuana:

> Q Would you tell the Court, would you describe to the Court what their appearance was on the day in question that led you to believe that they were dope haulers. . . .
> A Well, they just look like dope haulers.
> Q Okay.
> A I got my own way of telling. . . .

[5]Michael Lipsky, *Street-Level Bureaucracy* (New York: Russell Sage, 1980), p. 3.
[6]Ibid.
[7]See the *New York Times*, August 4, 1986, p. 22.

Q . . .When in your State Police School did they tell you how to identify dope haulers?

A No, like I said, it comes with experience.

Q I see. Was it their age?

A No, I didn't know how old they was.

Q Okay, was it the length of their hair?

A No.

Q Was it the clothes they were wearing?

A No. It was the way they acted. Like I said, I got my own way of telling which you wouldn't have.

Q Okay.

A You know, I can't explain it to you.[8]

Even though the officer could not explain why he thought the car was carrying marihuana, he was correct in his assessment. But was he constitutional?

There is perhaps no proposition more fundamental to democratic constitutionalism in the United States than that government will be based on and subordinate to the rule of law. The Constitution is the "supreme law of the land." Governmental officials at all levels are required to swear or affirm their allegiance to it. All officials, including the President and his closest aides, are subject to constitutional and legal restrictions. Nobody is in any sense considered to be "above the law." This is the main reason why events such as the Watergate and Iran–Contra affairs are considered to constitute serious threats to American governance. But it is not always easy to square the rule of law with the exercise of unbridled discretion by public administrators or other government officials. Their actions should be directed by laws and rules, not personal judgments, prejudices, or intuition. As Justice Douglas vividly expressed it, "Yet if the individual is no longer to be sovereign, if the police can pick him up whenever they do not like the cut of his jib, if they can 'seize' and 'search' him in their discretion, we enter a new regime."[9]

Thus, the dilemma is that on the one hand, in order to do their jobs, street-level bureaucrats must often rely on their intuition (and they often are correct in so doing); while on the other hand, intuition, by its very nature, entails very broad discretion that cannot be assessed in rational terms by higher level officials and the courts. For every car hauling marihuana that is stopped by a particular police officer, an unknown number of others escape his or her detection. Others are mistakenly stopped, possibly in violation of their occupants' rights. *Delaware* v. *Prouse* (1979), Case 3.1, presented later in this chapter, addresses this dilemma.

MODEL II: RATIONAL COMPREHENSIVENESS

The rational-comprehensive decision-making model stands almost diametrically opposed to the exercise of intuition. It assumes that public administrators have

[8]*New Mexico v. Bloom*, 561 P.2d 925, 930 (1976).
[9]Dissent in *Terry v. Ohio*, 392 U.S. 1, 39 (1968).

the time, resources, and ability to analyze logically and comprehensively when making decisions. Rational comprehensiveness is the preferred model of orthodox and managerially oriented public administration. It relies on theory and organizational features, such as specialization and formalization, to enhance the rationality of administrative decisions.

In simplified form, the rational-comprehensive model consists of the following steps. First, in making decisions the public administrator must determine what are the objectives or ends of the public policy with which he or she is concerned. If the objectives are unclear, they should be clarified and expressed in operational terms; that is, in ways that can be observed and measured. For example, a policy such as equal employment opportunity is less operational than one of affirmative action, because the latter looks toward actual changes in the social composition of a work force rather than only changes in "opportunity," which are far more difficult to assess. Of course, the public administrator does not have a free hand in determining policy objectives. He or she is constrained by culture, socialization, training,[10] law, administrative regulations, hierarchical authority, jurisdictional specialization, and political factors, including checks and balances.

Second, once the objectives of public policy are established, various means for accomplishing them must be considered. If the requisite comprehensiveness is to be achieved, virtually all the potential means that can be identified must be analyzed. To be rational and comprehensive the public administrator must try to project *all* the consequences of each of the alternative means under consideration. This may require heavy reliance on theory, since it is highly unlikely that all the potential means have at one time or another been tested and evaluated in practice. Such analysis will often require the formulation of fundamental assumptions about how people behave and the use of simulations.

Third, the most appropriate means to the desired ends are chosen. Traditional public administrative theory favors the maximization of efficiency, economy, and effectiveness in the choice of means. If these core administrative values are not fully in harmony with one another, then some balance among them will be favored. Current approaches to public administration would also require that attention be paid to political and legal values, such as responsiveness and the protection of robust individual civil rights and liberties.

There has been a long-standing debate over whether the rational-comprehensive model can be widely used in American public administration.[11] In many cases, policy objectives are too unclear to be expressed in operational terms without losing significant political support for a program. Administrators do not necessarily have the time and resources to approach decisions in a dispassionate way and to engage in thorough analysis of alternative means and their appropriateness. More fundamentally, if one agrees with Simon that

[10]Charles Perrow, *Complex Organizations*, 3rd ed. (New York: Random House, 1986), pp. 129–30, discusses these constraints under the label of "premise controls."
[11]See Charles Lindblom, "The Science of 'Muddling Through,' " *Public Administrative Review*, 19 (Spring 1959), 79–88.

administrative rationality is "bounded," then the prospects for being fully, or even highly, rational are likewise limited.[12]

The rational-comprehensive model can also run into problems from a constitutional perspective. Its reliance on theory, particularly social scientific theory, leads to the use of categories, such as male and female, as a means of understanding and predicting how people behave. Such categories are common in political analysis, where familiar terms include the "Black" vote, "gender gap," and "labor" and "farm" vote. But the Constitution looks toward the individual, not the group to which he or she belongs, in determining rights and liberties. Broad social scientific generalizations may be constitutionally problematic as a basis for public policy, because by their very nature they are not intended to apply equally to each individual. By definition, they do not attempt to treat individuals on their own merits (see Case 5.2). Moreover, Equal Protection analysis under the Fourteenth and Fifth Amendments is skeptical of governmental action treating members of different social groups disparately. It considers some social scientific categorizations to be *suspect classifications* that can be constitutionally acceptable only if the government can show a compelling need for their use or, possibly, if the public policies based on them do not invidiously discriminate against any groups. For instance, any categorization based on race will be suspect, though some forms of affirmative action, which is not viewed as invidious or demeaning to any group, are constitutional.[13] Classifications that are not suspect, such as those based on age and, currently, sex, will be constitutionally deficient if the government cannot show an adequate rational basis for them. These constitutional requirements are discussed by the Supreme Court in Case 3.2, *Craig* v. *Boren* (1976), which is presented later in this chapter.

MODEL III: INCREMENTALISM

Incrementalism is a third common model of public administrative decision-making. It differs radically from the rational-comprehensive approach in its fundamental outlook. It assumes that the question for public administrators is more likely to be, "What should we do next?" rather than, "How should we maximize the attainment of our objectives?" Incrementalism proceeds step by step, often without a very clear or agreed on objective, in an effort to use whatever resources are available to further a program's general mission. It recognizes that in a pluralistic political system, characterized by fragmented power, the objectives of public policy must often necessarily be stated in vague and politically appealing terms in order to win sufficient support for a program or course of action. Lack of specificity is frequently the price of compromise and coalition building. Examples abound, but perhaps none is clearer than the Federal Communication Commission's charge to regulate the nation's airwaves in "the public convenience,

[12]Herbert Simon, *Models of Man* (New York: Wiley, 1957).
[13]*United States* v. *Paradise*, 94 L.Ed. 2d 203 (1987).

interest, or necessity." None of these terms has been precisely defined comprehensively, and each may conflict with the other two on occasion. But such language enables a broad majority of legislators and interested parties to support government regulation of radio and television broadcasting without having to agree on specific regulatory standards. Instead, the overall content of regulatory policy will be an outgrowth of numerous decisions by the FCC.

At the first stage of an incremental decision, ends and means are treated as a package rather than as distinct from one another. Since the ends of public policies are viewed as ill-defined and undefinable without jeopardizing political support, the decision-maker considers some plausible steps that might be taken to improve the conditions for which the program under his or her jurisdiction bears responsibility. The decision-maker recognizes that alternative steps may ultimately lead to different definitions of what the general policy will be.

After a few possible courses of action are identified and considered, one is selected. The main criterion is likely to be agreement or consensus among those concerned that the proposed step is desirable. Since the incremental approach is generally sensitive politics, a decision that generates support will be viewed as "good," whereas one that begets substantial opposition will typically be avoided. Again, the model enables concerned interests to agree on the next move even though they may differ substantially in their understandings of the overall policy's proper objectives.

Analysis tends to be more limited in the incremental appproach than in the rational-comprehensive model. A few means–ends packages are considered. One that is *satisfactory* is chosen. Little or no effort is made to reach an optimum decision that maximizes all the pertinent values. Moreover, in practice, reliance on theory is downgraded because incrementalism does not seek to be comprehensive, to maximize, or to predict the long-term consequences of decisions. Policy grows out of a succession of choices among limited means–ends packages and can be corrected whenever it appears to be on the wrong course.

Like the intuitive and rational-comprehensive models, the incremental approach has some political and constitutional pitfalls. By definition, it is conservative because its effort to change the status quo is incremental. Consequently, it is not suited to decisions regarding the adoption of fundamentally new policy directions or innovations. Since it is not comprehensive, it may neglect important political values and policy alternatives. Proceeding step by step, without a map, can lead decision-makers to an unexpected (and undesirable) place. Moreover, if an incremental decision-making process fails to take constitutional values into account in selecting its steps, the resulting policy may be unconstitutional. This possibility is illustrated by Case 3.3, *Hawkins* v. *Town of Shaw* (1971), the last case presented in this chapter. It shows that while each individual decision the town made in developing its infrastructure and economic base might have been constitutional and sensible on its own particular merits, taken together, the net result of a series of such decisions was to create such a broad disparity in public spending between White and Black neighborhoods as to violate the Equal Protection Clause of the Fourteenth Amendment. Similarly, it is easy to conceive of a series of incremental decisions maintaining de facto racial segregation in public schools and constitutionally inadequate conditions in public mental health facilities and prisons.[14]

Delaware v. *Prouse* explains why intuition alone will often be an unconstitutional basis for taking action considered injurious to an individual's constitutional rights. *Craig* v. *Boren* considers the difficulties that broad social scientific generalizations about group behavior can present in terms of the Constitution's guarantee of equal protection of the laws. *Hawkins* v. *Town of Shaw* illustrates how unchecked incrementalism can lead to broad and unconstitutional disparities in the treatment of different social groups. In considering these cases, it will be useful to think about other ways in which the administrative decisions they involve could have been made. Each case is followed by a series of discussion questions intended to facilitate a deeper exploration of each of the decision-making models and the constitutional constraints on them. The next chapter, on administrative effectiveness, augments the analysis of decision-making by considering the problem of selecting constitutional administrative means for implementing objectives.

ADDITIONAL READING

LINDBLOM, CHARLES E. "The Science of 'Muddling Through,'" *Public Administration Review*, 19 (Spring 1959), 79–88.

SIMON, HERBERT. *Administrative Behavior*, 3rd ed. New York: Free Press, 1976.

[14]See, for example, *Swann* v. *Charlotte–Mecklenburg Board of Education*, 403 U.S. 912 (1971); *Wyatt* v. *Stickney*, 325 F. Supp. 781 (1971); and *Rhodes* v. *Chapman*, 452 U.S. 337 (1981) (dealing with how the totality of conditions, rather than a single condition, may trigger violations of the Eighth Amendment).

CASE 3.1:
ADMINISTRATIVE INTUITION

STATE OF DELAWARE, Petitioner,

v

WILLIAM J. PROUSE, III
440 US 648
[No. 77–1571]
Argued January 17, 1979.
Decided March 27, 1979.

Opinion

Mr. Justice **White** delivered the opinion of the Court.

The question is whether it is an unreasonable seizure under the Fourth and Fourteenth Amendments to stop an automobile, being driven on a public highway, for the purpose of checking the driving license of the operator and the registration of the car, where there is neither probable cause to believe nor reasonable suspicion that the car is being driven contrary to the laws governing the operation of motor vehicles or that either the car or any of its occupants is subject to seizure or detention in connection with the violation of any other applicable law.

I

At 7:20 p.m. on November 30, 1976, a New Castle County, Del., patrolman in a police cruiser stopped the automobile occupied by respondent. The patrolman smelled marihuana smoke as he was walking toward the stopped vehicle, and he seized marihuana in plain view on the car floor. Respondent was subsequently indicted for illegal posession of a controlled substance. At a hearing on respondent's motion to suppress the marihuana seized as a result of the stop, the patrolman testified that prior to stopping the vehicle he had observed neither traffic or equipment violations nor any suspicious activity, and that he made the stop only in order to check the driver's license and registration. The patrolman was not acting pursuant to any standards, guidelines or procedures pertaining to document spot checks, promulgated by either his department or the State Attorney General. Characterizing the stop as "routine," the patrolman explained, "I saw the car in the area and wasn't answering any complaints, so I decided to pull them off.". . . The trial court granted the motion to suppress, finding the stop and detention to have been wholly capricious and therefore violative of the Fourth Amendment.

The Delaware Supreme Court affirmed, noting first that "[t]he issue of the legal validity of systematic, roadblock-type stops of a number of vehicles for license and vehicle registration check is *not* now before the Court,". . . The court held that "a random stop of a motorist in the absence of specific articulable facts which justify the stop by indicating a reasonable suspicion that a violation of the law has occurred is constitutionally impermissible and violative of the Fourth and Fourteenth Amendments to the United States Constitution.". . . We granted certiorari to resolve the conflict between this decision, which is in accord with decisions in five other jurisdictions, and the contrary determination in six jurisdictions that the Fourth Amendment does not prohibit the kind of automobile stop that occurred here. . . .

*   *   *

III

The Fourth and Fourteenth Amendments are implicated in this case because stopping an automobile and detaining its occupants constitute a "seizure" within the meaning of those Amendments, even though the purpose of the stop is limited and the resulting detention quite brief. . . . The essential purpose of the proscriptions in the Fourth Amendment is to impose a standard of "reasonableness" upon the exercise of discretion by government officials, including law enforcement agents, in order " 'to safeguard the privacy and security of individuals against arbitrary invasions. . . .' " . . . Thus, the permissibility of a particular law enforcement practice is judged by balancing its intrusion on the individual's Fourth Amendment interests against its promotion of legitimate governmental interests. Implemented in this manner, the reasonableness standard usually requires, at a minimum, that the facts upon which an intrusion is based be capable of measurement against "an objective standard," whether this be probable cause or a less stringent test. In those situations in which the balance of interests precludes insistence upon "some quantum of individualized suspicion," other safeguards are generally relied upon to assure that the individual's reasonable expectation of privacy is not "subject to the discretion of the official in the field." . . .

In this case, however, the State of Delaware urges that patrol officers be subject to no constraints in deciding which automobiles shall be stopped for a license and registration check because the State's interest in discretionary spot checks as a means of ensuring the safety of its roadways outweighs the resulting intrusion on the privacy and security of the persons detained.

*   *   *

V

But the State of Delaware urges that even if discretionary spot checks such as occurred in this case intrude upon motorists as much as or more than do the roving patrols held impermissible in Brignoni-Ponce,* these stops are reasonable under the Fourth Amendment because the State's interest in the practice as a means of promoting public safety upon its roads more than outweighs the intrusion entailed. Although the record discloses no statistics concerning the extent of the problem of lack of highway safety, in Delaware or in the Nation as a whole, we are aware of the danger to life and property posed by vehicular traffic and of the difficulties that even a cautious and an experienced driver may encounter. We agree that the States have a vital interest in ensuring that only those qualified to do so are permitted to operate motor vehicles, that these vehicles are fit for safe opera-

tion, and hence that licensing, registration, and vehicle inspection requirements are being observed. Automobile licenses are issued periodically to evidence that the drivers holding them are sufficiently familiar with the rules of the road and are physically qualified to operate a motor vehicle. The registration requirement and, more pointedly, the related annual inspection requirement in Delaware are designed to keep dangerous automobiles off the road. Unquestionably, these provisions, properly administered, are essential elements in a highway safety program. Furthermore, we note that the State of Delaware requires a minimum amount of insurance coverage as a condition to automobile registration, implementing its legitimate interest in seeing to it that its citizens have protection when involved in a motor vehicle accident.

The question remains, however, whether in the service of these important ends the discretionary spot check is a sufficiently productive mechanism to justify the intrusion upon Fourth Amendment interests which such stops entail. On the record before us, that question must be answered in the negative. Given the alternative mechanisms available, both those in use and those that might be adopted, we are unconvinced that the incremental contribution to highway safety of the random spot check justifies the practice under the Fourth Amendment.

The foremost method of enforcing traffic and vehicle safety regulations, it must be recalled, is acting upon observed violations. Vehicle stops for traffic violations occur countless times each day; and on these occasions, licenses and registration papers are subject to inspection and drivers without them will be ascertained. Furthermore, drivers without licenses are presumably the less safe drivers whose propensities may well exhibit themselves.

---

*U.S. v. *Brignoni-Ponce*, 422 U.S. 873 (1975)—editors' note.

Absent some empirical data to the contrary, it must be assumed that finding an unlicensed driver among those who commit traffic violations is a much more likely event than finding an unlicensed driver by choosing randomly from the entire universe of drivers. If this were not so, licensing of drivers would hardly be an effective means of promoting roadway safety. It seems common sense that the percentage of all drivers on the road who are driving without a license is very small and that the number of licensed drivers who will be stopped in order to find one unlicensed operator will be large indeed. The contribution to highway safety made by discretionary stops selected from among drivers generally will therefore be marginal at best. Furthermore, and again absent something more than mere assertion to the contrary, we find it difficult to believe that the unlicensed driver would not be deterred by the possibility of being involved in a traffic violation or having some other experience calling for proof of his entitlement to drive but that he would be deterred by the possibility that he would be one of those chosen for a spot check. In terms of actually discovering unlicensed drivers or deterring them from driving, the spot check does not appear sufficiently productive to qualify as a reasonable law enforcement practice under the Fourth Amendment.

Much the same can be said about the safety aspects of automobiles as distinguished from drivers. Many violations of minimum vehicle-safety requirements are observable, and something can be done about them by the observing officer, directly and immediately. Furthermore, in Delaware, as elsewhere, vehicles must carry and display current license plates, which themselves evidence that the vehicle is properly registered; and, under Delaware law, to qualify for annual registration a vehicle must pass the annual safety inspection and be properly insured. It does not appear, therefore, that a stop of a Delaware-registered vehicle is necessary in order to ascertain compliance with the State's registration requirements; and because there is nothing to show that a significant percentage of automobiles from other States do not also require license plates indicating current registration, there is no basis for concluding that stopping even out-of-state cars for document checks substantially promotes the State's interest.

The marginal contribution to roadway safety possibly resulting from a system of spot checks cannot justify subjecting every occupant of every vehicle on the roads to a seizure—limited in magnitude compared to other intrusions but nonetheless constitutionally cognizable—at the unbridled discretion of law enforcement officials. To insist neither upon an appropriate factual basis for suspicion directed at a particular automobile nor upon some other substantial and objective standard or rule to govern the exercise of discretion "would invite intrusions upon constitutionally guaranteed rights based on nothing more substantial than inarticulate hunches. . . ." . . . By hypothesis, stopping apparently safe drivers is necessary only because the danger presented by some drivers is not observable at the time of the stop. When there is not probable cause to believe that a driver is violating any one of the multitude of applicable traffic and equipment regulations—or other articulable basis amounting to reasonable suspicion that the driver is unlicensed or his vehicle unregistered—we cannot conceive of any legitimate basis upon which a patrolman could decide that stopping a particular driver for a spot check would be more productive than stopping any other driver. This kind of standardless and unconstrained discretion is the evil the Court has discerned when in previous cases it has insisted that the discretion of the official in the field be circumscribed, at least to some extent. . . .

VI

The "grave danger" of abuse of discretion . . . does not disappear simply because the automobile is subject to state regulation resulting in numerous instances of police-citizen contact. . . . Only last Term we pointed out that "if the government intrudes . . . the privacy interest suffers whether the government's motivation is to investigate violations of criminal laws or breaches of other statutory or regulatory standards.". . . There are certain "relatively unique circumstances," . . . in which consent to regulatory restrictions is presumptively concurrent with participation in the regulated enterprise. . . . Otherwise, regulatory inspections unaccompanied by any quantum of individualized, articulable suspicion must be undertaken pursuant to previously specified "neutral criteria.". . .

An individual operating or traveling in an automobile does not lose all reasonable expectation of privacy simply because the automobile and its use are subject to government regulation. Automobile travel is a basic, pervasive, and often necessary mode of transportation to and from one's home, workplace, and leisure activities. Many people spend more hours each day traveling in cars than walking on the streets. Undoubtedly, many find a greater sense of security and privacy in traveling in an automobile than they do in exposing themselves by pedestrian or other modes of travel. Were the individual subject to unfettered governmental intrusion every time he entered an automobile, the security guaranteed by the Fourth Amendment would be seriously circumscribed. . . . [P]eople are not shorn of all Fourth Amendment protection when they step from their homes onto the public sidewalks. Nor are they shorn of those interests when they step from the sidewalks into their automobiles.

VII

Accordingly, we hold that except in those situations in which there is at least articulable and reasonable suspicion that a motorist is unlicensed or that an automobile is not registered, or that either the vehicle or an occupant is otherwise subject to seizure for violation of law, stopping an automobile and detaining the driver in order to check his driver's license and the registration of the automobile are unreasonable under the Fourth Amendment. This holding does not preclude the State of Delaware or other States from developing methods for spot checks that involve less intrusion or that do not involve the unconstrained exercise of discretion. Questioning of all oncoming trafic at roadblock-type stops is one possible alternative. We hold only that persons in automobiles on public roadways may not for that reason alone have their travel and privacy interfered with at the unbridled discretion of police officers. . . .

DISCUSSION QUESTIONS

1. It is difficult to ignore the fact that in Prouse, the police officer stopped a car in which a crime was occurring. In this sense, he was doing his job properly. The chances of randomly stopping someone smoking marihauna in a moving

vehicle in Delaware must be extremely remote. Since the officer was unable to provide even an articulable suspicion that such a crime was taking place, it appears that his decision to stop Prouse was intuitive. Thus, the facts of the case suggest that the patrolman's intuition worked well. Yet, the Supreme Court's opinion prohibits sole reliance on intuition in such circumstances because it is neither articulable nor, by definition, reasonable. Do you think street-level administrators can do their jobs properly without relying on intuition? Under what circumstances would intuition seem most important? Least important? If you were the administrative supervisor of officers, such as the one in Prouse, how would you recommend that your subordinates become "constitutionally competent" while doing their jobs well?

2. In dissent, Justice Rehnquist pointed out that because Justice White's opinion would allow the States to stop *all* cars at roadblocks for license and registration checks, the majority's fundamental concern was with the exercise of discretionary authority by police, rather than the intrusiveness of the stops themselves. Indeed, in some ways stopping all motorists is more intrusive than stopping only some. Why does the majority have greater difficulty with discretionary stops than it does with comprehensive stops? Do you find its argument convincing?

3. Suppose the officer had decided to stop Prouse on the basis of a written profile of a motorist likely to be smoking marihuana. What questions would you raise in addressing the administrative utility and constitutionality of reliance on such a profile? As a place to start your analysis, consider the practice at issue in *U.S.* v. *Brignoni–Ponce*, noted earlier in the chapter, of roving vehicle stops made by the U.S. Border Patrol partly on the basis that those being stopped "looked Mexican."

CASE 3.2:
RATIONAL-COMPREHENSIVE DECISIONS: SOCIAL SCIENTIFIC GENERALIZATION VERSUS EQUAL PROTECTION

CRAIG ET AL. *v.* BOREN, GOVERNOR OF OKLAHOMA, ET AL.
429 US 190
APPEAL FROM THE UNITED STATES DISTRICT COURT FOR THE WESTERN DISTRICT OF OKLAHOMA
No. 75-628. Argued October 5, 1976—Decided December 20, 1976

Opinion

MR. JUSTICE BRENNAN delivered the opinion of the Court.

The interaction of two sections of an Oklahoma statute, Okla. Stat., Tit. 37,

§§ 241 and 245 (1958 and Supp. 1976), prohibits the sale of "nonintoxicating" 3.2% beer to males under the age of 21 and to females under the age of 18. The question to be decided is whether such a gender-based differential constitutes a denial to males 18–20 years of age of the equal protection of the laws in violation of the Fourteenth Amendment.

*   *   *

[II] C

We accept for purposes of discussion the District Court's identification of the objective underlying §§ 241 and 245 as the enhancement of traffic safety. Clearly, the protection of public health and safety represents an important function of state and local governments. However, appellees' statistics in our view cannot support the conclusion that the gender-based distinction closely serves to achieve that objective and therefore the distinction cannot . . . withstand equal protection challenge.

The appellees introduced a variety of statistical surveys. First, an analysis of arrest statistics for 1973 demonstrated that 18–20-year-old male arrests for "driving under the influence" and "drunkenness" substantially exceeded female arrests for that same age period. Similarly, youths aged 17–21 were found to be overrepresented among those killed or injured in traffic accidents, with males again numerically exceeding females in this regard. Third, a random roadside survey in Oklahoma City revealed that young males were more inclined to drive and drink beer than were their female counterparts. Fourth, Federal Bureau of Investigation nationwide statistics exhibited a notable increase in arrests for "driving under the influence." Finally, statistical evidence gathered in other jurisdictions, particularly Minnesota and Michigan, was offered to corroborate Oklahoma's experience by indicating the pervasiveness of youthful participation in motor vehicle accidents following the imbibing of alcohol. Conceding that "the

case is not free from doubt," . . . the District Court nonetheless concluded that this statistical showing substantiated "a rational basis for the legislative judgment underlying the challenged classification.". . .

Even were this statistical evidence accepted as accurate, it nevertheless offers only a weak answer to the equal protection question presented here. The most focused and relevant of the statistical surveys, arrests of 18–20-year-olds for alcohol-related driving offenses, exemplifies the ultimate unpersuasiveness of this evidentiary record. Viewed in terms of the correlation between sex and the actual activity that Oklahoma seeks to regulate—driving while under the influence of alcohol—the statistics broadly establish that .18% of females and 2% of males in that age group were arrested for that offense. While such a disparity is not trivial in a statistical sense, it hardly can form the basis for employment of a gender line as a classifying device. Certainly if maleness is to serve as a proxy for drinking and driving, a correlation of 2% must be considered an unduly tenuous "fit." Indeed, prior cases have consistently rejected the use of sex as a decisionmaking factor even though the statutes in question certainly rested on far more predictive empirical relationships than this.

Moreover, the statistics exhibit a variety of other shortcomings that seriously impugn their value to equal protection analysis. Setting aside the obvious methodological problems, the surveys do not adequately justify the salient features of Oklahoma's gender-based traffic-safety law. None purports to measure the use and dangerousness of 3.2% beer as opposed to alcohol generally, a detail that is of particular importance since, in light of its low alcohol level, Oklahoma apparently considers the 3.2% beverage to be "nonintoxicating.". . . Moreover, many of the studies, while graphically documenting the unfortunate increase in driving while under the influence of alcohol, make no effort to relate their findings to age-sex differentials as involved here. Indeed, the only survey that explicitly centered its attention upon young drivers and their use of beer—albeit apparently not of the diluted 3.2% variety—reached results that hardly can be viewed as impressive in justifying either a gender or age classification.

There is no reason to belabor this line of analysis. It is unrealistic to expect either members of the judiciary or state officials to be well versed in the rigors of experimental or statistical technique. But this merely illustrates that proving broad sociological propositions by statistics is dubious business, and one that inevitably is in ten-

sion with the normative philosophy that underlies the Equal Protection Clause. Suffice to say that the showing offered by the appellees does not satisfy us that sex represents a legitimate accurate proxy for the regulation of drinking and driving. In fact, when it is further recognized that Oklahoma's statute prohibits only the selling of 3.2% beer to young males and not their drinking the beverage once acquired (even after purchase by their 18–20-year-old female companions), the relationship between gender and traffic safety becomes far too tenuous to satisfy . . . [the] requirement that the gender-based difference be substantially related to achievement of the statutory objective.

We hold, therefore, that . . . Oklahoma's 3.2% beer statute invidiously discriminates against males 18–20 years of age.

DISCUSSION QUESTIONS

1. The Court reasoned that "proving broad sociological propositions by statistics a . . . business . . . that inevitably is in tension with the normative philosophy that underlies the Equal Protection Clause." What is that philosophy and how is it related to the use of categories, such as female and male or White and Black, in social scientific analysis? What are the implications of the tension of which the Court speaks for the use of social science in public policy-making and implementation?

2. In a concurring opinion, Justice Stevens argued that ". . . the empirical data submitted by the State accentuate the unfairness of treating all 18–20-year-old males as inferior to their female counterparts. The legislation imposes a restraint on 100% of the males in the class allegedly because about 2% of them have probably violated one or more laws relating to the consumption of alcholic [sic] beverages. It is unlikely that this law will have a significant deterrent effect either on that 2% or on the law-abiding 98%. But even assuming some such slight benefit, it does not seem to me that an insult to all of the young men of the State can be justified by visiting the sins of the 2% on the 98%." How does this rejection of the classification by sex differ from that of the Court's majority opinion? What are the implications of Stevens's position for the use of social scientific generalizations in public policy?

3. In dissent, Justice Rehnquist maintained that "[t]he rationality of a statutory classification for equal protection purposes does not depend upon the statistical 'fit' between the class and the trait sought to be singled out. It turns on whether there may be a sufficiently higher incidence of the trait within the included class than in the excluded class to justify different treatment." How

does this dissenting position differ from those of the majority and Justice Stevens?

4. Assess the compatibility of each of the positions noted in the foregoing questions with rational-comprehensive decision-making.

**CASE 3.3:
INCREMENTALISM: NEGLECTING
IMPORTANT CONSTITUTIONAL
VALUES WITHOUT A MASTER PLAN**

Andrew HAWKINS et al., Plaintiffs,
Appellants,
v.
TOWN OF SHAW, MISSISSIPPI,
et al.,
Defendants-Appellees.
No. 29013.
United States Court of Appeals,
Fifth Circuit,
Jan. 23, 1971
437 F.2d 1286

Summary

The Court of Appeals, Tuttle, Circuit Judge, held that disparities in providing municipal services in that nearly 98% of all homes fronting on unpaved streets in town were occupied by blacks and 97% of homes not served by sanitary sewers were in black neighborhoods, and fact that all new mercury vapor street lighting fixtures had been installed in white neighborhoods resulted in denial of equal protection. . . .

Opinion

TUTTLE, Circuit Judge:
Referring to a portion of town or a segment of society as being "on the other side of the tracks" has for too long been a familiar expression to most Americans. Such a phrase immediately conjures up an area characterized by poor housing, overcrowded conditions and, in short, overall deterioration. While there may be many reasons why such areas exist in nearly all of our cities, one reason that cannot be accepted is the discriminatory provision of municipal services based on race. It is such a reason that is alleged as the basis of this action.

Appellants are Negro citizens of the Town of Shaw, Mississippi. They alleged that the town has provided various municipal services including street paving and street lighting, sanitary sewers, surface water drainage as well as water mains and fire hydrants in a discriminatory manner based on race. Appellants brought a class action seeking injunctive relief under 42 U. S .C. § 1983 against the town, the town's mayor, clerk and five aldermen. . . .

FACTS

The Town of Shaw, Mississippi, was incorporated in 1886 and is located in the

Mississippi Delta. Its population, which has undergone little change since 1930, consists of about 2,500 people—1,500 black and 1,000 white residents. Residential racial segregation is almost total. There are 451 dwelling units occupied by blacks in town, and, of these, 97% (439) are located in neighborhoods in which no whites reside. That the town's policies in administering various municipal services have led to substantially less attention being paid to the black portion of town is clear.

* * *

STREET PAVING

The undisputed evidence is that 97% of all those who live in homes fronting on unpaved streets are black. In attempting to justify this, the trial court stated:

"Initially, concrete paving was afforded to those streets serving commercial and industrial interests and to the areas nearest the town's center. In some cases this resulted in more street paving in white than Negro neighborhoods, but the paving actually done in the municipality was on the basis of general usage, traffic needs and other objective criteria. Residential neighborhoods not facing principal streets or thoroughfares long remained unpaved, regardless of their character as white or black neighborhoods."

The record simply does not support the justification that streets were built according to traffic needs and usage. The town's one engineer who made recommendation to defendants as to the priority of street paving projects testified that he had never surveyed the town to determine which streets were used the most. Nor did he compare the usage of streets in black neighborhoods. He even admitted that he was not familiar with the usage of streets in the Promised Land Addition, which is one of the oldest and largest black neighborhoods in Shaw.

The finding that many streets were paved in the business areas and that this resulted, "in some cases," in providing more paving in white rather than black neighborhoods, also fails to justify the existing disparities. As appellants point out, in 1956 when the first residential streets in black neighborhoods were paved, 96% of the white residents of Shaw already lived on paved streets, most of which had been paved during the 1930's. Many of these streets, however, were solely residential, and could not possibly serve commercial, industrial or any public buildings.

The trial court also found that many of the streets on which blacks live were too narrow to pave. The town engineer had testifed that streets in black neighborhoods had not been paved because they did not have the fifty foot right-of-way he considered necessary. However, as appellants point out, most of the streets in Shaw, in both black and white neighborhoods, have platted rights of way that range from 30 to 40 feet. Further, while most streets *under* 50 feet in white neighborhoods are paved, those in the black areas are not.

In short, even if we assume that such criteria as traffic usage, need and width constitute compelling state interests, they were not applied equally to both black and white neighborhoods. We are led to the inevitable conclusion that Shaw's policies, which have resulted in such significant disparities between the black and white portions of town, are, in no way justifiable.

STREET LIGHTS

The record clearly shows that absolutely no high power mercury vapor street lights have been installed in black residential areas. Only the much weaker bare bulb fixtures are to be found. The trial court stated that there was no showing that the lighting was inadequate and, in any event:

"The brighter lights are provided for those streets forming either a state highway, or serving commercial, industrial or special school needs, or otherwise carrying the heaviest traffic load."

The fact that there was no specific showing that lighting was not adequate is not significant. What is significant is that it is clear that all of the *better* lighting that exists in Shaw can be found *only* in the white parts of town. Surely, this cannot be justified merely on the ground that the bare bulb fixtures are not shown to be inadequate. One might readily assume, it seems, that the modern high intensity lights are *more* adequate from the fact of their use by the city. *Improvements* to existing facilities provided in a discriminatory manner may also constitute a violation of equal protection.

The other justifications accepted by the trial court again fail, for if the "special needs" criteria were applied equally for the benefit of both black and white citizens, all the high intensity lights would not be in only the white areas of town. For example, while streets with heavy traffic serving commercial and public centers, such as Gale Street, in black areas have only bare bulb fixtures, many little traveled streets in white neighborhoods have the high intensity variety. In short, we are again convinced that as with the paving of streets, the placement of new light fixtures only in the white portion of town cannot be justified.

SANITARY SEWERS

While 99% of white residents are served by a sanitary sewer system, nearly 20% of the black population is not so served. The trial court thought this was justified by noting that:

"Part of the problem in reaching all older unserved areas has been the necessity for bringing this service into newer subdivisions developed for both races and brought into the town, as it is the town's firm policy to make sewer installations for all such new areas."

It is not at all clear from the record that such a "firm policy" exists. However, even assuming that it does, the fact that extensions are now made to new areas in a non-discriminatory manner is not sufficient when the effect of such a policy is to "freeze in" the results of past discrimination. As this court stated [previously]. . . "a relationship otherwise rational may be insufficient in itself to meet constitutional standards—if its effect is to freeze-in past discrimination." We find that since over one-third of the black population was not served when the original sewer system was constructed and nearly twenty percent of this population remains unserved, a policy of serving only new areas would freeze in the results of past discrimination.

The trial court, however, also stated that:

"While the complaint about less than 100% sanitary sewage for all residences is certainly a real one, that condition arises basically from the fact that local law does not yet require indoor plumbing. The lack of sanitary sewers in certain areas of the town is not the result of racial discrimination in withholding a vital service: rather it is a consequence of *not* requiring through a proper housing code, certain minimal conditions for inhabited housing."

While we recognize that a proper housing code would help this situation, it is circular reasoning to argue that because indoor plumbing is not required, sewers are not provided. If sewers were provided, indoor plumbing could be more easily installed. Indeed, without it, black residents desiring such facilities are forced to incur the extra expense of installing individual sewage disposal apparatus. In short, the justifications offered for the disparities that exist in the town's sewerage system are not valid.

SURFACE WATER DRAINAGE

We do not doubt that as the trial court notes: "Having flat nonporous soil with slow run-off conditions, Shaw suffers from drainage problems common to the Delta area." Indeed, there are serious drainage problems in both the black and white sections of town. However, the record reveals that the problems of the black community are far more serious. Whereas, the white community has been provided with either underground storm sewers or a continuous system of drainage ditches, the black neighborhoods have been provided with a poorly maintained system of drainage ditches and, on many streets, none at all. The following testimony concerning the black portion of town is illustrative:

Q. What is the shape of the actual drainage ditches or absence of them within the area?
A. These vary, so greatly. In one section, for example, of Canaan Street where within the last week someone has come along and cleared a ditch. The ditch is in the shape of a spade; that is, it's one shovel wide and one shovel deep and whatever was in what is now the ditch is now heaped in a pile along the side and this in that area serve as a ditch.
On Lampton Street, back in the Gale Street area, the ditch is a major excavation being three or four feet deep and the course of it, for example, negotiating a turn by automobile traveling from Lampton Street and attempting to turn into one of the short streets such as Johnson Steet or Mose Street or Shaw Street is very precarious kind of

undertaking that requires backing up and adjusting several times so as to get the car down the street without leaving the car in the ditch.
Then in the Elm Street area there is no visible form of drainage.

Appellees point to various impediments to justify this disparity including haphazard subdividing, the absence of zoning regulations and rights of way of insufficient width. We have already dealt with the claim that roads in the black area are of insufficient width. Regarding the other impediments, we only note that they have been substantially overcome in white neighborhoods. We see no acceptable reason why they should not have been overcome in the black community as well.

WATER MAINS, FIRE HYDRANTS AND TRAFFIC CONTROL SIGNS

Although water is supplied to all residents of the town, the trial court found that "at all times water pressure is inadequate in certain localities, irrespective of their racial character." We agree that the record discloses inadequate water pressure, but disagree that it is not related to the racial make-up of the locality.

The record reveals that the two areas where water pressure is most inadequate are black and constitute 63% of the town's black population. As appellants note, in the Gale Street area, 211 homes are served by 4″ water mains while in the Promised Land, most of the 74 homes are served by 2″ or 1¼″ mains. Most of the white community is served by 6″ mains. The 4″ mains that do exist in the white portion of town serve, however, far fewer homes than the 4″ mains in the black section. In short, as with the previously examined municipal services, the town's policies have again created a situation in which the black portion of town is severely disadvantaged. An examination of the record regarding the placement of fire hydrants as well as the placement of any traffic control signs in black neighborhoods leads us to the same conclusion.

INTENT

Yet, despite the fact that we conclude that no compelling state interests can justify the disparities that exist in the black and white portions of town, it may be argued that this result was not intended. That is to say, the record contains no direct evidence aimed at establishing bad faith, ill will or an evil motive on the part of the Town of Shaw and its public officials. . . . Having determined that no compelling state interests can possibly justify the discriminatory *results* of Shaw's administration of municipal services, we conclude that a violation of equal protection has occurred.

DISCUSSION QUESTIONS

1. One of the outstanding aspects of the Hawkins case was that the disparities between the White and African-American neighborhoods developed in the absence of comprehensive zoning plans and housing codes. Step by step, the town demonstrated a marked preference for Whites in the allocation of street, lighting, sewer, drainage, and water improvements. Each step was accompanied by somewhat different rationales and/or rationalizations. Consequently, there was clearly a process of incremental discrimination, though, as the court noted, no comprehensive plan to treat Whites favorably was found in the case. In a subsequent ruling, *Washington* v. *Davis* (1976),[*] the Supreme Court rejected ". . . the proposition that a law or other official act, without regard to whether it reflects a racially discriminatory purpose, is unconstitutional *solely* because it has a racially disproportionate impact." It went on to hold that "[n]ecessarily, an invidious [racially] discriminatory purpose may often be inferred from the totality of the relevant facts, including the fact, if it is true, that the law bears more heavily on one race than another. It is also not infrequently true that the discriminatory impact . . . may for all practical purposes demonstrate unconstitutionality because in various circumstances the discrimination is difficult to explain on nonracial grounds." Based on your reading of the facts in the Hawkins case, do you think it can be inferred that the town's actions reflected an underlying invidious discriminatory purpose? Why or why not? What kinds of additional information, if any, would help you decide? Did the incremental decision-making described in Hawkins have any clear purposes? Consider the testimony of the town's engineer regarding street paving in addressing this question.

2. In a concurring opinion, Judge Bell noted that "since the Negro citizens obtained the right to vote some four years ago under the Voting Rights Act of 1965 and under the present government which took office in 1965, there has been a considerable improvement in most of the services rendered them by the city." This fact suggests that incremental decision-making is less likely to neglect important values when all major interests are represented in the policy-making process. Consider concrete ways in which public administrators can enhance their ability to recognize salient values and interests when

---

[*]426 U.S. 229.

engaging in incremental decision-making. For instance, would public opinion surveys or mechanisms for public participation be useful in this regard?

3. Beyond the Hawkins case, can you think of instances in which incremental decision-making has neglected important political and/or constitutional values? Would the federal deficit be an example of this problem?

4

ADMINISTRATIVE EFFECTIVENESS

Traditionally, public administration in the United States has been concerned primarily with the means of carrying out governmental action. Much of its historical thrust was to develop the capacity to implement successfully public policy by finding the best ways of organizing, selecting and managing personnel, and of budgeting. Today, operations management and a host of managerially oriented techniques, such as management by objectives (MBO) and program evaluation and review technique (PERT), are similarly used to enhance the means by which laws and policies are executed.[1] As Woodrow Wilson explained the means orientation of public administration in his classic essay "The Study of Administration":

> Public administration is detailed and systematic execution of public law. Every particular application of general law is an act of administration. The assessment and raising of taxes, for instance, the hanging of a criminal, the transportation and delivery of the mails, the equipment and recruiting of the army and navy, *etc.*, are all obvious acts of administration; but the general laws which direct these things to be done are as obviously outside and above administration. The broad plans of governmental action are not administrative; the detailed execution of such plans is administrative.[2]

[1]See Chester A. Newland, "Policy/Program Objectives and Federal Management: The Search for Government Effectiveness," *Public Administration Review,* 36 (January/February 1976), 20–27; and Stephen Rosenthal, *Managing Government Operations* (Glenview, Ill.: Scott, Foresman, 1982).

[2]Woodrow Wilson, "The Study of Administration," *Political Science Quarterly,* 56 (December 1941), 481–506 (originally published in 1887), at p. 496.

Wilson even argued that "The weightier debates of constitutional principle . . . are no longer of more immediate practical moment than questions of administration. It is getting to be harder to *run* a constitution than to frame one."[3] What Wilson and orthodox public administration tended to neglect, however, was that the Constitution places constraints on the means available to public administrators for implementing public policy. "Running" the Constitution is not divorced from debates—even weighty ones, at that—over constitutional principles.

At a minimum, constitutionally competent public administrators must be aware of how the Constitution limits the means available for implementing public policy. More broadly, though, as Constance Horner, former director of the federal Office of Personnel Management, noted, public administrators should be constitutionally literate so that they can effectively engage in debates over both means and ends. In her words, "I am calling . . . for a commitment to what might be termed *constitutional literacy*" because ". . . one antidote to growing specialization within the Federal executive service is to reinvigorate *constitutional* discourse, so we can meet once again on common ground. As Professor John Rohr puts it, we must 'create within the bureaucracy a community of moral discourse centered on fundamental constitutional values.' "[4]

CONSTITUTIONAL MEANS: A BRIEF HISTORY OF JUDICIAL APPROACHES

In some ways it is obvious that the Constitution limits the choice of means for achieving legitimate governmental ends. In principle, democratic constitutionalism must reject the premise that even laudable ends can justify unconstitutional means. In fact, Chief Justice John Marshall made this very point in one of the most famous passages in United States constitutional law. In *McCulloch* v. *Maryland* (1819), he wrote for the Court, "Let the end be legitimate, let it be within the scope of the Constitution, and all means which are appropriate, which are plainly adapted to that end, which are not prohibited, but consistent with the letter and spirit of the Constitution, are constitutional."[5] Conversely, means not meeting these tests would be unconstitutional. But precisely which administrative means are contrary to the letter and the spirit of the Constitution is not always clear.

Over the past century, the federal judiciary expressed three general moods in response to the need to develop guidelines for assessing the constitutionality of public administrative means. First, from the 1880s to the mid-1930s, it tended to oppose two types of administrative means, one on substantive grounds and the other for procedural reasons. Substantively, the judiciary was highly skeptical of any governmental interference in the functioning of free markets. For

[3]Ibid., p. 484.
[4]Constance Horner, "Remarks to FEI's [Federal Executive Institute's] 20th Anniversary Dinner," Charlottesville, Virginia, October 14, 1988, pp. 13–14.
[5]*McCulloch* v. *Maryland*, 4 Wheat. 316, 420 (1819).

instance, it overturned laws and/or administrative actions seeking to regulate wages and hours, railroad rates and conditions of service, and child labor.[6] Procedurally, the courts frowned on administrative adjudication, and to a lesser extent, rule-making on the grounds that both processes violated the constitutional separation of powers. Judges also tended to view the adjudicatory activities of public agencies as an infringement on constitutional due process. During this period, the judiciary generally paid little deference to administrative expertise. In fact, in 1890, the Supreme Court declared that the judiciary was the more appropriate body to engage in rate-setting, which is now considered a standard administrative activity.[7] In general, the judiciary's outlook placed a heavy burden of persuasion on public administrators who sought to defend the constitutionality of the means chosen to implement even those policies that the courts considered legitimate.

The period of judicial opposition came to a head during the early part of the New Deal. In response to the Great Depression, Congress delegated vast legislative authority to the executive branch. It sought to enable the president and federal agencies to intervene more readily in the economy in an effort to bring about a recovery. The judiciary perceived a greater threat to the separation of powers and free markets than it was willing to accept. According to Robert Jackson, a former Supreme Court Justice, in 1935–1936, " 'hell broke loose' in the lower [federal] courts. Sixteen hundred injunctions restraining officers of the Federal Government from carrying out acts of Congress were granted by federal judges."[8] In 1935, the Supreme Court undercut a major New Deal initiative, the National Industrial Recovery Act of 1933, by concluding, among other problems, that it involved an unconstitutional delegation of legislative power to the executive branch.[9] Earlier in 1935, the Court had overturned a scheme granting the president authority to regulate the petroleum industry.[10] President Franklin D. Roosevelt responded by asking Congress to increase the size of the Court so that he might be able to appoint enough new justices to create a majority in favor of his economic policies. The "Court Packing" plan was never enacted. Soon after it was introduced, Justice Owen Roberts switched his point of view and joined what had been a minority of four pro-New Deal justices, thereby establishing a majority of five. As time went on, Roosevelt made a number of appointments to the Court and the crisis passed. As part of the same effort to limit the judiciary's influence, the powers of individual district court judges to frustrate federal administration were weakened by the

---

[6]*Lochner* v. *New York,* 198 U.S. 45 (1905); *Chicago, Milwaukee, and St. Paul Railway Co.* v. *Minnesota,* 134 U.S. 418 (1890); *Hammer* v. *Dagenhart,* 247 U.S. 251 (1918). See David H. Rosenbloom, "Public Law and Regulation," pp. 523–75 in Jack Rabin, Gerald Miller, and Bart Hildreth, eds., *Handbook on Public Administration* (New York: Marcel Dekker, 1989), esp. pp. 532–39.
[7]*Chicago, Milwaukee, and St. Paul Railway Co.* v. *Minnesota,* 134 U.S. 418, 458 (1890).
[8]Robert H. Jackson, *The Struggle for Judicial Supremacy* (New York: Knopf, 1941), p. 115.
[9]*Schechter Poultry Corp.* v. *United States,* 295 U.S. 495 (1935).
[10]*Panama Refining Co.* v. *Ryan,* 293 U.S. 388 (1935).

Judiciary Act of 1937, which requires them to sit in panels of three, rather than alone, in cases seeking to enjoin the activities of federal officials on constitutional grounds.

A second judicial view of administrative means grew out of Roosevelt's ability to defeat the opposition to New Deal measures and eventually to make a large number of appointments to the federal bench. From the late 1930s to the mid-1950s, the judiciary acquiesced in administrative action. During this period, the courts did not simply rubber stamp administrative activities, but they did pay great deference to administrators' expertise and they seldom found administrative means to be unconstitutional. What C. Herman Pritchett wrote of the Supreme Court's record from 1941 to 1946 characterized the judicial mood generally: "A basic assumption of the Roosevelt Court has been that administrative agencies possess an expertness and a competence in economic and social fields which the Court does not share, and that consequently in areas where this expertness is relevant the Court will not disturb or contradict administrative conclusions."[11] The Court also remained committed to constitutional doctrines that had the effect of allowing administrative agencies to infringe on individuals' constitutional rights in the course of providing them with public services and benefits.[12] Consequently, even into the 1960s, it could be concluded, with Martin Shapiro, that:

> Judicial review of administrative decision making is . . . marginal in the sense that . . . policy differences are unlikely to arise in most instances in which review is theoretically possible. Thus most of the relations between agencies and courts are relations of acquiescence, consent, or compromise arrived at by anticipation of the other participant's position before even a tremor of conflict arises.[13]

However, by the 1950s, a major constitutional change was beginning and the current judicial perspective on administrative means was developing. As noted in Chapter 2, during the past three decades the judiciary has handed down a number of decisions and fashioned several doctrines that have broadly expanded the constitutional rights of individuals as they come into contact with public administration. Consequently, today public administrators are more constrained by the Constitution than ever before when dealing with clients, subordinate employees and applicants for civil service jobs, patients in public mental health facilities and inmates in prisons, and individuals involved in street-level administrative encounters.[14] This is precisely why public administrators must now have constitutional competence in the judiciary's view.

The contemporary judicial approach to public administration emerged in

[11]C. Herman Pritchett, *The Roosevelt Court* (New York: Macmillan, 1948), p. 172.
[12]See David H. Rosenbloom, *Public Administration and Law* (New York: Marcel Dekker, 1983), pp. 79–85, 115–20, for a discussion.
[13]Martin Shapiro, *The Supreme Court and Administrative Agencies* (New York: Free Press, 1968), p. 268.
[14]See Rosenbloom, *Public Administration and Law,* Chapters 3–5, and the discussion on intuition in Chapter 3 of this text.

response to a variety of actors. During the "red scare"[15] of the late 1940s and early 1950s, public employees were labeled disloyal and dismissed partly on the basis of activities such as favoring peace and civil liberties, racial equality, and desegregation. Such abuses led the courts to reassess and to reject the historic concept that governmental benefits were "privileges" to which almost any conditions could be attached without violating the Constitution.[16] Eventually, clients and employees of public agencies were afforded considerable procedural and substantive constitutional protections against the erosion of their rights through their dependency on the government for benefits or jobs.[17] By 1954, the Supreme Court unanimously concluded that legally enforced racial segregation of public schools was an unconstitutional denial of equal protection of the laws.[18] Thereafter, equal protection was applied to the distribution of other public services as well. Prisons and other public institutions were also desegregated and a broadly, though loosely, connected movement for sweeping constitutionally based reforms of correctional and public mental health facilities developed.[19]

GENERAL CONSTITUTIONAL RESTRICTIONS ON ADMINISTRATIVE MEANS TODAY

The vast expansion of individuals' rights vis-à-vis public administration since the 1950s has been accompanied by the formulation of constitutional doctrines and judicial approaches that place general constraints on administrators' choice of means for implementing public policies. The three most general limitations of this kind are (a) due process as a protection against arbitrary or capricious administrative actions, (b) utilization of the "least restrictive alternative" when infringing on individuals' rights for constitutionally permissible governmental purposes, and (c) using "narrow tailoring" when employing racial classifications in constitutionally acceptable ways. Narrow tailoring, which developed with regard to affirmative action-like measures, is intended to balance governmental interests in promoting equal opportunity for minorities with its interests in not doing so at the expense of the constitutional rights of nonminorities. It applies to the use of any "suspect classification," such as one based on race, for which there must be a compelling state interest; and perhaps to some nonsuspect classifications, such as those based on sex, as well.

[15]The "red scare," also called the McCarthy period after Senator Joseph McCarthy (R-Wis.), was characterized by a widespread belief that communists had infiltrated the governmental and cultural institutions of the United States and that they were subverting public policy and promoting communistic values. The federal government and many states and localities established loyalty-security programs to screen out employees and applicants who might advance communist causes.
[16]See David H. Rosenbloom, *Federal Service and the Constitution* (Ithaca: Cornell University Press, 1971), Chapters 6–7.
[17]William Van Alstyne, "The Demise of the Right–Privilege Distinction in Constitutional Law," *Harvard Law Review*, 81 (1968), 1439–64.
[18]*Brown* v. *Board of Education of Topeka*, 347 U.S. 483 (1954).
[19]Rosenbloom, *Public Administration and Law*, Chapter 5.

Due Process

It is axiomatic, as Chief Marshall indicated in *McCulloch* v. *Maryland,* that administrative means or actions must bear a direct and strong relationship to the achievement of legitimate governmental objectives. Thus, means that are not logically related to the policy objectives being sought and those that are based on inaccurate premises or conclusions are vulnerable to successful legal challenge in court.[20] Similarly, by definition, means that are arbitrary or capricious do not connect administrative actions to their intended purposes in a successful fashion. The Due Process Clause of the Fifth and Fourteenth Amendments is a generalized check on the use of such arbitrary or capricious administrative means that infringe on individuals' constitutionally protected rights. Substantively, due process requires that administrative means be rationally related to the ends they intend to promote. Procedurally, it protects individuals from unfair denials of their interests in life, liberty, or property. For instance, at a minimum, procedural due process usually requires that an individual be notified of administrative decisions that will abridge his or her liberty or property interests and that he or she be given an opportunity to respond to the administrative information, charges, and rationale. More elaborately, it may require trial-like hearings. At a very broad level, even a law or regulation that encourages arbitrary or capricious administrative implementation may be considered an unconstitutional violation of due process. *Kolender* v. *Lawson,* excerpt following, discusses due process at this general level. Cases discussing the more specific requirements of due process are presented in Chapter 5 (Cases 5.1 and 5.2).

The Least Restrictive Alternative

The least restrictive alternative doctrine places constraints on administrative means that infringe on individuals' substantive constitutional rights. Although rights such as freedom of speech, association, and exercise of religion are not ordinarily considered absolute, contemporary constitutional law prohibits their gratuitous or unnecessary abridgment. In order to infringe on these rights constitutionally, the government must have a compelling interest *and* it must choose the method for achieving its purpose that is least restrictive of the individual's opportunity to exercise his or her constitutional rights. Importantly, the least restrictive standard focuses on the damage that alternative means do to individuals' rights, rather than on the economic costs of the various alternatives or the administrative ease with which they can be implemented. As one court forcefully stated its premise in a case involving prisons, "inadequate resources can never be an adequate justification for the state's depriving any person of his constitutional rights. If the state cannot obtain the resources to detain persons awaiting trial in accordance with minimum constitutional standards, then the

---

[20]*Federal Trade Commission* v. *Sperry and Hutchinson,* 405 U.S. 233 (1972); *Industrial Union Department, AFL-CIO* v. *American Petroleum Institute,* 448 U.S. 607 (1980); *Motor Vehicles Manufacturers Association* v. *State Farm,* 463 U.S. 29 (1983).

state simply will not be permitted to detain such persons."[21] The vigor with which the courts apply the least restrictive alternative approach will vary with the scope of administrative infringement on individuals' rights. However, as discussed in *Elrod* v. *Burns* (Case 4.2) the approach is a useful guide for administrators seeking to be constitutionally competent.

Narrow Tailoring

Narrow tailoring places a similar type of constraint on public administrative means seeking to use racial classifications as a way of promoting equal opportunity without violating the Fourteenth Amendment's Equal Protection Clause. The concept of narrow tailoring is clearly discussed in *United States* v. *Paradise,* the last of this chapter's cases.

In reading the cases that follow, consider the administrative means at issue from the following perspectives: What purposes do they seek to achieve? How well adapted to those purposes are they? Are they the best means? What are the constitutional constraints that they must satisfy?

Each of the cases is followed by discussion questions. The next three chapters, on efficiency, standardization, and economy, further promote constitutional competence by moving the analysis of public administration and the Constitution from the broad general concerns of decision-making and effectiveness to the more specific common tensions between administrative and constitutional values.

ADDITIONAL READING

ROSENTHAL, STEPHEN. *Managing Government Operations.* Glenview, Ill.: SCOTT FORESMAN, 1982.

WHOLEY, JOSEPH S. *Evaluation and Effective Public Management.* Boston: Little, Brown, 1983.

[21]*Hamilton* v. *Love,* 328 U.S. 1194 (1971).

CASE 4.1:
DUE PROCESS VERSUS ARBITRARY MEANS

KOLENDER, CHIEF OF POLICE
OF SAN DIEGO,
et al.

v

LAWSON
461 US 352
Appeal from the United States
Court of Appeals for the Ninth
Circuit
No. 81-1320.
Argued November 8,
1982—Decided May 2, 1983

Summary

A California statute requires persons who loiter or wander on the streets to identify themselves and to account for their presence when requested by a peace officer. The California Court of Appeal has construed the statute to require a person to provide "credible and reliable" identification when requested by a police officer who has reasonable suspicion of criminal activity sufficient to justify a stop under the standards of *Terry v. Ohio*, 392 U.S. 1. The California court has defined "credible and reliable" identification as "carrying reasonable assurance that the identification is authentic and proving means for later getting in touch with the person who has identified himself." Appellee, who had been arrested and convicted under the statute, brought an action in Federal District Court challenging the statute's constitutionality. The District Court held the statute unconstitutional and enjoined its enforcement, and the Court of Appeals affirmed.

Held: The statute, as drafted and as construed by the state court, is unconstitutionally vague on its face within the meaning of the Due Process Clause of the Fourteenth Amendment by failing to clarify what is contemplated by the requirement that a suspect provide a "credible and reliable" identification. As such, the statute vests virtually complete discretion in the hands of the police to determine whether the suspect has satisfied the statute and must be permitted to go on his way in the absence of probable cause to arrest.

Opinion

JUSTICE O'CONNOR delivered the opinion of the Court.

This appeal presents a facial challenge to a criminal statute that requires persons who loiter or wander on the streets to provide a "credible and reliable" identification and to account for their presence when requested by a peace officer under circumstances that would justify a stop under the standards of *Terry* v. *Ohio*, 392 U.S. 1 (1968). We conclude that the statute as it has been construed is unconstitutionally vague within the meaning of the Due Process Clause of the Fourteenth Amendment by failing to clarify what is contemplated by the requirement that a suspect provide a "credible and reliable" identification. Accordingly, we affirm the judgment of the court below.

I

Appellee Edward Lawson was detained or arrested on approximately 15 occasions between March 1975 and January 1977 pursuant to Cal. Penal Code Ann. § 647(e) (West 1970). Lawson was prosecuted only twice, and was convicted once. The second charge was dismissed.

Lawson then brought a civil action in the District Court for the Southern District of California seeking a declaratory judgment that § 647(e) is unconstitutional, a mandatory injunction to restrain enforcement of the statute, and compensatory and punitive damages against the various officers who detained him. The District Court found that § 647(e) was overbroad because "a person who is stopped on less than probable cause cannot be punished for failing to identify himself." . . . The District Court enjoined enforcement of the statute. . . .

Appellant H. A. Porazzo, Deputy Chief Commander of the California Highway Patrol, appealed the District Court decision to the Court of Appeals for the Ninth Circuit. . . . The Court of Appeals affirmed the District Court determination as to the unconstitutionality of § 647(e). . . . The appellate court determined that the statute was unconstitutional in that it violates the Fourth Amendment's proscription against unreasonable searches and seizures, it contains a vague enforcement standard that is susceptible to arbitrary enforcement, and it fails to give fair and adequate notice of the type of conduct prohibited. . . .

The officers appealed to this Court. . . .

*   *   *

II

Our Constitution is designed to maximize individual freedoms within a framework of ordered liberty. Statutory limitations on those freedoms are examined for substantive authority and content as well as for definiteness or certainty of expression. . . .

As generally stated, the void-for-vagueness doctrine requires that a penal statute define the criminal offense with sufficient definiteness that ordinary people can understand what conduct is prohibited and in a manner that does not encourage arbitrary and discriminatiory enforcement. . . . Although the doctrine focuses both on actual notice to citizens and arbitrary enforcement, we have recognized recently that the more important aspect of the vagueness doctrine "is not actual notice, but the other principal element of the doctrine—the requirement that a legislature establish minimal guidelines to govern law enforcement.". . . Where the legislature fails to provide such minimal guidelines, a criminal statute may permit "a standardless sweep [that] allows policemen, prosecutors, and juries to pursue their personal predilections.". . .

Section 647(e), as presently drafted and as construed by the state courts, contains no standard for determining what a suspect has to do in order to satisfy the requirement to provide a "credible and reliable" identification. As such, the statute vests virtually complete discretion in the hands of the police to determine whether the suspect has satisfied the statute and must be permitted to go on his way in the absence of probable cause to arrest. An individual, who police may think is suspicious but do not have probable cause to believe has committed a crime, is entitled to continue to walk the public streets "only at the whim of any police officer" who happens to stop that individual under § 647(e). . . . Our concern here is based upon the "potential for arbitrarily suppressing First Amendment liberties. . . ." . . . In addition, § 647(e) implicates consideration of the constitutional right to freedom of movement. . . .

Section 647(e) is not simply a "stop-and-identify" statute. Rather, the statute requires that the individual provide a "credible and reliable" identification that carries a "reasonable assurance" of its authenticity, and that provides "means for later getting in touch with the person who has identified himself." . . .

In addition, the suspect may also have to account for his presence "to the extent it assists in producing credible and reliable identification." . . .

At oral argument, the appellants confirmed that a suspect violates § 647(e) unless "the officer [is] satisfied that the identification is reliable." . . . In giving examples of how suspects would satisfy the requirement, appellants explained that a jogger, who was not carrying identification, could, depending on the particular officer, be required to answer a series of questions concerning the route that he followed to arrive at the place where the officers detained him, or could satisfy the identification requirement simply by reciting his name and address. . . .

It is clear that the full discretion accorded to the police to determine whether the suspect has provided a "credible and reliable" identification necessarily

"entrust[s] lawmaking 'to the moment-to-moment judgment of the policeman on his beat.' ". . . Section 647(e) "furnishes a convenient tool for 'harsh and discriminatory enforcement by local prosecuting officials, against particular groups deemed to merit their displeasure,' ". . . and "confers on police a virtually unrestrained power to arrest and charge persons with a violation.". . . In providing that a detention under § 647(e) may occur only where there is the level of suspicion sufficient to justify a *Terry* stop, the State ensures the existence of "neutral limitations on the conduct of individual officers.". . .

Although the initial detention is justified, the State fails to establish standards by which the officers may determine whether the suspect has complied with the subsequent indentification requirement.

Appellants stress the need for strengthened law enforcement tools to combat the epidemic of crime that plagues our Nation. The concern of our citizens with curbing criminal activity is certainly a matter requiring the attention of all branches of government. As weighty as this concern is, however, it cannot justify legislation that would otherwise fail to meet constitutional standards for definiteness and clarity. . . . Section 647(e), as presently construed, requires that "suspicious" persons satisfy some undefined identification requirement, or face criminal punishment. Although due process does not require "impossible standards" of clarity, this is not a case where further precision in the statutory language is either impossible or impractical.

DISCUSSION QUESTIONS

1. There is more to *Kolender* v. *Lawson* than meets the eye. In part, the majority opinion holds the regulation unconstitutional because it encourages arbitrary enforcement. But it is possible to apply the regulation in nonarbitrary ways as well. For instance, Justice White speculated in dissent that an individual

might answer, "Who I am is just none of your business." Would an arrest for failing to comply with the regulation be arbitrary under such circumstances? According to the Court's logic, does the constitutional requirement that a criminal statute be definite and clear rule out even the nonarbitrary application of vague statutes? What does the *Kolender* ruling suggest in terms of enforcing administrative rules?

2. The Court maintains that ". . . this is not a case where further precision in the statutory language is either impossible or impractical." Try to draft a statute that would accomplish the purposes sought by California while meeting the constitutional standards for definiteness and clarity.

3. Accounting for one's presence creates a logical difficulty, since everyone must always be *someplace*. Can you think of times when your answer to a police officer's question, "Why are you here?" might "inadequately" account for your presence? Does the legitimacy of one's presence depend on the time and circumstances? In short, does the statute demand a high degree of social conformity in order to assure compliance at all times?

4. In a concurring opinion, Justice Brennan noted that failure to comply with the California regulations might ". . . subject [a pedestrian] to arrest and all that goes with it: new acquaintances among jailers, lawyers, prisoners, and bail bondsmen, firsthand knowledge of local jail conditions, a 'search incident to arrest,' and the expense of defending against a possible prosecution." Do you think that in practical terms, such penalties are disproportionate to the offense of failing to provide adequate identification or an account of one's presence?

CASE 4.2:
THE LEAST RESTRICTIVE
ALTERNATIVE

ELROD, SHERIFF, ET AL.

v.

BURNS ET AL.
427 US 347
CERTIORARI TO THE UNITED
STATES COURT OF APPEALS
FOR THE SEVENTH CIRCUIT
No. 74-1520. Argued April 19,
1976—Decided June 28, 1976

Summary

Respondents, Republicans who are non-civil-service employees of the Cook County, Ill., Sheriff's Office, brought this suit as a class action for declaratory, injunctive, and other relief against petitioners, including the newly elected Sheriff, a Democrat, and county Democratic organizations, alleging that in violation of the First and Fourteenth Amendments and various statutes, including the Civil Rights Act of 1871, respondents were discharged or (in the case of one respondent) threatened with discharge for the sole reason that they were not affiliated with or sponsored by the Democratic Party. Finding that respondents had failed to show irreparable injury, the District Court denied their motion for a preliminary injunction and ultimately dismissed their complaint for failure to state a claim upon which relief could be granted. The Court of Appeals reversed and remanded with instructions to enter appropriate preliminary injunctive relief. *Held*: The judgment is affirmed.

Opinion

Mr. Justice Brennan announced the judgment of the Court and delivered an opinion in which Mr. Justice White and Mr. Justice Marshall joined.

This case presents the question whether public employees who allege that they were discharged or threatened with discharge solely because of their partisan political affiliation or nonaffiliation state a claim for deprivation of constitutional rights secured by the First and Fourteenth Amendments.

*   *   *

II

In December 1970, the Sheriff of Cook County, a Republican, was replaced by Richard Elrod, a Democrat. At that time, respondents, all Republicans, were employees of the Cook County Sheriff's Office. They were non-civil-service employees and, therefore, not covered by any statute, ordinance, or regulation protecting them from arbitrary discharge. One respondent, John Burns, was Chief Deputy of the Process Division and supervised all Departments of the Sheriff's Office working on the seventh floor of the building housing that office. Frank Vargas was a bailiff and security guard at the Juvenile Court of Cook County. Fred L. Buckley

was employed as a process server in the office. Joseph Dennard was an employee in the office.

It has been the practice of the Sheriff of Cook County, when he assumes office from a Sheriff of a different political party, to replace non-civil-service employees of the Sheriff's Office with members of his own party when the existing employees lack or fail to obtain requisite support from, or fail to affiliate with, that party. Consequently, subsequent to Sheriff Elrod's assumption of office, respondents, with the exception of Buckley, were discharged from their employment solely because they did not support and were not members of the Democratic Party and had failed to obtain the sponsorship of one of its leaders. Buckley is in imminent danger of being discharged solely for the same reasons. Respondents allege that the discharges were ordered by Sheriff Elrod under the direction of the codefendants in this suit.

*   *   *

IV

The Cook County Sheriff's practice of dismissing employees on a partisan basis is but one form of the general practice of political patronage. The practice also includes placing loyal supporters in government jobs that may or may not have been made available by political discharges. Nonofficeholders may be the beneficiaries of lucrative government contracts for highway construction, buildings, and supplies. Favored wards may receive improved public services. Members of the judiciary may even engage in the practice through the appointment of receiverships, trusteeships, and refereeships. Although political patronage comprises a broad range of activities, we are here concerned only with the constitutionality of dismissing public employees for partisan reasons.

Patronage practice is not new to American politics. It has existed at the federal level at least since the Presidency of Thomas Jefferson, although its popularization and legitimation primarily occurred later, in the Presidency of Andrew Jackson. The practice is not unique to American politics. It has been used in many European countries, and in darker times, it played a significant role in the Nazi rise to power in Germany and other totalitarian states. More recent times have witnessed a strong decline in its use, particularly with respect to public employment. Indeed, only a few decades after Andrew Jackson's administration, strong discontent with the corruption and inefficiency of the patronage system of public employment eventuated in the Pendleton Act, the foundation of modern civil service. And on the state and local levels, merit systems have increasingly displaced the practice. This trend led the Court to observe in *CSC* v. *Letter Carriers* . . . (1973), that "the judgment of Congress, the Executive, and the country appears to have been that partisan political activities by federal employees must be limited if the Government is to operate effectively and fairly, elections are to play their proper part in representative government, and employees themselves are to be sufficiently free from improper influences."

The decline of patronage employment is not, of course, relevant to the question of its constitutionality. It is the practice itself, not the magnitude of its occurrence, the constitutionality of which must be determined. Nor for that matter does any unacceptability of the practice signified by its decline indicate its unconstitutionality. Our inquiry does not begin

with the judgment of history, though the actual operation of a practice viewed in retrospect may help to assess its workings with respect to constitutional limitations. . . . Rather, inquiry must commence with identification of the constitutional limitations implicated by a challenged governmental practice.

V

The cost of the practice of patronage is the restraint it places on freedoms of belief and association. In order to maintain their jobs, respondents were required to pledge their political allegiance to the Democratic Party, work for the election of other candidates of the Democratic Party, contribute a portion of their wages to the Party, or obtain the sponsorship of a member of the Party, usually at the price of one of the first three alternatives. Regardless of the incumbent party's identity, Democratic or otherwise, the consequences for association and belief are the same. An individual who is a member of the out-party maintains affiliation with his own party at the risk of losing his job. He works for the election of his party's candidates and espouses its policies at the same risk. The financial and campaign assistance that he is induced to provide to another party furthers the advancement of that party's policies to the detriment of his party's views and ultimately his own beliefs, and any assessment of his salary is tantamount to coerced belief.

Even a pledge of allegiance to another party, however ostensible, only serves to compromise the individual's true beliefs. Since the average public employee is hardly in the financial position to support his party and another, or to lend his time to two parties, the individual's ability to act according to his beliefs and to associate with others of his political persuasion is constrained, and support for his party is diminished.

It is not only belief and association which are restricted where political patronage is the practice. The free functioning of the electoral process also suffers. Conditioning public employment on partisan support prevents support of competing political interests. Existing employees are deterred from such support, as well as the multitude seeking jobs. As government employment, state or federal, becomes more pervasive, the greater the dependence on it becomes, and therefore the greater becomes the power to starve political opposition by commanding partisan support, financial and otherwise. Patronage thus tips the electoral process in favor of the incumbent party, and where the practice's scope is substantial relative to the size of the electorate, the impact on the process can be significant.

Our concern with the impact of patronage on political belief and association does not occur in the abstract, for political belief and association constitute the core of those activities protected by the First Amendment. Regardless of the nature of the inducement, whether it be by the denial of public employment or, as in *Board of Education* v. *Barnette*. . . (1943), by the influence of a teacher over students, "[i]f there is any fixed star in our constitutional constellation, it is that no official, high or petty, can prescribe what shall be orthodox in politics, nationalism, religion, or other matters of opinion or force citizens to confess by word or act their faith therein.". . . And, though freedom of belief is central, "[t]he First Amendment protects political association as well as political expression.". . . "There can no longer be any doubt that freedom to associate with others for the common advancement of

political beliefs and ideas is a form of 'orderly group activity' protected by the First and Fourteenth Amendments. . . . The right to associate with the political party of one's choice is an integral part of this basic constitutional freedom."

These protections reflect our "profound national commitment to the principle that debate on public issues should be uninhibited, robust, and wide-open," . . . a principle itself reflective of the fundamental understanding that "[c]ompetition in ideas and governmental policies is at the core of our electoral process. . . ." . . . Patronage, therefore, to the extent it compels or restrains belief and association, is inimical to the process which undergirds our system of government and is "at war with the deeper traditions of democracy embodied in the First Amendment."

* * *

VI

Although the practice of patronage dismissals clearly infringes First Amendment interests, our inquiry is not at an end, for the prohibition on encroachment of First Amendment protections is not an absolute. Restraints are permitted for appropriate reasons. . . .

* * *

. . . It is firmly established that a significant impairment of First Amendment rights must survive exacting scrutiny. . . . "This type of scrutiny is necessary even if any deterrent effect on the exercise of First Amendment rights arises, not through direct government action, but indirectly as an unintended but inevitable result of the government's conduct. . . ." . . . Thus encroachment "cannot be justified upon a mere showing of a legitimate state interest." . . .

The interest advanced must be paramount, one of vital importance, and the burden is on the government to show the existence of such an interest. . . . In the instant case, care must be taken not to confuse the interest of partisan organizations with governmental interests. Only the latter will suffice. Moreover, it is not enough that the means chosen in furtherance of the interest be rationally related to that end. . . . The gain to the subordinating interest provided by the means must outweigh the incurred loss of protected rights . . . and the government must "emplo[y] means closely drawn to avoid unnecessary abridgment. . . ." . . . "[A] State may not choose means that unnecessarily restrict constitutionally protected liberty. 'Precision of regulation must be the touchstone in an area so closely touching our most precious freedoms.' If the State has open to it a less drastic way of satisfying its legitimate interests, it may not choose a legislative scheme that broadly stifles the exercise of fundamental personal liberties." . . . In short, if conditioning the retention of public employment on the employee's support of the in-party is to survive constitutional challenge, it must further some vital government end by a means that is least restrictive of freedom of belief and association in achieving that end, and the benefit gained must outweigh the loss of constitutionally protected rights.

One interest which has been offered in justification of patronage is the need to insure effective government and the efficiency of public employees. It is argued that employees of political persuasions not the same as that of the party in control of public office will not have the incentive to work effectively and may even be motivated to subvert the incumbent administration's efforts to govern effectively. We are not persuaded. The inefficiency resulting from the wholesale replacement of large numbers of public employees every time political office changes hands belies this justification. And the prospect of dismissal after an election in which the incumbent party has lost is only a disincentive to good work. Further, it is not clear that dismissal in order to make room for a patronage appointment will result in replacement by a person more qualified to do the job since appointment often occurs in exchange for the delivery of votes, or other party service, not job capability. More fundamentally, however, the argument does not succeed because it is doubtful that the mere difference of political persuasion motivates poor performance; nor do we think it legitimately may be used as a basis for imputing such behavior. The Court has consistently recognized that mere political association is an inadequate basis for imputing disposition to ill-willed conduct. . . .

Even if the first argument that patronage serves effectiveness and efficiency be rejected, it still may be argued that patronage serves those interests by giving the employees of an incumbent party the incentive to perform well in order to insure their party's incumbency and thereby their jobs. Patronage, according to the argument, thus makes employees highly accountable to the public. But the ability of officials more directly accountable to the electorate to discharge employees for cause and the availability of merit systems, growth in the use of which has been quite significant, convince us that means less intrusive than patronage still exist for achieving accountability in the public work force and, thereby, effective and efficient government. The greater effectiveness of patronage over these less drastic means, if any, is at best marginal, a gain outweighed by the absence of intrusion on protected interests under the alternatives. . . .

A second interest advanced in support of patronage is the need for political loyalty of employees, not to the end that effectiveness and efficiency be insured, but to the end that representative government not be undercut by tactics obstructing the implementation of policies of the new administration, policies presumably sanctioned by the electorate. The justification is not without force, but is nevertheless inadequate to validate patronage wholesale. Limiting patronage dismissals to policymaking positions is sufficient to achieve this governmental end. Nonpolicymaking individuals usually have only limited responsibility and are therefore not in a position to thwart the goals of the in-party. . . .

It is argued that a third interest supporting patronage dismissals is the preservation of the democratic process. According to petitioners, " 'we have contrived no system for the support of party that does not place considerable reliance on patronage. The party organization makes a democratic government work and charges a price for its services.' " The argument is thus premised on the centrality of partisan politics to the democratic process.

Preservation of the democratic process is certainly an interest protection of which may in some instances justify limitations on First Amendment freedoms. . . . But however important preservation of the two-party system or any system involving a fixed number of parties may or may not be, we are not persuaded that the elimination of patronage practice or, as is specifically involved here, the interdiction of patronage dismissals, will bring about the demise of party politics. Political parties existed in the absence of active patronage practice prior to the administration of Andrew Jackson, and they have survived substantial reduction in their patronage power through the establishment of merit systems.

Patronage dismissals thus are not the least restrictive alternative to achieving the contribution they may make to the democratic process. The process functions as well without the practice, perhaps even better, for patronage dismissals clearly also retard that process. Patronage can result in the entrenchment of one or a few parties to the exclusion of others. And most indisputably, as we recognized at the outset, patronage is a very effective impediment to the associational and speech freedoms which are essential to a meaningful system of democratic government. Thus, if patronage contributes at all to the elective process, that contribution is diminished by the practice's impairment of the same. . . .

*   *   *

In summary, patronage dismissals severely restrict political belief and association. Though there is a vital need for government efficiency and effectiveness, such dismissals are on balance not the least restrictive means for fostering that end. There is also a need to insure that policies which the electorate has sanctioned are effectively implemented. That interest can be fully satisfied by limiting patronage dismissals to policymaking positions. Finally, patronage dismissals cannot be justified by their contribution to the proper functioning of our democratic process through their assistance to partisan politics since political parties are nurtured by other, less intrusive and equally effective methods. More fundamentally, however, any contribution of patronage dismissals to the democratic process does not suffice to override their severe encroachment on First Amendment freedoms. We hold, therefore, that the practice of patronage dismissals is unconstitutional under the First and Fourteenth Amendments, and that respondents thus stated a valid claim for relief.

DISCUSSION QUESTIONS

1. Justice Brennan's plurality opinion identifies three governmental objectives allegedly served by patronage dismissals and concludes that such dismissals are not the means least restrictive of constitutional rights for achieving any of them. Consider each of the objectives mentioned and less restrictive means that could be employed to promote them. Are the means you choose more or less effective than patronage dismissals?

2. Justice Powell dissented in an opinion joined by Chief Justice Burger and Justice Rehnquist. He noted that "The Court holds unconstitutional a practice as old as the Republic. . . ." Does the *Elrod* decision suggest: (a) that the judiciary is free to declare any practice implicating constitutional rights to which it is opposed to be unconstitutional regardless of the history of that practice; (b) that the Constitution is continually being adapted to changing political, economic, and social circumstances; and/or (c) that the constitutional requirements are constant and the courts simply articulate them when the opportunity and need arises (in other words, patronage was always unconstitutional, but the Court was never presented with the opportunity to rule on it prior to the *Elrod* case)? What are the full implications of each of these three possible interpretations for choosing administrative means that are constitutional? For achieving constitutional competence generally?

3. In *Branti* v. *Finkel*, 445 U.S. 506 (1980), the Supreme Court modified the constitutional barrier to patronage dismissals by indicating that ". . . the ultimate inquiry is not whether the label 'policymaker' or 'confidential' fits a particular position; rather, the question is whether the hiring authority can demonstrate that party affiliation is an appropriate requirement for the effective performance of the public office involved." Can you think of an administrative position for which patronage dismissals could be successfully defended under this standard? Under the least restrictive alternative test? Would a department head or budget director fill such a position? A city manager? The U.S. Secretary of State? What criteria, if any exist, would such a position have to meet?

CASE 4:3:
NARROW TAILORING

UNITED STATES, Petitioner

v

PHILLIP PARADISE, Jr., et al
480 US—, 94 L Ed 2d 203
[No. 85–999]
Argued November 12, 1986.
Decided February 25, 1987.

Summary

In 1972, in an action brought by, among others, a class of black plaintiffs to challenge the long-standing practice of the Alabama Department of Public Safety (department) of excluding blacks from employment, the United States District Court for the Middle District of Alabama found that the department had engaged in a pattern of discrimination in hiring, ordered it to hire one black trooper for each white trooper hired until blacks constituted approximately 25% of the state trooper force, and enjoined the department from engaging in any discrimination in its employment practices, including promotions. . . . In 1974, the District Court found that the department had delayed or frustrated full relief to the plaintiff class by artificially restricting the size of the trooper force and the number of new troopers hired and that there was a disproportionate failure of blacks hired to achieve permanent trooper status; the court reaffirmed its 1972 hiring order and enjoined attempts by the department to delay or frustrate compliance. In 1977, the plaintiffs sought supplemental relief from the District Court on the question of the department's promotion practices. In 1979, in a partial consent decree*approved by the court, the department agreed (1) to develop within 1 year a promotion procedure that would be fair to all applicants and have little or no adverse impact on blacks seeking promotion to corporal, and (2) that the promotion procedure would conform with [equal employment opportunity guidelines]. The 1979 decree required that once such a procedure was in place for the rank of corporal, the department was to develop similar procedures for the other upper ranks. In a second consent decree approved by the District

Court in 1981, the department reaffirmed its 1979 commitment to implement a promotion procedure with little or no adverse impact on blacks; the parties agreed to the administration of the proposed procedure and that its results would be reviewed to determine whether it had an adverse impact on black applicants. In a test administered to 262 applicants of whom 60 were blacks, only 5 blacks were in the top half of the promotion register, and the highest black candidate was number 80. The department then declared that there was an immediate need to make between 8 and 10 promotions to corporal and announced its intention to promote between 16 and 20 individuals. The United States objected to any use of the promotion list, and no promotions were made. In 1983, the plaintiffs asked the District Court to require the department to promote blacks to corporal at the same rate at which they have been hired, one for one, until the department implemented a valid promotion procedure. Finding that the department's selection procedure had an adverse impact on blacks, the District Court ordered the department to submit a plan to promote to corporal, from qualified candidates, at least 15 persons in a manner that would not have an adverse racial impact. The department then proposed to promote 15 persons, of whom four would be black. The District Court granted the plaintiffs' motion to enforce the 1979 and 1981 decrees and, noting that 12 years after it had condemned the racially discriminatory policies and practices of the department, the effects of those policies and practices remained pervasive and conspicuous at all ranks above the entry-level position, the court held that for a period of time, at least 50% of the promotions to corporal should be awarded to black troopers, if qualified black candidates were available; the court

---

*Editors' note; According to *Black's Law Dictionary* (fifth edition), a consent decree is an "agreement by defendant to cease activities asserted as illegal by government" or "a decree entered in an equity suit on consent of both parties." A consent decree is binding on the parties, but not the court. When a defendant enters into such an agreement, the government drops its action against that party.

also (1) imposed a 50% promotional quota in the upper ranks, but only if there were qualified black candidates, if the rank were less than 25% black, and if the department had not developed and implemented a promotion plan without adverse impact for the relevant rank, and (2) ordered the department to submit within 30 days a schedule for the development of promotion procedures for all ranks above the entry-level. . . . After the department promoted eight blacks and eight whites to corporal and submitted for the court's approval its proposed procedures for promotions to corporal and sergeant, the District Court suspended application of the one-for-one requirement for that purpose and ruled that the department could promote up to 13 troopers to corporal by utilizing this procedure. The United States Court of Appeals for the Eleventh Circuit affirmed, stating that the relief at issue was designed to remedy the present effects of past discrimination and was deemed to extend no further than necessary to accomplish the objective of remedying the egregious and long-standing racial imbalances in the upper ranks of the department. . . .

On certiorari, the United States Supreme Court affirmed. Although unable to agree on an opinion, five members of the court agreed that the judgment of the Court of Appeals affirming the order of the District Court should be affirmed.

Opinion

Justice **Brennan** announced the judgment of the Court and delivered an opinion in which Justice **Marshall,** Justice **Blackmun,** and Justice **Powell** join.

The question we must decide is whether relief awarded in this case, in the form of a one-black-for-one-white promo-

tion requirement to be applied as an interim measure to state trooper promotions in the Alabama Department of Public Safety (Department), is permissible under the Equal Protection guarantee of the Fourteenth Amendment.

In 1972 the United States District Court for the Middle District of Alabama held that the Department had systematically excluded blacks from employment in violation of the Fourteenth Amendement. Some 11 years later, confronted with the Department's failure to develop promotion procedures that did not have an adverse impact on blacks, the District Court ordered the promotion of one black trooper for each white trooper elevated in rank, as long as qualified black candidates were available, until the Department implemented an acceptable promotion procedure. The United States challenges the constitutionality of this order.

*   *   *

II

The United States maintains that the race-conscious relief ordered in this case violates the Equal Protection Clause of the Fourteenth Amendment to the Constitution of the United States.

It is now well established that government bodies, including courts, may constitutionally employ racial classifications essential to remedy unlawful treatment of racial or ethnic goups subject to discrimination. . . . But although this Court has consistently held that some elevated level of scrutiny is required when a racial or ethnic distinction is made for remedial purposes, it has yet to reach consensus on the appropriate constitutional analysis. We need not do so in this case, however, because we conclude that the relief ordered survives even strict scrutiny analysis: it is "narrowly tailored" to serve a "compelling governmental purpose."

*   *   *

III

While conceding that the District Court's order serves a compelling interest, the Government insists that it was not narrowly tailored to accomplish its purposes—to remedy past discrimination and eliminate its lingering effects, to enforce compliance with the 1979 and 1981 Decrees by bringing about the speedy implementation of a promotion procedure that would not have an adverse impact on blacks, and to eradicate the ill effects of the Department's delay in producing such a procedure. We cannot agree.

In determining whether race-conscious remedies are appropriate, we look to several factors, including the necessity for the relief and the efficacy of alternative remedies, the flexibility and duration of the relief, including the availability of waiver provisions; the relationship of the numerical goals to the relevant labor market; and the impact of the relief on the rights of third parties . . . . When considered in light of these factors, it was amply established, and we find that the one-for-one promotion requirement was narrowly tailored to serve its several purposes, both as applied to the initial set of promotions to the rank of corporal and as a continuing contigent order with respect to the upper ranks.

*   *   *

IV

The remedy imposed here is an effective, temporary and flexible measure. It applies only if qualified blacks are available, only if the Department has an objective need to make promotions, and only if the Department fails to implement a promotion procedure that does not have an adverse impact on blacks. The one-for-one requirement is the product of the considered judgment of the District Court which, with its knowledge of the parties and their resources, properly determined that strong measures were required in light of the Department's long and shameful record of delay and resistance. The race-conscious relief imposed here was amply justified, and narrowly tailored to serve the legitimate and laudable purposes of the District Court.

*   *   *

Justice **Powell,** concurring.

In determining whether an affirmative action remedy is narrowly drawn to achieve its goal, I have thought that five factors may be relevant: (i) the efficacy of alternative remedies; (ii) the planned duration of the remedy; (iii) the relationship between the percentage of minority workers to be employed and the percentage of minority group members in the relevant population or work force; (iv) the availablity of waiver provisions if the hiring plan could not be met; and (v) the effect of the remedy upon innocent third parties. . . .

The District Court imposed the one-for-one promotion requirement only on one occasion, when it ordered the promotion of eight blacks and eight whites to the rank of corporal in February 1984. Because the Department urgently needed at least fifteen additional corporals, . . . there appears to have been no alternative remedy that would have met the then-existing need. Given the findings of persistent discrimination, the Department's longstanding resistance to necessary remedies, and the exigent circumstances presented to the District Court, the imposition of a one-for-one requirement for the particular promotions at issue did not violate the Equal Protection Clause.

The District Court's order contains significant elements of flexibility and fairness. First, it applies only if qualified black candidates are available for promotion. Second, the court suspended the order when the Department proposed procedures that appeared likely to have no adverse impact on minority applicants. It thus appears that the court's order is based upon "realistic expectations," and that the one-for-one requirement is likely to be, as the court intended, a "one-time occurrence.". . . The court's actions indicate that the order will be enforced in a constitutional manner if it is reimposed. . . . Although the burden of a narrowly pre-

scribed promotion goal, as in this case, is not diffused among society generally, the burden is shared by the nonminority employees over a period of time. As noted above, only qualified minority applicants are eligible for promotion, and qualified nonminority applicants remain eligible to compete for the available promotions. Although some white troopers will have their promotions delayed, it is uncertain whether any individual trooper, white or black, would have achieved a different rank, or would have achieved it at a different time, but for the promotion requirement.

In view of the purpose and indeed the explicit language of the Equal Protection Clause, court-ordered or government-adopted affirmative action plans must be most carefully scrutinized. The Court, in its opinion today, has done this. I therefore join the opinion.

DISCUSSION QUESTIONS

1. Consider alternative means for remedying the past violations of African-Americans' Equal Protection rights by the Alabama Department of Public Safety. Evaluate each in terms of meeting the five factors comprising narrow tailoring mentioned by Justice Powell. For instance, would a means requiring the promotion of African-Americans only, or the dismissal of Whites to make room for African-Americans, be narrowly tailored? Is there a trade-off between narrow tailoring and effective affirmative action?

2. In dissent, Justice O'Connor, joined by Chief Justice Rehnquist and Justice Scalia, suggested that it would have been more appropriate for the district court to have fined the Public Safety Department for contempt of court for its failure to comply with earlier consent decrees. From the perspective of a public administrator involved in such a case, identify the advantages and disadvantages of the imposition of (a) fines and (b) the district court's affirmative action plan.

5

EFFICIENCY

According to the classical approach to public administration, "The fundamental objective of the science of administration is the accomplishment of the work in hand with the least expenditure of man-power and materials. Efficiency is thus axiom number one in the value scale of administration."[1] Indeed, the importance of administrative efficiency is almost self-evident. As the scope of the administrative state grew, the potential impact of waste through inefficiencies became tremendous. For example, today, if each federal employee wasted but one-half hour every workday in the year, the total lost time would be equivalent to employing 175,000 workers for a year—more than the number of civil servants in the Departments of State, Labor, Energy, Housing and Urban Development, and Commerce combined. However, efficiency, like other administrative values, must often be subordinated to constitutional values. The constitutionally competent public administrator can no longer assume that efficiency is the "basic 'good' "[2] of his or her work.

EFFICIENCY DEFINED

Public administrative efficiency is usually defined analogously to mechanical efficiency. It is a ratio of outputs to inputs. The outputs can be any units of service or constraints delivered or applied through public administrative operations. The number of tons of garbage collected, miles of streets snowplowed,

[1]Luther Gulick and L. Urwick, eds., *Papers on the Science of Administration* (New York: Institute of Public Administration, 1937), p. 192.
[2]Ibid.

square miles patrolled by police, and restaurants inspected are examples of outputs. The inputs include personnel, equipment, supplies, materials, buildings, and the overhead administrative activities used to obtain and/or maintain them. The greater the outputs, relative to the inputs, the more efficient public administration is considered to be.

Although the concept of administrative efficiency is related to economy, it is analytically distinct. Efficiency seeks to use a given level of inputs to produce more outputs. It looks toward better management, training, organization of work, and technology as means of obtaining more output with the same (or less) input. Economy, which is the subject of Chapter 7, by contrast, is concerned with the *cost* per unit of output. Economy seeks to reduce the cost of the output, rather than the effort, energy, and time required to produce it. Of course, efficiency and economy may overlap, but the distinction between the two is illustrated by any number of technologies that are both more efficient and more expensive. For instance, memos, reports, and letters can be printed on typewriters and duplicated through the use of carbon paper. These technologies are cheaper to purchase, maintain, and perhaps operate than word processors and copy machines. Depending on the amount of printing and copying involved, typewriters and carbon paper may also be less costly per page. However, they are also clearly less efficient in terms of the speed and effort with which the output can be produced.

Generally, administrative agencies are organized in a way that is intended to promote efficiency. They rely on specialization, or a division of labor because it promotes efficiency. As Adam Smith observed in *The Wealth of Nations* (1776), the same number of workers can produce more pins or other products per unit of time if each specializes in the creation of part of the item rather than if each worker is expected to produce it entirely by himself or herself. Assembly line production is an embodiment of this idea. Administrative organizations typically use hierarchy to coordinate the specialized functions so that the desired outputs are produced. Further, these organizations emphasize hiring and promoting the most capable workers.

It is important to bear in mind that the concept of efficiency does not directly concern the value of the outputs. Efficiency is not a ratio of benefits to inputs: administrative ". . . efficiency takes the output you intend to produce as given; it does not question the output's benefit."[3] Consequently, the emphasis on efficiency may beg the larger question of the purposes to which public administrative activity ought to be devoted.

EFFICIENCY AS A MORAL VALUE

Although efficiency is instrumental because it is not concerned with the ultimate purposes or objectives of public administration, it has frequently been treated as

---

[3]George Downs and Patrick Larkey, *The Search for Government Efficiency* (New York: Random House, 1986), p. 6.

an end in itself. Because it is the antithesis of waste, which is considered by many to be immoral, efficiency has often been thought of as a moral good. As Robert Simmons and Eugene Dvorin note, according to classical administrative theory,

> The "goodness" or "badness" of a particular organizational pattern was a mathematical relationship of "inputs" to "outputs." Where the latter was maximized and the former minimized, a moral "good" resulted. Where the situation was reversed, a moral "bad" resulted. Virtue or "goodness" was therefore equated with the relationship of these two factors, that is, "efficiency" or "inefficiency." Mathematics was transformed into ethics.[4]

But, as Dwight Waldo, a major critic of the traditional approach, argued in his classic book, *The Administrative State*, ". . . efficiency cannot *itself* be a 'value.'. . . Things are not simply 'efficient' or 'inefficient.' They are efficient or inefficient for given purposes, and efficiency for one purpose may mean inefficiency for another."[5] For example, consider the question of whether the bicameral legislatures found in the federal government and forty-nine of the fifty states (Nebraska being the sole exception) are efficient. Certainly, the Senate and House (or assembly) have overlapping responsibilities. They could even be considered redundant, especially at the state level where the upper and lower houses are both apportioned on the basis of population. The legislative process is generally slow, cumbersome, and subject to numerous barriers. It is stalemated unless both houses agree, by majority vote, to pass a bill. Consequently, on the surface, and from an organizational perspective, bicameralism looks inefficient as a means of processing proposals for legislation. However, as a structural arrangement for representing constituencies, deliberating over public policy, and placing checks and balances on elected legislators, bicameralism may be highly efficient.

Moreover, seeking efficiency with regard to some governmental purposes may be of secondary concern. Generally speaking, although a lot of lip service is paid to efficiency, American political culture does not place the highest premium on it. As Chief Justice Burger wrote in *Immigration and Naturalization Service* v. *Chadha* (1983), presented in Chapter 1, "with all the obvious flaws of delay, untidiness, and potential for abuse, we have not yet found a better way to preserve freedom than by making the exercise of power subject to the carefully crafted restraints spelled out in the Constitution."[6] Consequently, to the extent that public administration is intertwined or infused with politics, it may be inappropriate to emphasize efficiency as "axiom number one." Even Luther Gulick, who believed that efficiency could be the basis of a science of administration, noted that "There are . . . highly inefficient arrangements like citizen boards and small local governments which may be necessary in a democ-

---

[4]Robert Simmons and Eugene Dvorin, *Public Administration* (Port Washington, N.Y.: Alfred Publishers, 1977), p. 217.

[5]Dwight Waldo, *The Administrative State*, 2nd ed. (New York: Holmes and Meier, 1984), p. 193.

[6]*Immigration and Naturalization Service* v. *Chadha*, 462 U.S. 919, 959 (1983).

racy. . . ."[7] One of the most common disparities between political and administrative outlooks is manifested in the tension between accountability and efficiency. Accountability requires *red tape*—vouchers, forms, approvals, oversight—which clearly militates against administrative efficiency.[8]

EFFICIENCY WITHIN THE CONSTITUTIONAL FRAMEWORK

Public administrators must be aware of at least four broad constitutional values that help determine the appropriateness of efforts to maximize efficiency. These are: constitutional integrity (already discussed in Chapter 1); due process; robust individual civil rights and liberties; and equal protection of the laws. Together, these concerns provide a framework that can guide constitutionally competent public administrators in their pursuit of efficiency.

The Fifth and Fourteenth Amendments provide that the government shall not deprive any person of "life, liberty, or property, without due process of law." The essence of due process is fundamental fairness. In the public administrative context, it often requires procedures, such as hearings, that are at odds with managerial efficiency. Moreover, the importance of due process in public administration has expanded considerably in the past two decades because the courts have treated governmental benefits, such as public employment and welfare payments, as "property interests" that are protected by it. The case of *Loudermill* v. *Cleveland Board of Education* (1985), which follows, well conveys recent constitutional concepts regarding the application and procedural requirements of due process in routine public administration. In considering the constitutionality of the dismissal of a public employee, the Supreme Court assesses the three standard factors, first established in *Mathews* v. *Eldridge* (1976),[9] which must be taken into account when public administrators are depriving individuals of governmental benefits. These are: ". . . first, the private interest that will be affected by the official action; second, the risk of an erroneous deprivation of such interest through the procedures used, and the probable value, if any, of additional or substitute procedural safeguards; and finally, the Government's interest, including the function involved and the fiscal and administrative burdens that the additional or substitute procedural requirement would entail."[10] The *Loudermill* case also discusses the constitutional importance of providing individuals, who stand to be deprived of liberty or property interests, notice of the impending action and an opportunity to respond to the information or charges on which it is based. Although the decision applies specifically to dismissal from public employment, the Court's

---

[7]Gulick and Urwick, *Papers on the Science of Administration,* pp. 192–93. See Waldo, *The Administrative State,* 2nd ed., Chapter 10 for a strong critique of classical public administration on these points.

[8]Herbert Kaufman, *Red Tape* (Washington: Brookings Institution, 1977).

[9]*Mathews v. Eldridge,* 424 U.S. 319 (1976).

[10]*Ibid.* at 335.

discussion of due process is broad enough to encompass other administrative actions as well.

Another aspect of due process is illustrated by *Cleveland Board of Education* v. *LaFleur* (1974) (Case 5.2). There, the Supreme Court discusses two interrelated aspects of due process: (a) the Constitution's distaste for conclusive, or irrebuttable, harmful presumptions about individuals, and (b) its strong preference for individualized treatment of persons whose liberty or property interests may be abridged by administrative action. However, avoiding generalized presumptions and assessing each case on its own merits can interfere with efficiency, as in *LaFleur.*

The high value placed by the Constitution on individual civil rights and liberties can also place constraints on administrative efficiency. *Rankin* v. *McPherson* (1987), Case 5.3, deals with a relatively common administrative issue: When can public employees' public remarks be the basis for adverse actions, including dismissals, intended to promote the efficiency of the civil service? In reaching its startling conclusion that McPherson had a constitutionally protected right to say of an assassination attempt on President Reagan, "shoot, if they go for him again, I hope they get him," the Supreme Court broadly explains how the government's concern with efficiency must be balanced against public employees' countervailing interests in freedom of speech.

Another aspect of the tension between administrative efficiency and public employees' constitutional rights is the focus of *O'Connor* v. *Ortega* (1987), Case 5.4, which deals with the right to privacy. Although the Supreme Court was unable to reach a majority opinion, its lead opinion, by Justice O'Connor, clearly explains how the right to privacy is structured in general. Her opinion also suggests how public administrators should balance the need for efficiency against the right of public employees to privacy. The Court's discussion in *Ortega* provides the basis for analyzing the constitutionality of mandatory drug testing of public employees.[11]

Finally, *Baker* v. *City of St. Petersburg* (1968), Case 5.5, provides an illustration of how and why administrative claims for greater efficiency must be subordinated to the requirements of the Equal Protection Clause of the Fourteenth Amendment.

ADDITIONAL READING

DOWNS, GEORGE, and PATRICK LARKEY. *The Search for Government Efficiency.* New York: Random House, 1986.

GULICK, LUTHER, and L. URWICK, eds. *Papers on the Science of Administration.* New York: Institute of Public Administration, 1937.

WALDO, DWIGHT. *The Administrative State,* 2nd ed. New York: Holmes and Meier, 1984.

[11]*National Treasury Employees Union* v. *Von Raab,* 103 L. Ed. 2d 685 (1989).

CASE 5.1:
DUE PROCESS AND EFFICIENT
PROCESS

CLEVELAND BOARD OF
EDUCATION v.
LOUDERMILL ET AL.
470 US 532
CERTIORARI TO THE UNITED
STATES COURT OF APPEALS
FOR
THE SIXTH CIRCUIT
No. 83-1362. Argued December 3,
1984—Decided March 19, 1985[*]

Summary

In No. 83-1362, petitioner Board of Education hired respondent Loudermill as a security guard. On his job application Loudermill stated that he had never been convicted of a felony. Subsequently, upon discovering that he had in fact been convicted of grand larceny, the Board dismissed him for dishonesty in filling out the job application. He was not afforded an opportunity to respond to the dishonesty charge or to challenge the dismissal. Under Ohio law, Loudermill was a "classified civil servant," and by statute, as such an employee, could be terminated only for cause and was entitled to administrative review of the dismissal. He filed an appeal with the Civil Service Commission, which, after hearings before a referree and the Commission, upheld the dismissal some nine months after the appeal had been filed. Although the Commission's decision was subject to review in the state courts, Loudermill instead filed suit in Federal District Court, alleging that the Ohio stat-

ute providing for administrative review was unconstitutional on its face because it provided no opportunity for a discharged employee to respond to charges against him prior to removal, thus depriving him of liberty and property without due process. It was also alleged that the statute was unconstitutional as applied because discharged employees were not given sufficiently prompt postremoval hearings. The District Court dismissed the suit for failure to state a claim on which relief could be granted, holding that because the very statute that created the property right in continued employment also specified the procedures for discharge, and because those procedures were followed, Loudermill was, by definition, afforded all the process due; that the post-termination hearings also adequately protected Loudermill's property interest; and that in light of the Commission's crowded docket the delay in processing his appeal was constitutionally acceptable. In No. 83-1363, petitioner Board of Education fired respondent Donnnelly from his job as a bus mechanic because he had failed an eye examination. He appealed to the Civil Service Commission, which ordered him reinstated, but without backpay. He then filed

[*]Together with No. 83-1363, *Parma Board of Education* v. *Donnelly et al.*, and No. 83-6392, *Loudermill* v. *Cleveland Board of Education et al.*, also on certiorari to the same court.

a complaint in Federal District Court essentially identical to Loudermill's, and the court dismissed for failure to state a claim. On a consolidated appeal, the Court of Appeals reversed in part and remanded, holding that both respondents had been deprived of due process and that the compelling private interest in retaining employment, combined with the value of presenting evidence prior to dismissal, outweighed the added administrative burden of a pretermination hearing. But with regard to the alleged deprivation of liberty and Loudermill's 9-month wait for an administrative decision, the court affirmed the District Court, finding no constitutional violation.

Held: All the process that is due is provided by a pretermination opportunity to respond, coupled with post-termination administrative procedures as provided by the Ohio statute; since respondents alleged that they had no chance to respond, the District Court erred in dismissing their complaints for failure to state a claim.

Opinion

JUSTICE WHITE delivered the opinion of the Court.

In these cases we consider what pretermination process must be accorded a public employee who can be discharged only for cause.

I

In 1979 the Cleveland Board of Education, petitioner in No. 83-1362, hired respondent James Loudermill as a security guard. On his job application, Loudermill stated that he had never been convicted of a felony. Eleven months later, as part of a routine examination of his employment records, the Board discovered that in fact Loudermill had been convicted of grand larceny in 1968. By letter dated November 3, 1980, the Board's Business Manager informed Loudermill that he had been dismissed because of his dishonesty in filling out the employment application. Loudermill was not afforded an opportunity to respond to the charge of dishonesty or to challenge his dismissal. On November 13, the Board adopted a resolution officially approving the discharge.

Under Ohio law, Loudermill was a "classified civil servant.". . . Such employees can be terminated only for cause, and may obtain administrative review if discharged. . . . Pursuant to this provision, Loudermill filed an appeal with the Cleveland Civil Service Commission on November 12. The Commission appointed a referee, who held a hearing on January 29, 1981. Loudermill arued that he had thought that his 1968 larceny conviction was for a misdemeanor rather than a felony. The referee recommended reinstatement. On July 20, 1981, the full Commission heard argument and orally announced that it would uphold the dismissal. Proposed findings of fact and conclusions of law followed on August 10, and Loudermill's attorneys were advised of the result by mail on August 21.

*   *   *

The other case before us arises on similar facts and followed a similar course. Respondent Richard Donnelly was a bus mechanic for the Parma Board of Education. In August 1977, Donnelly was fired because he had failed an eye examination. He was offered a chance to retake the examination but did not do so. Like Loudermill, Donnelly appealed to the Civil Service Commission. After a year of wrangling about the timeliness of his appeal, the Commission heard the case. It ordered

Donnelly reinstated, though without back-pay. In a complaint essentially identical to Loudermill's, Donnelly challenged the constitutionality of the dismissal procedures.

*   *   *

II

Respondents' federal constitutional claim depends on their having had a property right in continued employment. . . . If they did, the State could not deprive them of this property without due process. . . .

Property interests are not created by the Constitution, "they are created and their dimensions are defined by existing rules or understandings that stem from an independent source such as state law. . . .". . . The Ohio statute plainly creates such an interest. Respondents were "classified civil service employees," entitled to retain their positions "during good behavior and efficient service," who could not be dismissed "except . . . for . . . misfeasance, malfeasance, or nonfeasance in office.". . . The statute plainly supports the conclusion, reached by both lower courts, that respondents possessed property rights in continued employment. Indeed, this question does not seem to have been disputed below.

The Parma Board argues, however, that the property right is defined by, and conditioned on, the legislature's choice of procedures for its deprivation. . . . The Board stresses that in addition to specifying the grounds for termination, the statute sets out procedures by which termination may take place. The procedures were adhered to in these cases. According to petitioner, "[t]o require additional procedures would in effect expand the scope of the property interest itself.". . .

*   *   *

. . . [I]t is settled that the "bitter with the sweet" approach [argued by the Parma Board] misconceives the constitutional guarantee. If a clearer holding is needed, we provide it today. The point is straightforward: the Due Process Clause provides that certain substantive rights—life, liberty, and property—cannot be deprived except pursuant to constitutionally adequate procedures. The categories of substance and procedure are distinct. Were the rule otherwise, the Clause would be reduced to a mere tautology. "Property" cannot be defined by the procedures provided for its deprivation any more than can life or liberty. The right to due process "is conferred, not by legislative grace, but by constitutional guarantee. While the legislature may elect not to confer a property interest in [public] employment, it may not constitutionally authorize the depriviation of such an interest, once conferred, without appropriate procedural safeguards.". . .

In short, once it is determined that the Due Process clause applies, "the question remains what process is due.". . . The answer to that question is not to be found in the Ohio statute.

III

An essential principle of due process is that a deprivation of life, liberty, or property "be preceded by notice and opportunity for hearing appropriate to the nature of the case.". . . We have described "the root requirement" of the Due Process Clause as being "that an individual be given an opportunity for a hearing *before* he is deprived of any significant property interest.". . . This principle requires "some kind of a hearing" prior to the discharge of an employee who has a constitutionally protected property interest in his employment. . . . Even decisions finding no constitutional violation in termination procedures have relied on the existence of some pretermination opportunity to respond. . . .

The need for some form of pretermination hearing . . . is evident from a balancing of the competing interests at stake. These are the private interest in retaining employment, the governmental interest in the expeditious removal of unsatisfactory employees and the avoidance of administrative burdens, and the risk of an erroneous termination. See *Mathews* v. *Eldridge*, 424 U.S. 319, 335 (1976).

First, the significance of the private interest in retaining employment cannot be gainsaid. We have frequently recognized the severity of depriving a person of the means of livelihood. . . . While a fired worker may find employment elsewhere, doing so will take some time and is likely to be burdened by the questionable circumstances under which he left his previous job. . . .

Second, some opportunity for the employee to present his side of the case is recurringly of obvious value in reaching an accurate decison. Dismissals for cause will often involve factual disputes. . . . Even where the facts are clear, the appropriateness or necessity of the discharge may not be; in such cases, the only meaningful opportunity to invoke the discretion of the decisionmaker is likely to be before the termination takes effect. . . .

The cases before us illustrate these considerations. Both respondents had plausible arguments to make that might have prevented their discharge. The fact that the Commission saw fit to reinstate Donnelly suggests that an error might have been avoided had he been provided an opportunity to make his case to the Board. As for Loudermill, given the Commission's ruling we cannot say that the discharge was mistaken. Nonetheless, in light of the referee's recommendation, neither can we say that a fully informed decisionmaker might not have exercised its discretion and decided not to dismiss him, notwithstanding its authority to do so. In any event, the termination involved arguable issues, and the right to a hearing does not depend on a demonstration of certain success. . . .

The governmental interest in immediate termination does not outweigh these interests. As we shall explain, affording the employee an opportunity to respond prior to termination would impose neither a significant administrative burden nor intolerable delays. Furthermore, the employer shares the employee's interest in avoiding disruption and erroneous decisions; and until the matter is settled, the employer would continue to receive the benefit of the employee's labors. It is preferable to keep a qualified employee on than to train a new one. A governmental employer also has an interest in keeping citizens usefully employed rather than taking the possibly erroneous and counterproductive step of forcing its employees onto the welfare rolls. Finally, in those situations where the employer perceives a significant hazard in keeping the employee on the job, it can avoid the problem by suspending with pay.

IV

The foregoing considerations indicate that the pretermination "hearing," though necessary, need not be elaborate. We have pointed out that "[t]he formality and procedural requisites for the hearing can vary, depending upon the importance of the interests involved and the nature of the subsequent proceedings." . . . In general, "something less" than a full evidentiary hearing is sufficient prior to adverse administrative action. . . . Under state law, respondents were later entitled to a full administrative hearing and judical review. The only question is what steps were required before the termination took effect.

In only one case, *Goldberg* v. *Kelly* . . . (1970), has the court required a full adversarial evidentiary hearing prior to adverse governmental action. However, . . . that case presented significantly different considerations than are present in the context of public employment.* Here, the pretermination hearing need not definitively resolve the propriety of the discharge. It should be an initial check against mistaken decisions—essentially, a determination of whether there are reasonable grounds to believe that the charges against the employee are true and support the proposed action. . . .

The essential requirements of due process, and all that respondents seek or

_____
*Editors' note: Goldberg involved the termination of a welfare benefit, upon which the individual allegedly depended for his immediate survival.

the Court of Appeals required, are notice and an opportunity to respond. The opportunity to present reasons, either in person or in writing, why proposed action should not be taken is a fundamental due process requirement.

The tenured public employee is entitled to oral or written notice of the charges against him, an explanation of the employer's evidence, and an opportunity to present his side of the story. . . . To require more than this prior to termination would intrude to an unwarranted extent on the government interest in quickly removing an unsatisfactory employee.

V

Our holding rests in part on the provisions in Ohio law for a full post-termination hearing. . . .

VI

We concluded that all the process that is due is provided by a pretermination opportunity to respond, coupled with post-termination administrative procedures as provided by the Ohio statute. . . .

DISCUSSION QUESTIONS

1. Consider the extent to which administrative efficiency may be compromised by the due process requirement that those public employees who have a property interest in their jobs be afforded notice and an opportunity to respond to information against them prior to termination. For instance, will agency lawyers ordinarily review the wording of the information prior to its transmission to the employee? Will higher level administrators have to sign off on the information? Does the right to respond implicitly include a right to have the response considered seriously?

2. The Court's decision clearly rests, in part, on the availability of a post-termination hearing procedure. Presumably, such a hearing would be before an impartial examiner, referee, or administrative law judge, and the employee would have the right to bring counsel as well as to confront and cross-examine adverse witnesses. Would such hearings undercut administrative efficiency? Would pretermination hearings be significantly more burdensome to efficient administration? Consider the interest of the government,

the employee, and the employee's supervisor in responding to these questions.

3. In a dissenting opinion, Justice Rehnquist stated:

This customary "balancing" inquiry conducted by the Court in these cases reaches a result that is quite unobjectionable, but it seems to me that it is devoid of any principles which will either instruct or endure. The balance is simply an ad hoc weighing which depends to a great extent upon how the Court subjectively views the underlying interests at stake.

Do you think that the three-factor test prescribed by *Mathews* v. *Eldridge,* as elaborated on in *Loudermill,* provides public administrators with sufficient guidance regarding the applicability and requirements of due process? Can you suggest a better test?

CASE 5.2:
PRESUMPTIONS, INDIVIDUALIZED DETERMINATIONS, AND EFFICIENCY

CLEVELAND BOARD OF
EDUCATION et al.
v.
LaFLEUR et al.
414 US 632
CERTIORARI TO THE UNITED
STATES COURT OF APPEALS
FOR THE SIXTH CIRCUIT
No. 72-777. Argued October 15,
1973—Decided January 21, 1974*

Summary

Pregnant public school teachers brought these actions under 42 U. S. C. § 1983 challenging the constitutionality of mandatory maternity leave rules of the Cleveland, Ohio (No. 72-777), and Chesterfield County, Virginia (No. 72-1129), School Boards. The Cleveland rule requires a pregnant school teacher to take unpaid maternity leave five months before the expected childbirth, with leave application to be made at least two weeks before her departure. Eligibility to return to work is not accorded until the next regular semester after her child is three months old. The Chesterfield County rule requires the teacher to leave work at least four months, and to give notice at least six months, before the anticipated childbirth. Reemployment is guaranteed no later than the first day of the school year after the date she is declared re-eligible. Both schemes require a physicians' certificate of physical fitness prior to the teacher's return. Each Court of Appeals reversed the court below, one holding the Chesterfield County maternity leave rule constitutional,

*Together with No. 72–1129, *Cohen v. Chesterfield County School Board et al.,* on certiorari to the United States Court of Appeals for the Fourth Circuit.

the other holding the Cleveland rule unconstitutional. *Held:*

1. The mandatory termination provisions of both maternity rules violate the Due Process Clause of the Fourteenth Amendment.

2. The Cleveland three-month return provision also violates due process, being both arbitrary and irrational. It creates an irrebuttable presumption that the mother (whose good health must be medically certified) is not fit to resume work, and it is not germane to maintaining continuity of instruction, as the precise point a child will reach the relevant age will occur at a different time throughout the school year for each teacher.

3. The Chesterfield County return rule, which is free of any unnecessary presumption, comports with due process requirements.

Opinion

Mr. Justice Stewart delivered the opinion of the Court.

The respondents in No. 72-777 and the petitioner in No. 72-1129 are female public school teachers. During the 1970–1971 school year, each informed her local school board that she was pregnant; each was compelled by a mandatory maternity leave rule to quit her job without pay several months before the expected birth of her child. These cases call upon us to decide the constitutionality of the school boards' rules.

I

Joe Carol LaFleur and Ann Elizabeth Nelson, the respondents in No. 72-777, are junior high school teachers employed by the Board of Education of Cleveland, Ohio. Pursuant to a rule first adopted in 1952, the school board requires every pregnant school teacher to take maternity leave without pay, beginning five months before the expected birth of her child. Appplication for such leave must be made no later than two weeks prior to the date of departure. A teacher on maternity leave is not allowed to return to work until the beginning of the next regular school semester which follows the date when her child attains the age of three months. A doctor's certificate attesting to the health of the teacher is a prerequisite to return; an additional physical examination may be required. The teacher on maternity leave is not promised re-employment after the birth of the child; she is merely given priority in reassignment to a position for which she is qualified. Failure to comply with the mandatory maternity leave provisions is ground for dismissal.

Neither Mrs. LaFleur nor Mrs. Nelson wished to take an unpaid maternity leave; each wanted to continue teaching until the end of the school year. Because of the mandatory maternity leave rule, however, each was required to leave her job in March 1971. The two women then filed separate suits in the United States District Court for the Northern District of Ohio under 42 U. S. C. § 1983, challenging the constitutionality of the maternity leave rule. The District Court tried the cases together, and rejected the plaintiffs' arguments. . . . A divided panel of the United States Court of Appeals for the Sixth Circuit reversed, finding the Cleveland rule in violation of the Equal Protection Clause of the Fourteenth Amendment. . . .

The petitioner in No. 72-1129, Susan Cohen, was employed by the School Board of Chesterfield County, Virginia. That school board's maternity leave regulation requires that a pregnant teacher leave work at least four months prior to the expected birth of her child. Notice in writing must be given to the school board at least six months prior to the expected birth date. A teacher on maternity leave is declared re-eligible for employment when she submits written notice from a physician that she is physically fit for re-employment, and when she can give assurance that care of the child will cause only minimal interference with her job responsibilities. The teacher is guaranteed re-employment no later than the first day of the school year following the date upon which she is declared re-eligible.

Mrs. Cohen informed the Chesterfield County School Board in November 1970, that she was pregnant and expected the birth of her child about April 28, 1971. She initially requested that she be permitted to continue teaching until April 1, 1971. The school board rejected the request, as it did Mrs. Cohen's subsequent suggestion that she be allowed to teach until January 21, 1971, the end of the first school semester. Instead, she was required to leave her teaching job on December 18, 1970. She subsequently filed this suit under 42 U. S. C. § 1983 in the United States District Court for the Eastern District of Virginia. The District Court held that the school board regulation violates the Equal Protection Clause, and granted appropriate relief. . . . A divided panel of the Fourth Circuit affirmed, but, on rehearing en banc[*] the Court of Appeals upheld the constitutionality of the challenged regulation in a 4–3 decision. . . .

We granted certiorari in both cases . . . in order to resolve the conflict between the Courts of Appeals regarding the constitutionality of such manadatory maternity leave rules for public school teachers.

II

This Court has long recognized that freedom of personal choice in matters of marriage and family life is one of the liberties protected by the Due Process Clause of the Fourteenth Amendment. . . .

[T]here is a right "to be be free from unwarranted governmental intrusion into matters so fundamentally affecting a person as the decision whether to bear or beget a child."

By acting to penalize the pregnant teacher for deciding to bear a child, overly restrictive maternity leave regulations can constitute a heavy burden on the exercise of these protected freedoms. Because public school maternity leave rules directly affect "one of the basic civil rights of man," the Due Process Clause of the Fourteenth Amendment requires that such rules must not needlessly, arbitrarily, or capriciously impinge upon this vital area of a teacher's constitutional liberty. The question before us in these cases is whether the interests advanced in support of the rules of the Cleveland and Chesterfield County School boards can justify the particular procedures they have adopted.

The school boards in these cases have offered two essentially overlapping explanations for their mandatory maternity leave rules. First, they contend that the firm cutoff dates are necessary to maintain continuity of classroom instruction, since advance knowledge of when a pregnant teacher must leave facilitates the finding and hiring of a qualified substitute. Secondly, the school boards seek to justify their maternity rules by arguing that at least some teachers become physically

---

[*]**Editors' note:** A rehearing *en banc* is one in which all the judges of a Circuit Court of Appeals are eligible to participate. The procedure is generally used sparingly and only in cases of extraordinary importance.

incapable of adequately performing certain of their duties during the latter part of pregnancy. By keeping the pregnant teacher out of the classroom during these final months, the maternity leave rules are said to protect the health of the teacher and her unborn child, while at the same time assuring that students have a physically capable instructor in the classroom at all times.

It cannot be denied that continuity of instruction is a significant and legitimate educational goal. Regulations requiring pregnant teachers to provide early notice of their condition to school authorities undoubtedly facilitate administrative planning toward the important objective of continuity. But, as the Court of Appeals for the Second Circuit noted in *Green* v. *Waterford Board of Education*, . . .

"Where a pregnant teacher provides the Board with a date certain for commencement of leave . . . that value [continuity] [sic] is preserved; an arbitrary leave date at the end of the fifth month is no more calculated to facilitate a planned and orderly transition between the teacher and a substitute than is a date fixed closer to confinement. Indeed, the latter . . . would afford the Board more, not less, time to procure a satisfactory long-term substitute." . . .

Thus, while the advance-notice provisions in the Cleveland and Chesterfield County rules are wholly rational and may well be necessary to serve the objective of continuity of instruction, the absolute requirements of termination at the end of the fourth or fifth month of pregnancy are not. Were continuity the only goal, cutoff dates much later during pregnancy would serve as well as or better than the challenged rules, providing that ample advance notice requirements were retained. Indeed, continuity would seem just as well attained if the teacher herself were allowed to choose the date upon which to commence her leave, at least so long as the decision were required to be made and notice given of it well in advance of the date selected.

In fact, since the fifth or sixth month of pregnancy will obviously begin at different times in the school year for different teachers, the present Cleveland and Chesterfield Country rules may serve to hinder attainment of the very continuity objectives that they are purportedly designed to promote. For example, the beginning of the fifth month of pregnancy for both Mrs. LaFleur and Mrs. Nelson occurred during March of 1971. Both were thus required to leave work with only a few months left in the school year, even though both were fully willing to serve through the end of the term. Similarly, if continuity were the only goal, it seems ironic that the Chesterfield County rule forced Mrs. Cohen to leave work in mid-December 1970 rather than at the end of the semester in January, as she requested.

We thus conclude that the arbitrary cutoff dates embodied in the mandatory leave rules before us have no rational relationship to the valid state interest of preserving continuity of instruction. As long as the teachers are required to give substantial advance notice of their condition, the choice of firm dates later in pregnancy would serve the boards' objectives just as well, while imposing a far lesser burden on the women's exercise of constitutionally protected freedom.

The question remains as to whether the cutoff dates at the beginning of the fifth and sixth months can be justified on the other ground advanced by the school boards—the necessity of keeping physically unfit teachers out of the classroom. There can be no doubt that such an objective is perfectly legitimate, both on educational and safety grounds. And, despite the plethora of conflicting medical testimony in these cases, we can assume, *arguendo,* that at least some teachers become physically disabled from effectively performing their duties during the latter stages of pregnancy.

The mandatory termination provisions of the Cleveland and Chesterfield County rules surely operate to insulate the classroom from the presence of potentially incapacitated pregnant teachers. But the question is whether the rules sweep too broadly. . . . That question must be answered in the affirmative, for the provisions amount to a conclusive presumption that every pregnant teacher who reaches the fifth or sixth month of pregnancy is physically incapable of continuing. There is no individualized determination by the teacher's doctor—or the school board's—as to any particular teacher's ability to continue at her job. The rules contain an irrebuttable presumption of physical incompetency, and that presumption applies even when the medical evidence as to an individual woman's physical status might be wholly to the contrary.

As the Court noted last Term . . . "permanent irrebuttable presumptions have long been disfavored under the Due Process Clauses of the Fifth and Fourteenth Amendments."

* * *

While the medical experts in these cases differed on many points, they unanimously agreed on one—the ability of any particular pregnant woman to continue at work past any fixed time in her pregnancy is very much an individual matter. Even assuming, *arguendo,* that there are some women who would be physically unable to work past the particular cutoff dates embodied in the challenged rules, it is evident that there are large numbers of teachers

who are fully capable of continuing work for longer than the Cleveland and Chesterfield County regulations will allow. Thus, the conclusive presumption embodied in these rules is neither "necessarily [nor] universally true," and is violative of the Due Process Clause.

The school boards have argued that the mandatory termination dates serve the interest of administrative convenience, since there are many instances of teacher pregnancy, and the rules obviate the necessity for case-by-case determinations. Certainly, the boards have an interest in devising prompt and efficient procedures to achieve their legitimate objectives in this area. But, as the Court stated in *Stanley* v. *Illinois* [1972],

"[T]he Constitution recognizes higher values than speed and efficiency. Indeed, one might fairly say of the Bill of Rights in general, and the Due Process Clause in particular, that they were designed to protect the fragile values of a vulnerable citizenry from the overbearing concern for efficiency and efficacy that may characterize praiseworthy government officials no less, and perhaps more, than mediocre ones." . . .

While it might be easier for the school boards to conclusively presume that all pregnant women are unfit to teach past the fourth or fifth month or even the first month, of pregnancy, administrative convenience alone is insufficient to make valid what otherwise is a violation of due process of law. The Fourteenth Amendment requires the school boards to employ alternative administrative means, which do not so broadly infringe upon basic constitutional liberty, in support of their legitimate goals.

We conclude, therefore, that neither the necessity for continuity of instruction nor the state interest in keeping physically unfit teachers out of the classroom can justify the sweeping mandatory leave regulations that the Cleveland and Chesterfield County School Boards have adopted. While the regulations no doubt represent a good-faith attempt to achieve a laudable goal, they cannot pass muster under the Due Process Clause of the Fourteenth Amendment, because they employ irrebuttable presumptions that unduly penalize a female teacher for deciding to bear a child.

III

In addition to the mandatory termination provisions, both the Cleveland and Chesterfield County rules contain limitations upon a teacher's eligibility to return to work after giving birth. Again, the school boards offer two justifications for the return rules—continuity of instruction and the desire to be certain that the teacher is physically competent when she returns to work. As is the case with the leave provisions, the question is not whether the school board's goals are legitimate, but rather whether the particular means chosen to achieve those objectives unduly infringe upon the teacher's constitutional liberty.

Under the Cleveland rule, the teacher is not eligible to return to work until the beginning of the next regular school semester following the time when her child attains the age of three months. A doctor's certificate attesting to the teacher's health is required before return; an additional physical examination may be required at the option of the school board.

The respondents in No. 72-777 do not seriously challenge either the medical requirements of the Cleveland rule or the policy of limiting eligibility to return to the next semester following birth. The provisions concerning a medical certificate or supplemental physical examination are narrowly drawn methods of protecting the school board's interest in teacher fitness; these requirements allow an individualized decision as to the teacher's condition, and thus avoid the pitfalls of the presumptions inherent in the leave rules. Similarly, the provision limiting eligibility to return to the semester following delivery is a precisely drawn means of serving the school board's interest in avoiding unnecessary changes in classroom personnel during any one school term.

The Cleveland rule, however, does not simply contain these reasonable medical and next-semester eligibility provisions. In addition, the school board requires the mother to wait until her child reaches the age of three months before the return rules begin to operate. The school board has offered no reasonable justification for this supplemental limitation, and we can perceive none. To the extent that the three-month provision reflects the school board's thinking that no mother is fit to return until that point in time, it suffers from the same constitutional deficiencies that plague the irrebuttable presumption in the termination rules. The presumption, moreover, is patently unnecessary, since the requirement of a physician's certificate or a medical examination fully protects the school's interests in this regard. And finally, the three-month provision simply has nothing to do with continuity of instruction, since the precise point at which the child will reach the relevant age will obviously occur at a different point throughout the school year for each teacher.

Thus, we conclude that the Cleveland return rule, insofar as it embodies the three-month age provision, is wholly arbitrary and irrational, and hence violates the Due Process Clause of the Fourteenth Amendment. The age limitation serves no legitimate state interest, and unnecessarily penalizes the female teacher for asserting her right to bear children.

We perceive no such constitutional infirmities in the Chesterfield County rule. In that school system, the teacher becomes eligible for re-employment upon submission of a medical certificate from her physician; return to work is guaranteed no later than the beginning of the next school year following the eligibility determination. The medical certificate is both a reasonable and narrow method of protecting the school board's interest in teacher fitness, while the possible deferring of return until the next school year serves the goal of preserving continuity of instruction. In short, the Chesterfield County rule manages to serve the legitimate state interests here without employing unnecessary presumptions that broadly burden the exercise of protected constitutional liberty.

IV

For the reasons stated, we hold that the mandatory termination provisions of the Cleveland and Chesterfield County maternity regulations violate the Due Process Clause of the Fourteenth Amendment, because of their use of unwarranted conclusive presumptions that seriously burden the exercise of protected constitutional liberty. For similar reasons, we hold the three-month provisions of the Cleveland return rule unconstitutional.

DISCUSSION QUESTIONS

1. Does the Court's opinion fully identify all the administrative interests of the school boards in enforcing the mandatory maternity leave policies at issue? For instance, would it be more efficient and effective to be able to hire a long-term replacement for a pregnant teacher as of a particular date, known in advance, rather than as of the day the teacher is no longer able to continue in her job based on an individualized medical determination? What other administrative interests might be involved? Do you think the Court's opinion deals with these adequately?

2. The lower courts decided these cases under the Equal Protection Clause. In a concurring opinion, Justice Powell argued that the Supreme Court should have done the same. Discuss how you would decide the cases under equal protection. What might be the advantages for public administrators if equal protection analysis, rather than that of irrebuttable presumptions, were used? Consider how administrative (or legislative) classifications are treated by each approach.

3. Aside from the issue raised in Question 1, would the individualized medical determinations called for by the Court reduce efficiency? How and/or how not?

CASE 5.3:
PUBLIC EMPLOYEES' FREEDOM OF SPEECH AND ADMINISTRATIVE EFFICIENCY

Walter H. RANKIN, etc., et
al., Petitioners
v.
Ardith McPHERSON.
No. 85-2068.
Argued March 23, 1987.
Decided June 24, 1987.
107 S. Ct. 2891

Summary

Former clerical employee in county constable's office brought suit against constable and county, alleging that she was denied her First and Fourteenth Amendments rights when she was fired by constable for political remark made to coemployee during private conversation. The United States District Court for the Southern District of Texas entered summary judgment in favor of constable and county, and, after remand . . . the Court . . . entered judgment for constable and county, and deputy appealed. The Court of Appeals for the Fifth Circuit . . . reversed and remanded, and certiorari was granted. The Supreme Court, Justice Marshall, held that: (1) statement by employee, made in course of conversation with coemployee addressing policies of President's administration, that, "if they go for him again, I hope they get him" dealt with matter of public concern, and (2) constable's interest in discharging clerical employee in constable's office for making statement did not outweigh employee's rights under First Amendment.

Opinion

Justice MARSHALL delivered the opinion of the Court.

The issue in this case is whether a clerical employee in a county constable's office was properly discharged for remarking, after hearing of an attempt on the life of the President, "If they go for him again, I hope they get him."

I

On January 12, 1981, respondent Ardith McPherson was appointed a deputy in the office of the constable of Harris County, Texas. The constable is an elected official who functions as a law enforcement officer. At the time of her appointment, McPherson, a black woman, was 19 years old and had attended college for a year, studying secretarial science. Her appointment was conditional for a 90-day probationary period.

Although McPherson's title was "deputy constable," this was the case only because all employees of the constable's office, regardless of job function, were deputy constables. . . . She was not a commissioned peace officer, did not wear a uniform, and was not authorized to make arrests or permitted to carry a gun. McPherson's duties were purely clerical. Her work station was a desk at which there was no telephone, in a room to which the public did not have ready access. Her job was to type data from court papers into a computer that maintained an automated record of the status of civil process in the county. Her training consisted of two days of instruction in the operation of her computer terminal.

On March, 30, 1981, McPherson and some fellow employees heard on a office radio that there had been an attempt to assassinate the President of the United States. Upon hearing that report, McPherson engaged a co-worker, Lawrence Jackson, who was apparently her boyfriend, in a brief conversation, which according to McPherson's uncontroverted testimony went as follows:

"Q: What did you say?
"A: I said I felt that that would happen sooner or later.
"Q: Okay. And what did Lawrence say?
"A: Lawrence said, yeah, agreeing with me.
"Q: Okay. Now, when you—after Lawrence spoke, then what was your next comment?
"A: Well, we were talking—it's a wonder why they did that. I felt like it would be a black person that did that, because I feel like most of my kind is on welfare and CETA, and they use medicaid, and at the time, I was thinking that's what it was.
"... But then after I said that, and then Lawrence said, yeah, he's cutting back medicaid and food stamps. And I said, yeah, welfare and CETA. I said, shoot, if they go for him again, I hope they get him."

McPherson's last remark was overheard by another deputy constable, who, unbeknownst to McPherson, was in the room at the time. The remark was reported to Constable Rankin, who summoned McPherson. McPherson readily admitted that she had made the statement, but testified that she told Rankin, upon being asked if she made the statement, "Yes, but I didn't mean anything by it." ... After their discussion, Rankin fired McPherson.

McPherson brought suit in the United States District Court for the Southern District of Texas under 42 U.S.C. § 1983, alleging that petitioner Rankin, in discharging her, had violated her constitutional rights under color of state law. She sought reinstatement, back pay, costs and fees, and other equitable relief.

* * *

II

It is clearly established that a State may not discharge an employee on a basis that infringes that employee's constitutionally protected interest in freedom of speech. ... Even though McPherson was merely a probationary employee, and even if she could have been discharged for any reason or for no reason at all, she may nonetheless be entitled to reinstatement if she was discharged for exercising her constitutional right to freedom of expression. ...

The determination whether a public employer has properly discharged an employee for engaging in speech requires "a balance between the interests of the [employee], [*sic*] as a citizen, in commenting upon matters of public concern and the interest of the State, as an employer, in promoting the efficiency of the public services it performs through its employees.". ... This balancing is necessary in order to accommodate the dual role of the public employer as a provider of public services and as a government entity operating under the constraints of the First Amendment. On one hand, public employers are *employers*, concerned with the efficient function of their operations: review of every personnel decision made by a public employer could, in the long run, hamper the performance of public functions. On the other hand, "the threat of dismissal from public employment is . . . a potent means of inhibiting speech." . . . Vigilance is necessary to ensure that public employers do not use authority over employees to silence discourse, not because it hampers public functions but simply because superiors disagree with the content of employees' speech.

A

The threshold question in applying this balancing test is whether McPherson's speech may be "fairly characterized as constituting speech on a matter of public concern." . . . "Whether an employee's speech addresses a matter of public concern must be determined by the content, form, and context of a given statement, as revealed by the whole record." . . . The District Court apparently found that McPherson's speech did not address a matter of public concern. The Court of Appeals rejected this conclusion, finding that "the life and death of the President are obviously matters of public concern." . . .

Considering the statement in context . . . discloses that it plainly dealt with a matter of public concern. The statement was made in the course of a conversation addressing the policies of the President's administration. It came on the heels of a news bulletin regarding what is certainly a matter of heightened public attention: an attempt on the life of the President. While a statement that amounted to a threat to kill the President would not be protect by the First Amendment, the District Court concluded, and we agree, that McPherson's statement did not amount to a threat. . . . The inappropriate or controversial character of a statement is irrelevant to the question whether it deals with a matter of public concern. "[D]ebate on public issues should be uninhibited, ro-

bust, and wide-open, and . . . may well include vehement, caustic, and sometimes unpleasantly sharp attacks on government and public officials." . . .

"Just as erroneous statements must be protected to give freedom of expression the breathing space it needs to survive, so statements criticizing public policy and the implementation of it must be similarly protected."

B

Because McPherson's statement addressed a matter of public concern, [precedent] next requires that we balance McPherson's interest in making her statement against "the interest of the State, as an employer, in promoting the efficiency of the public services it performs through its employees." . . . The State bears a burden of justifying the discharge on legitimate grounds. . . .

In performing the balancing, the statement will not be considered in a vacuum; the manner, time, and place of the employee's expression are relevant, as is the context in which the dispute arose. . . .

We have previously recognized as pertinent considerations whether the statement impairs discipline by superiors or harmony among coworkers, has a detrimental impact on close working relationships for which personal loyalty and confidence are necessary, or impedes the performance of the speaker's duties or interferes with the regular operation of the enterprise. . . .

These considerations, and indeed the very nature of the balancing test, make apparent that the state interest element of the test focuses on the effective functioning of the public employer's enterprise. Interference with work, personnel relations, or the speaker's job performance can detract from the public employer's function; avoiding such interference can be a strong state interest. From this perspective, however, petitioner fails to demonstrate a state interest that outweighs McPherson's First Amendment rights. While McPherson's statement was made at the workplace, there is no evidence that it interfered with the efficient functioning of the office. The Constable was evidently not afraid that McPherson had disturbed or interrupted other employees—he did not inquire to whom respondent had made the remark and testified that he "was not concerned who she had made it to," . . . In fact, Constable Rankin testified that the possibility of interference with the functions of the Constable's office had *not* been a consideration in his discharge of respondent and that he did not even inquire whether the remark had disrupted the work of the office.

Nor was there any danger that McPherson had discredited the office by making her statement in public. McPherson's speech took place in an area to which there was ordinarily no public access; her remark was evidently made in a private conversation with another employee. There is no suggestion that any member of the general public was present or heard McPherson's statement. Nor is there any evidence that employees other than Jackson who worked in the room even heard the remark. Not only was McPherson's discharge unrelated to the functioning of the office, it was not based on any assessment by the constable that the remark demonstrated a character trait that made respondent unfit to perform her work.

While the facts underlying Rankin's discharge of McPherson are, despite extensive proceedings in the District Court, still somewhat unclear, it is undisputed that he fired McPherson based on the *content* of her speech. Evidently because McPherson had made the statement and because the Constable believed that she "meant it," he decided that she was not a suitable employee to have in a law enforcement agency. But in weighing the State's interest in discharging an employee based on any claim that the content of a statement made by the employee somehow undermines the mission of the public employer, some attention must be paid to the responsibilities of the employee within the agency. The burden of caution employees bear with respect to the words they speak will vary with the extent of authority and public accountability the employee's role entails. Where, as here, an employee serves no confidential, policymaking, or public contact role, the danger to the agency's successful function from that employee's private speech is minimal. We cannot believe that every employee in Constable Rankin's office, whether computer operator, electrician, or file clerk, is equally required, on pain of discharge, to avoid any statement susceptible of being interpreted by the Constable as an indication that the employee may be unworthy of employment in his law enforcement agency. At some point, such concerns are so removed from the effective function of the public employer that they cannot prevail over the free speech rights of the public employee.

This is such a case. McPherson's employment-related interaction with the Constable was apparently negligible. Her duties were purely clerical and were limited solely to the civil process function of the constable's office. There is no indication that she would ever be in a position to further—or indeed to have any involvement with—the minimal law enforcement activity engaged in by the Constable's office. Given the function of the agency,

McPherson's position in the office, and the nature of her statement, we are not persuaded that Rankin's interest in discharging her outweighed her rights under the First Amendment.

DISCUSSION QUESTIONS

1. In a strongly worded dissent, Justice Scalia, joined by Chief Justice Rehnquist and Justices White and O'Connor, argued that McPherson's speech was not on "a matter of 'public' concern." Do you agree with the majority or the dissent on this point? What guidance does the majority opinion offer public administrators in identifying speech on a matter of public concern? Do you think its guidance is adequate?

2. Even if a public employee's speech is on a matter of public concern, a public employer may be allowed to discipline him or her for it in the interests of government efficiency. What are the factors that must be considered in deciding whether such speech can constitutionally be the basis of an adverse action? Based on these factors, do you think that Rankin should have known that McPherson's speech was protected? Or, do you agree with the dissent that "It boggles the mind to think that she has such a right [of free speech on the job]"?

3. Suppose, on hearing the remark, a fellow employee harshly criticized McPherson for her comment and a great deal of ill-will developed and, in consequence, smooth working relationships were threatened. Based on the Court's reasoning, does the constitutional protection afforded to public employees's speech depend, in part, on how those hearing their remarks react? If so, can you envision any difficulties not considered by the Court?

4. In *Rankin*, a majority of the justices agreed that ". . . a purely private statement on a matter of public concern will rarely, if ever, justify discharge of a public employee." Can you think of any circumstances in which such remarks might hamper administrative efficiency? For example, suppose an employee at an off-the-job gathering made a racial slur regarding Justice Marshall that was overheard by another employee who subsequently was unable to work with him or her.

CASE 5.4:
PUBLIC EMPLOYEES' PRIVACY AND ADMINISTRATIVE EFFICIENCY

Dennis M. O'CONNOR, et al.,
Petitioners
v.
Magno J. ORTEGA.
No. 85-530.
Argued Oct. 15, 1986.
Decided March 31, 1987
107 S. Ct. 1492

Summary

Former chief of professional education at state hospital brought action against various state hospital officials, alleging claims under § 1983 and state law. On cross motions for summary judgment, the United States District Court for the Northern District of California, John P. Vucasin, Jr., J., granted summary judgment against plaintiff, and he appealed. The Court of Appeals . . . affirmed in part and reversed and remanded with instructions in part, and officials petitioned for certiorari. The Supreme Court, Justice O'Connor, held that: (1) public employers' intrusions on constitutionally protected privacy interest of government employees for noninvestigatory, work-related purposes, as well as for investigations of work-related misconduct, should be judged by standard of reasonableness under all the circumstances, and (2) whether public employer's search of hospital supervisor's office was reasonable, both in its inception and in its scope, presented factual question precluding summary judgment.

Opinion

Justice O'CONNOR announced the judgment of the Court and delivered an opinion in which THE CHIEF JUSTICE, Justice WHITE, and Justice POWELL join.

This suit under 42 U.S.C. § 1983 presents two issues concerning the Fourth Amendment rights of public employees. First, we must determine whether the respondent, a public employee, had a reasonable expectation of privacy in his office, desk, and file cabinets at his place of work. Second, we must address the appropriate Fourth Amendment standard for a search conducted by a public employer in areas in which a public employee is found to have a reasonable expectation of privacy.

I

Dr. Magno Ortega, a physician and psychiatrist, held the position of Chief of Professional Education at Napa State Hospital (Hospital) for 17 years, until his dismissal from that position in 1981. As Chief of Professional Education, Dr. Ortega had primary responsibility for training young physicians in psychiatric residency programs.

In July 1981, Hospital officials, including Dr. Dennis O'Connor, the Executive Director of the Hospital, became concerned about possible improprieties in Dr. Ortega's management of the residency program. In particular, the Hospital officials were concerned with Dr. Ortega's acquisition of an Apple II computer for use in the residency program. The officials thought that Dr. Ortega may have misled Dr. O'Connor into believing that the computer had been donated, when in fact the computer had been financed by the possibly coerced contributions of residents. Additionally, the Hospital officials were concerned with charges that Dr. Ortega had sexually harassed two female Hospital employees, and had taken inappropriate disciplinary action against a resident.

On July 30, 1981, Dr. O'Connor requested that Dr. Ortega take paid administrative leave during an investigation of these charges. At Dr. Ortega's request, Dr. O'Connor agreed to allow Dr. Ortega to take two weeks vacation instead of administrative leave. Dr. Ortega, however, was requested to stay off Hospital grounds for the duration of the investigation. On August 14, 1981, Dr. O'Connor informed Dr. Ortega that the investigation had not yet been completed, and that he was being placed on paid administrative leave. Dr. Ortega remained on administrative leave until the Hosptial terminated his employment on September 22, 1981.

Dr. O'Connor selected several Hospital personnel to conduct the investigation, including an accountant, a physician, and a Hospital security officer. Richard Friday, the Hospital Administrator, led this "investigative team." At some point during the investigation, Mr. Friday made the decision to enter Dr. Ortega's office. The specific reason for the entry into Dr. Ortega's office is unclear from the record. The petitioners claim that the search was conducted to secure state property. Initially, petitioners contended that such a search was pursuant to a Hospital policy of conducting a routine inventory of state prop-

erty in the office of a terminated employee. At the time of the search, however, the Hospital had not yet terminated Dr. Ortega's employment; Dr. Ortega was still on administrative leave. Apparently, there was no policy of inventorying the offices of those on administrative leave. Before the search had been initiated, however, the petitioners had become aware that Dr. Ortega had taken the computer to his home. Dr. Ortega contends that the purpose of the search was to secure evidence for use against him in administrative disciplinary proceedings.

The resulting search of Dr. Ortega's office was quite thorough. The investigators entered the office a number of times and seized several items from Dr. Ortega's desk and file cabinets, including a Valentine's card, a photograph, and book of poetry all sent to Dr. Ortega by a former resident physician. These items were later used in a proceeding before a hearing officer of the California State Personnel Board to impeach the credibility of the former resident, who testified on Dr. Ortega's behalf. The investigators also seized billing documentation of one of Dr. Ortega's private patients under the California Medicaid program. The investigators did not otherwise separate Dr. Ortega's property from state property because, as one investigator testified, "[t]rying to sort State from non-State, it was too much to do, so I gave it up and boxed it up." . . . Thus, no formal inventory of the property in the office was ever made. Instead, all the papers in Dr. Ortega's office were merely placed in boxes, and put in storage for Dr. Ortega to retrieve.

Dr. Ortega commenced this action against the petitioners in Federal District Court under 42 U.S.C. § 1983, alleging that the search of his office violated the Fourth Amendment.

*   *   *

II

*   *   *

The Fourth Amendment protects the "right of the people to be secure in their persons, houses, papers, and effects, against unreasonable searches and seizures. . . ." Our cases establish that Dr. Ortega's Fourth Amendment rights are implicated only if the conduct of the Hospital officials at issue in this case infringed "an expectation of privacy that society is prepared to consider reasonable." . . . We have no talisman that determines in all cases those privacy expectations that society is prepared to accept as reasonable. Instead, "the Court has given weight to such factors as the intention of the Framers of the Fourth Amendment, the uses to which the individual has put a location, and our societal understanding that certain areas deserve the most scrupulous protection from government invasion." . . .

Because the reasonableness of an expectation of privacy, as well as the appropriate standard for a search, is understood to differ according to context, it is essential first to delineate the boundaries of the workplace context. The workplace includes those areas and items that are related to work and are generally within the employer's control. At a hospital, for example, the hallways, cafeteria, offices, desks, and file cabinets, among other areas, are all part of the workplace. These areas remain part of the workplace context even if the employee has placed personal items in them, such as a photograph placed in a desk or a letter posted on an employee bulletin board.

Not everything that passes through the confines of the business address can be considered part of the workplace context, however. An employee may bring closed luggage to the office prior to leaving on a trip, or a handbag or briefcase each workday. While whatever expectation of privacy the employee has in the existence and the outward appearance of the luggage is affected by its presence in the workplace, the employee's expectation of privacy in the *contents* of the luggage is not affected in the same way. The appropriate standard for a workplace search does not necessarily apply to a piece of closed personal luggage, a handbag or a briefcase that happens to be within the employer's business address.

Within the workplace context, this Court has recognized that employees may have a reasonable expectation of privacy against intrusions by police. . . .

Given the societal expectations of privacy in one's place of work expressed in [previous decisions], we reject the contention that public employees can never have a reasonable expectation of privacy in their place of work. Individuals do not lose Fourth Amendment rights merely because they work for the government instead of a private employer. The operational realities of the workplace, however, may make *some* employees' expectations of privacy unreasonable when an intrusion is by a supervisor rather than a law enforcement official. Public employees' expectations of privacy in their offices, desks, and file cabinets, like similar expectations of employees in the private sector, may be reduced by virtue of actual office practices and procedures, or by legitimate regulation. . . . The employee's expectation of privacy must be assesssed in the context of the employment relation. An office is seldom a private enclave free from entry by supervisors, other employees and business and personal invitees. Instead, in many cases offices are continually entered by fellow employees and other visitors during the workday for conferences, consultations, and other work-related visits. Simply put, it is the nature of government offices that others—such as fellow employees, supervisors, consensual visitors, and the general public—may have frequent access to an individual's office. . . . [S]ome government offices may be so open to fellow employees or the public that no expectation of privacy is reasonable. . . . Given the great variety of work environments in the public sector, the question of whether an employee has a reasonable expectation of privacy must be addressed on a case-by-case basis.

. . . [R]egardless of any legitimate right of access the Hospital staff may have had to the office as such, we recognize that the undisputed evidence suggests that Dr. Ortega had a reasonable expectation of privacy in his desk and file cabinets. The undisputed evidence discloses that Dr. Ortega did not share his desk or file cabinets with any other employees. Dr. Ortega had occupied the office for 17 years and he kept materials in his office, which included personal correspondence, medical files, and correspondence from private patients unconnected to the Hospital, personal financial records, teaching aids and notes, and personal gifts and mementos. . . . The files on physicians in residency training were kept outside Dr. Ortega's office. . . . Indeed, the only items found by the investigators were apparently personal items because, with the exception of the items seized for use in the administrative hearings, all the papers and effects found in the office were simply placed in boxes and made available to Dr. Ortega. . . . Finally, we note that there was no evidence that the Hospital had established any reasonable regulation or policy discouraging employees such as Dr. Ortega from storing personal papers and effects in their desks or file cabinets, . . .

although the absence of such a policy does not create an expectation of privacy where it would not otherwise exist.

*   *   *

III

Having determined that Dr. Ortega had a reasonable expectation of privacy in his office, . . . we must determine the appropriate standard of reasonableness applicable to the search. A determination of the standard of reasonableness applicable to a particular class of searches requires "balanc[ing] the nature and quality of the intrusion on the individual's Fourth Amendment interests against the importance of the governmental interests alleged to justify the intrusion." . . . In the case of searches conducted by a public employer, we must balance the invasion of the employees' legitimate expectations of privacy against the government's need for supervision, control and the efficient operation of the workplace.

There is surprisingly little case law on the appropriate Fourth Amendment standard of reasonableness for public employer's work-related search of its employee's offices, desks, or file cabinets. . . .

The legitimate privacy interests of public employees in the private objects they bring to the workplace may be substantial. Against these privacy interests, however, must be balanced the realities of the workplace, which strongly suggests that a warrant requirement would be unworkable. While police, and even administrative enforcement personnel, conduct searches for the primary purpose of obtaining evidence for use in criminal or other enforcement proceedings, employers most frequently need to enter the offices and desks of their employees for legitimate work-related reasons wholly unrelated to illegal conduct. Employers and supervisors are focused primarily on the need to complete the government agency's work in a prompt and efficient manner. An employer may have need for correspondence, or a file or report available only in an employees' office while the employee is away from the office. Or, as is alleged to have been the case here, employers may need to safeguard or identify state property or records in an office in connection with a pending investigation into suspected employee misfeasance.

In our view, requiring an employer to obtain a warrant whenever the employer wished to enter an employee's office, desk, or file cabinets for a work-related purpose would seriously disrupt the routine conduct of business and would be unduly burdensome. Imposing unwieldy warrant procedures in such cases upon supervisors, who would otherwise have no reason to be familiar with such procedures, is simply unreasonable. In contrast to other circumstances in which we have required warrants, supervisors in offices such as at the Hospital are hardly in the business of investigating the violation of criminal laws. Rather, work-related searches are merely incident to the primary business of the agency. Under these circumstances, the imposition of a warrant requirement would conflict with "the common-sense realization that government offices could not function if every employment decision became a constitutional matter." . . .

Whether probable cause is an inappropriate standard for public employer searches of their employees' offices presents a more difficult issue. . . .

As an initial matter, it is important to recognize the plethora of contexts in which employers will have an occasion to intrude to some extent on an employee's expectation of privacy. Because the parties in this case have alleged that the search was either a noninvestigatory work-related intrusion or an investigatory search for evidence of suspected work-related employee misfeasance, we undertake to determine the appropriate Fourth Amendment standard of reasonableness *only* for these two types of employer intrusions and leave for another day inquiry into other circumstances.

The governmental interest justifying work-related intrusions by public employers is the efficient and proper operation of the workplace. Government agencies provide myriad services to the public, and the work of these agencies would suffer if employers were required to have probable cause before they entered an employee's desk for the purpose of finding a file or piece of office correspondence. Indeed, it is difficult to give the concept of probable cause, rooted as it is in the criminal investigatory context, much meaning when the purpose of a search is to retrieve a file for work-related reasons. Similarly, the concept of probable cause has little meaning for a routine inventory conducted by public employers for the purpose of securing state property. . . . To ensure the efficient and proper operation of the agency, therefore, public employers must be given wide latitude to enter employee offices for work-related, noninvestigatory reasons.

We come to a similar conclusion for searches conducted pursuant to an investigation of work-related employee misconduct. Even when employers conduct an investigation, they have an interest substantially different from "the normal need for law enforcement." . . . Public employers have an interest in ensuring that their agencies operate in an effective and efficient manner, and the work of these agencies inevitably suffers from the inefficiency, incompetence, mismanagement or other work-related misfeasance of its employees. Indeed, in many cases, public employees are entrusted with tremendous responsibility, and the consequences of their misconduct or incompetence to both the agency and the public interest can be severe. In contrast to law enforcement officials, therefore, public employers are not enforcers of the criminal law; instead, public employers have a direct and overriding interest in ensuring that the work of the agency is conducted in a proper and efficient manner. In our view, therefore, a probable cause requirement for searches of the type at issue here would impose intolerable burdens on public employers. The delay in correcting the employee misconduct caused by the need for probable cause rather than reasonable suspicion will be translated into tangible and often irreparable damage to the agency's work, and ultimately to the public interest. . . . Additionally, while law enforcement officials are expected to "schoo[l] themselves in the niceties of probable cause," . . . no such expectation is generally applicable to public employers, at least when the search is not used to gather evidence of a criminal offense. It is simply unrealistic to expect supervisors in most government agencies to learn the subtleties of the probable cause standard. . . .

Balanced against the substantial government interests in the efficient and proper operation of the workplace are the privacy interests of government employees in their place of work which, while not insubstantial, are far less than those found at home or in some other contexts. . . . Government offices are provided to employees for the sole purpose of facilitating the work of an agency. The employee may avoid exposing personal belongings at work by simply leaving them at home.

In sum, we conclude that the "special needs, beyond the normal need for law enforcement make the . . . probable-cause requirement impracticable," . . . for legitimate work-related, noninvestigatory intrusions as well as investigations of work-related misconduct. A standard of reasonableness will neither unduly burden the efforts of government employers to ensure the efficient and proper operation of the workplace, nor authorize arbitrary intrusions upon the privacy of public employees. We hold, therefore, that public employer intrusions on the constitutionally protected privacy interests of government employees for noninvestigatory, work-related purposes, as well as for investigations of work-related misconduct, should be judged by the standard of reasonableness under all the circumstances. Under this reasonableness standard, both the inception and the scope of the intrusion must be reasonable: . . .

Ordinarily, a search of an employee's office by a supervisor will be "justified at its inception" when there are reasonable grounds for suspecting that the search will turn up evidence that the employee is guilty of work-related misconduct, or that the search is necessary for a noninvestigatory work-related purpose such as to retrieve a needed file. Because the petitioners had an "individualized suspicion" of misconduct by Dr. Ortega, we need not decide whether individualized suspicion is an essential element of the standard of reasonableness that we adopt today. . . .

IV

In the procedural posture of this case, we do not attempt to determine whether the search of Dr. Ortega's office and the seizure of his personal belongings, satisfy the standard of reasonableness we have articulated in this case. No evidentiary hearing was held in this case because [of the way it was heard at the lower court levels].

*　　*　　*

On remand, therefore, the District Court must determine the justification for the search and seizure, and evaluate the reasonableness of both the inception of the search and its scope.

DISCUSSION QUESTIONS

1. In retrospect, how could Dr. Dennis O'Connor have undertaken the search of Dr. Ortega's office with greater certainty that it would comport with constitutional standards? Make a list of the specific issues Dr. O'Connor should have addressed before authorizing the search.

2. The plurality opinion states that "Given the great variety of work environments in the public sector, the question of whether an employee has a reasonable expectation of privacy must be addressed on a case-by-case basis." Assess the impact of such an approach on efficient public administration. How would you go about determining whether any given public employee has "a reasonable expectation of privacy"?

3. In a concurring opinion, Justice Scalia contended that the plurality created " . . . a standard so devoid of content that it produces rather than eliminates uncertainty in this field" of searches. Restate the plurality's standard for the constitutionality of searches of public employees by their employers and consider whether its content provides public administrators with enough guidance to be constitutionally competent.

4. The Court was able to avoid deciding "whether an individualized suspicion is an essential element of the standard of reasonableness" that it adopted in *Ortega*. Assess the impact requiring individualized suspicion might have on administrative efficiency and the impact that *not* requiring it might have on public employees' privacy in the workplace. How would the requirement of an individualized suspicion, or the lack thereof, affect the drug testing of public employees?

CASE 5.5:
EQUAL PROTECTION AND EFFICIENCY

Adam BAKER et al., Appellants,

v.

CITY OF ST. PETERSBURG et al.,
Appellees.
No. 23720.
United States Court of Appeals
Fifth Circuit.
Aug. 1, 1968.
400 F.2d 294

Summary

Twelve Negro police officers brought action attacking validity of certain practices of police department allegedly based on classification by race. The United States District Court for the Middle District of Florida . . . held in favor of police department, and the Negro police officers appealed. The Court of Appeals, Wisdom, Circuit Judge, held that police department practice of assigning only Negro policemen solely on basis of race to patrol Negro residential district patrol zone and never assigning Negro policemen to patrol any other zones offended equal protection clause of Fourteenth Amendment.

Opinion

WISDOM, Circuit Judge:

We are asked to apply the law of equal protection to a factual situation not previously presented to the courts. Twelve Negro officers on the police force of St. Petersburg, Florida, attack the validity of certain practices of the city's police department which are allegedly based on classification by race. . . .

I.

The police department of St. Petersburg has 254 police officers, of whom 14 are Negro. Until 1950, there were no Negroes on the force. In that year, the City hired four Negro officers and assigned them to patrolling the Negro areas of the city. Since that time, more Negroes have been added to the force, but they are largely restricted in their duties to policing Negro citizens. The Chief of Police, Harold C. Smith, testified that the force is short of its authorized strength by several men, and that he has actively tried to recruit both Negro and white men to fill these vacancies. The Department is divided into three major divisions, Uniform, Detective, and Service, with several subdivisions. Two Negro officers are assigned to the Detective Division, two to Service, and the rest to Uniform, also referred to as Patrol. One of the Negro patrol officers is

a sergeant, but none of the other Negroes is . . . in a command position. The sergeant and the detectives are not named plaintiffs in this action, but since it is a class action their rights are involved to the extent that they are members of the class.

For the purpose of police patrol, the city is divided into 16 zones. Each zone is patrolled during three shifts daily by one radio car. The zones vary in size and character, and are designed to equalize the complaint load for each patrol car—except for Zone 13.

Zone 13 is unique in shape and area. It is irregular in shape, and as Harold Smith, Chief of Police, testified, that zone was designed to encompass the principal Negro residential and business districts. Zone 13 is entirely overlapped by other Zones, chiefly by Zone 12, and in smaller areas by Zones 1, 10, 11, and 14, so that every part of Zone 13 is also in another zone. With these exceptions, there are no other overlapping patrol zones in the city. The police administrators assert that the purpose of this overlapping is to equalize the complaint load per patrol car. Since Zone 13 has approximately twice the number of complaints as the other zones, it is given twice the patrol strength through this double coverage. Of course, this same result could have been achieved by dividing the area covered by Zone 13 into several smaller zones.

Zone 13 is also unique in its patrol force; no white officer is ever assigned to Zone 13. No Negro officer is ever assigned to any other zone, including Zone 12, which duplicates Zone 13 for about 75 percent of its area. The district court found that "the assignment of Negro officers to the predominantly Negro Zone 13 was not done for the purpose of discrimination but for the purpose of effective administration" in that "in the opinion of the Chief of Police, they are better able to cope with the inhabitants of that zone, who on occasion become abusive and aggressive toward police officers during a disturbance; and, further, that they are able to communicate with the inhabitants of the Negro area better than white officers and are better able to identify Negroes and investigate criminal activities in that zone more effectively than white officers." The record discloses no evidence in support of Chief Smith's opinion.

*   *   *

Of course, if police efficiency were an end in itself, the police would be free to put an accused on the rack. Police efficiency must yield to constitutional rights. "In a government of laws, existence of government will be imperilled if it fails to observe the law scrupulously."

III.

The district court erred in holding that the racial classification was *merely* for the purpose of police efficiency. The exclusion of Negroes from participation in law enforcement was part of the now-rejected pattern of excluding Negroes from positions of power and influence. Not until 1950 did the City of St. Petersburg hire Negro policemen. The first Negro officers were restricted in their duties to policing the Negro areas of the city, and were instructed to call for the assistance of a white officer if they found it necessary to arrest a white person. Before the institution of the zone postal system, the Negro officers were assigned to a particular patrol car, colloquially referred to in the department as the "colored car," and restricted to patrolling the Negro areas of the city. While many of the restrictions on

the Negro officers have been removed, their numbers on the force remain very small; there is but the one Negro sergeant on the force; and Zone 13 remains a unique zone in the St. Petersburg police system. What the St. Petersburg Police Department did was to superimpose on natural geographic zones an artificial zone that rests on the Department's judgment of Negroes as a class. The Department concluded that Negroes as a class are suitable only for the zone appropriately numbered 13. This is the kind of badge of slavery the Thirteenth Amendment condemns. . . . However, in this case it is necessary to hold only that a Department's practice of assigning Negroes solely on the basis of race to a Negro enclave offends the equal protection clause of the Fourteenth Amendment.

We do not hold that the assignment of a Negro officer to a particular task because he is a Negro can never be justified. It is clear, however, that, with due respect for the good faith of the Chief of Police, his opinion that Negro officers are better able to police Negro citizens cannot justify the blanket assignment of *all* Negroes, and *only* Negroes to patrol Zone 13. While strict equality is not and should not be compelled, Negro officers should be rotated among the various patrol zones of the city, in the same manner as white officers insofar as ability, available work force, and other variables permit.

Racial gerrymandering of political boundaries is clearly unconstitutional. . . . We do not hold, however, that the drawing of Zone 13 so as to encompass most of the Negro community is invalid on its face. On remand, the burden will be on the defendants to prove that the purposes sought to be achieved by the pattern of the zone could not be achieved without the overt racial classification.

DISCUSSION QUESTIONS

1. The assertion by Chief Smith that African-American police officers were better able to identify African-Americans in the community than were White officers sounds racist. However, suppose it were actually true and relevant. How could a constitutionally competent public administrator deal with the Whites' inadequacy in this regard? Would whatever method you select be more or less efficient than the course of action undertaken by Chief Smith?

2. When might the assignment of a particular police officer on the basis of race be constitutionally permissible? Under the principles of narrow tailoring discussed in Chapter 4, what criteria would have to be met in order for such an assignment to be legitimate?

3. Can you think of any administrative purpose that is a constitutionally acceptable basis for constructing an administrative zone, such as Zone 13, that is *intended* to include members of one race only? How about one ethnic group, whose primary language is not English?

6

ADMINISTRATIVE STANDARDIZATION

Public administration often promotes conformity or uniformity among individuals in an attempt to treat them in a standardized fashion. As in the case of other administrative values, constitutionally competent public administrators must be aware of tensions between efforts to standardize their treatment of clients, public employees, and other individuals, and the constitutional rights of these people. Standardization serves two main purposes. First, it enhances efficiency. Max Weber (1864–1921), who is generally considered the foremost analyst of bureaucracy, considered standardization in the form of "dehumanization" (impersonality) of bureaucrats to be the "special virtue" of bureaucratized administration.[1] In his view, dehumanization eliminates ". . . all purely personal, irrational, and emotional elements . . ." from official business.[2] Accordingly, in a fully developed bureaucracy, ". . . the professional bureaucrat is chained to his activity by his entire material and ideal existence. In the great majority of cases, he is only a single *cog* in an ever-moving mechanism which prescribes to him an essentially fixed route of march."[3] Partly as a result, in terms of efficiency, such a ". . . bureaucratic mechanism compares with other organizations exactly as does the machine with the non-mechanical modes of production."[4]

Several modern scholars have agreed with Weber's assessment. For in-

[1]Max Weber, *From Max Weber: Essays in Sociology*, trans. and ed. by H.H. Gerth and C.W. Mills (New York: Oxford University Press, 1958), p. 216.
[2]Ibid.
[3]Ibid., p. 228.
[4]Ibid., p. 214.

stance, Peter Blau and Marshall Meyer also claim that "efficiency . . . suffers when emotions or personal considerations influence administrative decisions."[5] Although many administrators will resist the idea that they are merely standardized "cogs," civilian bureaucracies in the United States are based on positions (or "slots" in language suitable to the "cog theory") rather than built around individual persons. Thus, ever since 1920, the fundamentals of position classification have held that:

1. Positions and not individuals should be classified;
2. The individual characteristics of an employee occupying a position should have no bearing on the classification of the position; and
3. Persons holding positions in the same class should be considered equally qualified for any other position in that class.[6]

Clients of public administrative agencies may also be standardized for the sake of efficiency. Generally, the individual client must be transformed from a person into a case before he or she can be processed. Administrative forms are the main vehicle for this transformation. They elicit only the information that the administrators need to categorize the person and decide on his or her status (for example, "eligible" or "ineligible"). Everything about the individual that does not appear on the form is extraneous and irrelevant to the bureaucrat. In fact, sometimes a clerk at an intake window helps the individual transmute himself or herself into a case, which will subsequently be dealt with by another administrator who has never even seen or spoken to the client. The administrative logic of such standardization is well expressed by Ralph Hummel:

> The bureaucrat has no time and no permission to become involved in the personal problems of clients. From his point of view the more he can depersonalize the client into a thing devoid of unique features the more easily and smoothly he will be able to handle the cases before him.[7]

Where the "clients" are really "inmates" confined to prisons or public mental health facilities, such standardization may be very extreme, as Erving Goffman explains:

> . . . [A] further set of characteristic problems is found in the constant conflict between humane standards on the one hand and institutional efficiency on the other. . . . The personal possessions of an individual are an important part of the materials out of which he builds a self, but as an inmate the ease with which he can be managed by staff is likely to increase with the degree to which he is dispossessed. The remarkable efficiency with which a mental-hospital ward can adjust to a daily shift in number of resident patients is related to the fact that the comers and leavers do not come or leave with any properties but themselves and do not have any right

[5]Peter Blau and Marshall Meyer, *Bureaucracy in Modern Society*, 2nd ed. (New York: Random House, 1971), p. 9.

[6]Jay M. Shafritz, Albert C. Hyde, and David H. Rosenbloom, *Personnel Management in Government* 3rd ed. (New York: Marcel Dekker, 1986), p. 118.

[7]Ralph Hummel, *The Bureaucratic Experience* (New York: St. Martin's Press, 1977), p. 56.

to choose where they will be located. Further, the efficiency with which the clothes of these patients can be kept clean and fresh is related to the fact that everyone's soiled clothing can be indiscriminately placed in one bundle, and laundered clothing can be redistributed not according to ownership but according to approximate size. . . .

Just as personal possesions may interfere with the smooth running of an institutional operation and be removed for this reason, so parts of the body may conflict with efficient management and the conflict may be resolved in favor of efficiency. If the heads of inmates are to be kept clean, and the possessor easily categorized, then a complete head shave is efficacious, despite the damage this does to appearance. On similar grounds, some mental hospitals have found it useful to extract the teeth of "biters," give hysterectomies to promiscuous female patients, and perform lobotomies on chronic fighters.[8]

As organizational theorist, Victor Thompson, reminds us, "Nearly all administrative organizations . . . must resort to some of the 'stripping' tactics of the more total institutions."[9]

A second purpose of standardization is to assure procedural equality. In theory, individuals who fall into the same categories will be treated identically by public administrators regardless of their extraneous personal characteristics or of any personal biases the officials may have. For example, standardization is a barrier to racial discrimination in administration or favoritism based on personal connections. As Thompson puts it in the title of a book, contemporary administration should be *Without Sympathy or Enthusiasm*, because we ". . . are proud of the fact that modern administration, as compared with administration in the past, is relatively free or . . . 'particularistic' behavior and is 'universalistic' instead."[10] Indeed, ". . . we believe in 'universalistic' norms of administration . . ." precisely because they promote procedural equality and efficiency simultaneously.[11]

Yet, despite its administrative virtues and its congruence with some aspects of the Constitution's commitment to equality, standardization is nevertheless frequently in tension with three fundamental constitutional values of which the constitutionally competent public administrator must be cognizant. These are diversity, equity, and individuation.

CONSTITUTIONAL VALUES

A. Diversity

Individual political, economic (property), and social diversity lies at the heart of the pluralistic government chartered by the Constitution. Diversity of

---

[8]Erving Goffman, *Assylums* (Garden City, N.Y.: Anchor, 1961), pp. 78–79.
[9]Victor Thompson, *Without Sympathy or Enthusiasm* (University, Alabama: University of Alabama Press, 1975), p. 41.
[10]Ibid., p. 17.
[11]Ibid., p. 18.

representation is built into the scheme by which the House of Representatives represents the people by districts within the various states, the Senate represents them by state, and the president, in a sense, does so nationwide. The different terms of office for these officials are also intended to assure that changing points of view are represented and that no short-lived popular passion will take hold of the entire government in one fell swoop. In *Federalist Number 10,* James Madison argued that according to the theory behind the newly drafted Constitution, the protection of the diverse and individual "faculties of men" was "the first object of government."[12] He wrote, "From the protection of different and unequal faculties of acquiring property, the possession of different degrees and kinds of property immediately results; and from the influence of these on the sentiments and views of the respective proprietors ensues a division of the society into different interests and parties."[13] Madison viewed such divisions, based on individual diversity, as a strong barrier against the development of a majority faction ". . . who are united and actuated by some common impulse of passion, or of interest, adverse to the rights of other citizens, or to the permanent and aggregate interests of the community."[14] The Bill of Rights specifically protects personal diversity in matters of religion, property, and speech. Its protections of privacy have been interpreted to seek to guarantee individuals a sphere of autonomy, within which they can develop their personalities and make personal choices, free of governmental intrusion. The Equal Protection Clause of the Fourteenth Amendment also protects diversity by outlawing discrimination against members of social groups who in one way or another do not conform or fit into the categories favored by the government. Case 6.1, *Goldman* v. *Weinberger* (1986), illustrates a fundamental clash between the Air Force's demand for standardized uniforms and an individual's interest in religious freedom.

B. Equity

The Constitution also values equity, or the judiciary's power ". . . to dispense with the harsh rigor of general laws in particular cases."[15] As Gary McDowell explains, "Equity was necessary, in many cases, to fulfill the law. The law, being by its nature general in scope and application, always admits of exceptions."[16] Thus, whereas administrative theory and practice often look on exceptions to standardization as improper or even corrupt, constitutional values sometimes require that exceptions be made in order to prevent the misapplication of its general principles. This is a constitutional concern that goes beyond

[12]*The Federalists Papers,* ed. by Clinton Rossiter (New York: New American Library, 1961), p. 78.

[13]Ibid.

[14]Ibid.

[15]Gary L. McDowell, *Equity and the Constitution* (Chicago: University of Chicago Press, 1982), p. 5.

[16]Ibid.

the exercise of equity powers in a technical sense. For instance, in *Sherbert* v. *Verner* (1963), Case 7.2, the Supreme Court held that it was unconstitutional to deny an individual unemployment compensation benefits on the basis that she voluntarily took herself out of the work force by refusing, for religious reasons, to work on Saturdays. From an administrative perspective, an exception made for a Seventh Day Adventist would have to be made for a Moslem who refused to work on Fridays as well as anyone else who claimed a religious basis for refusing to work on a weekday. An exception for one individual could lead to exceptions for everyone, which would leave the administrative scheme in disarray. But from the constitutional perspective, the failure to make an exception in the case of sincere religious belief constituted undue governmental interference with the individual's free exercise of religion. (But compare the aforementioned *Goldman* v. *Weinberger,* in which the Court did not find the case for making an exception compelling enough.)

C. Individuation

Finally, constitutional values, as reflected in contemporary constitutional law, often favor individuation, or the treatment of an individual as a distinct entity rather than as a member of a group or category of persons. For instance, as is evidenced in *Craig* v. *Boren* (Case 3.3) and *Cleveland Board of Education* v. *LaFleur* (Case 5.2), the Supreme Court has expressed doubt about applying broad social scientific or biological generalizations to specific individuals.[17] Moreover, cases alleging unconstitutional action by public administrators may turn not only on the specifics of what occurred, but also on the intentions and motives of the individual officials involved. Both general criminal and civil law likewise place great importance on individual state of mind in some circumstances.

The cases that follow illustrate important aspects of the tension between administrative standardization and constitutional values. They discuss the importance of standardization for administration and for procedural equality, and also how these values must be balanced against the need to protect diversity, to make appropriate exceptions, and to take individuation into account. The Goldman case (Case 6.1) has already been introduced. Case 6.2, *Leonard* v. *City of Columbus* (1983), presents a similar clash between standardization and freedom of expression. *Zobel* v. *Williams* (1982), Case 6.3, primarily concerns equal protection and will enhance the reader's understanding of that constitutional provision. However, the concurring opinion by Justice Brennan discusses the problem of administrative or legislative schemes that use a measure, such as number of years of residence, as a proxy for a specific individual's personal qualities. Both the majority and concurring opinions consider the problem of lumping individuals into categories as a matter of public policy; that is, the issue of individuation.

[17]See also *McCleskey* v. *Kemp,* 107 S.Ct. 1756 (1987).

ADDITIONAL READING

GOODSELL, CHARLES. *The Case for Bureaucracy.* 2nd ed. Chatham, N.J.: Chatham House, 1985.

HUMMEL, RALPH. *The Bureaucratic Experience,* 3rd ed. New York: St. Martin's Press, 1987.

THOMPSON, VICTOR. *Without Sympathy or Enthusiasm: The Problem of Administrative Compassion.* University, Ala.: University of Alabama Press, 1975.

CASE 6.1:
CONFORMITY VERSUS PLURALISM

S. SIMCHA GOLDMAN, Petitioner

v

CASPAR W. WEINBERGER,
Secretary of Defense, et al.
475 US 503
[No. 84-1097]
Argued January 14, 1986. Decided
March 25, 1986.

Summary

An Air Force regulation relating to uniforms prohibits members of the Air Force from wearing headgear while indoors, except for headgear for armed security police in the performance of their duties. An Air Force officer who was serving as a clinical psychologist at a mental health clinic on an Air Force base, and who was an Orthodox Jew and an ordained rabbi, had been wearing a yarmulke (skullcap) while he was on duty indoors, and he had been wearing a service cap over his yarmulke while he was outdoors. The officer was informed by his hospital commander that wearing a yarmulke while on duty indoors was a violation of an Air Force regulation relating to uniforms, the officer was ordered to discontinue wearing a yarmulke while on duty indoors, and the officer was warned that failure to obey the regulation could subject him to a court-martial. In the United States District Court for the District of Columbia, the officer brought suit against the Secretary of Defense and others, claiming that application of the Air Force regulation to prevent him from wearing his yarmulke infringed on his First Amendment right to free exercise of religion. The District Court granted the officer injunctive relief against application of the regulation to his wearing of a yarmulke (530 F Supp 12), but the United States Court of Appeals for the District of Columbia Circuit reversed, holding that the Air Force's interest in uniformity rendered the strict enforcement of its regulation permissible (236 App DC 248, 734 F2d 1531), and the Court of Appeals denied a petition for rehearing en banc (238 App DC 267, 739 F2d 657).

On certiorari, the United States Supreme Court affirmed.

Opinion

Justice Rehnquist delivered the opinion of the Court.

Petitioner S. Simcha Goldman contends that the Free Exercise Clause of the First Amendment to the United States Constitution permits him to wear a yarmulke while in uniform, notwithstanding an Air Force regulation mandating uniform dress for Air Force personnel. The District Court for the District of Columbia permanently enjoined the Air Force from enforcing its regulation against petitioner and from penalizing him for wearing his yarmulke. The Court of Appeals for the District of Columbia Circuit reversed on the ground that the Air Force's strong interest in discipline justified the strict enforcement of its uniform dress requirements. We granted certiorari because of the importance of the question. . . .

Petitioner Goldman is an Orthodox Jew and ordained rabbi. In 1973, he was accepted into the Armed Forces Health Professions Scholarship Program and placed on inactive reserve status in the Air Force while he studied clinical psychology at Loyola University of Chicago. During his three years in the scholarship program, he received a monthly stipend and an allowance for tuition, books, and fees. After completing his Ph.D. in psychology, petitioner entered active service in the United States Air Force as a commissioned officer, in accordance with a requirement that participants in the scholarship program serve one year of active duty for each year of subsidized education. Petitioner was stationed at March Air Force Base in Riverside, California, and served as a clinical psychologist at the mental health clinic on the base.

Until 1981, petitioner was not prevented from wearing his yarmulke on the base. He avoided controversy by remaining close to his duty station in the health clinic and by wearing his service cap over the yarmulke when out of doors. But in April 1981, after he testified as a defense witness at a court-martial wearing his yarmulke but not his service cap, opposing counsel lodged a complaint with Colonel Joseph Gregory, the Hospital Commander, arguing that petitioner's practice of wearing his yarmulke was a violation of Air Force Regulation (AFR) 35-10. This regulation states in pertinent part that "[h]eadgear will not be worn . . . [w]hile indoors except by armed security police in the performance of their duties." AFR 35-10, ¶ 1-6.h(2)(f) (1980).

Colonel Gregory informed petitioner that wearing a yarmulke while on duty does indeed violate AFR 35-10, and ordered him not to violate this regulation outside the hospital. Although virtually all of petitioner's time on the base was spent in the hospital, he refused. Later, after petitioner's attorney protested to the Air Force General Counsel, Colonel Gregory revised his order to prohibit petitioner from wearing the yarmulke even in the hospital. Petitioner's request to report for duty in civilian clothing pending legal resolution of the issue was denied. The next day he received a formal letter of reprimand, and was warned that failure to obey AFR 35-10 could subject him to a court-martial. Colonel Gregory also withdrew a recommendation that petitioner's application to extend the term of his active service be approved, and substituted a negative recommendation.

Petitioner then sued respondent Secretary of Defense and others, claiming that the application of AFR 35-10 to prevent him from wearing his yarmulke infringed upon his First Amendment freedom to exercise his religious beliefs.

* * *

Our review of military regulations challenged on First Amendment grounds is far more deferential than constitutional review of similar laws or regulations designed for civilian society. The military need not encourage debate or tolerate protest to the extent that such tolerance is required of the civilian state by the First Amendment; to accomplish its mission the military must foster instinctive obedience, unity, commitment, and esprit de corps. . . . The essence of military service "is the subordination of the desires and interests of the individual to the needs of the service."

These aspects of military life do not, of course, render entirely nugatory in the military context the guarantees of the First Amendment. . . . But "within the military community there is simply not the same [individual] autonomy as there is in the larger civilian community." . . . In the context of the present case, when evaluating whether military needs justify a particular restriction on religiously motivated conduct, courts must give great deference to the professional judgment of military authorities concerning the relative importance of a particular military interest. . . . Not only are courts " 'ill-equipped to determine the impact upon discipline that any particular intrusion upon military authority might have,' " . . . but the military authorities have been charged by the Executive and Legislative Branches with carrying out our Nation's military policy. "[J]udicial deference . . . is at its apogee when legislative action under the congressional authority to raise and support armies and make rules and regulations for their governance is challenged." . . .

The considered professional judgment of the Air Force is that the traditional outfitting of personnel in standardized uniforms encourages the subordination of personal preferences and identities in favor of the overall group mission. Uniforms encourage a sense of hierarchial unity by tending to eliminate outward individual distinctions except for those of rank. The Air Force considers them as vital during peacetime as during war because its personnel must be ready to provide an effec-

tive defense on a moment's notice; the necessary habits of discipline and unity must be developed in advance of trouble. We have acknowledged that "[t]he inescapable demands of military discipline and obedience to orders cannot be taught on battlefields; the habit of immediate compliance with military procedures and orders must be virtually reflex with no time for debate or reflection." . . .

To this end, the Air Force promulgated AFR 35-10, a 190-page document, which states that "Air Force members will wear the Air Force uniform while performing their military duties, except when authorized to wear civilian clothes on duty." AFR § 35-10, ¶ 1-6 (1980). The rest of the document describes in minute detail all of the various items of apparel that must be worn as part of the Air Force uniform. It authorizes a few individualized options with respect to certain pieces of jewelry and hair style, but even these are subject to severe limitations. See AFR 35-10, Table 1-1, and ¶ 1-12.b(1)(b) (1980). In general, authorized headgear may be worn only out of doors. See AFR § 35-10, ¶ 1-6.h (1980). Indoors, "[h]eadgear [may] not be worn . . . except by armed security police in the performance of their duties." AFR 35-10, ¶ 1-6.h(2)(f) (1980). A narrow exception to this rule exists for headgear worn during indoor religious ceremonies. See AFR 35-10, ¶ 1-6.h(2)(d) (1980). In addition, military commanders may in their discretion permit visible religious headgear and other such apparel in designated living quarters and nonvisible items generally. See Department of Defense Directive 1300.17 (June 18, 1985).

Petitioner Goldman contends that the Free Exercise Clause of the First Amendment requires the Air Force to make an exception to its uniform dress requirements for religious apparel unless the accouterments create a "clear danger" of undermining discipline and esprit de corps. He asserts that in general, visible but "unobtrusive" apparel will not create such a danger and must therefore be accommodated. He argues that the Air Force failed to prove that a specific exception for his practice of wearing an unobtrusive yarmulke would threaten discipline. He contends that the Air Force's assertion to the contrary is mere ipse dixit, with no support from actual experience or a scientific study in the record, and is contradicted by expert testimony that religious exceptions to AFR 35-10 are in fact desirable and will increase morale by making the Air Force a more humane place. . . .

. . . The Air Force has drawn the line essentially between religious apparel that is visible and that which is not, and we hold that those portions of the regulations challenged here reasonably and evenhandedly regulate dress in the interest of the military's perceived need for uniformity. The First Amendment therefore does not prohibit them from being applied to petitioner even though their effect is to restrict the wearing of the headgear required by his religious beliefs.

Separate Opinions

Justice **Stevens**, with whom Justice **White** and Justice **Powell** join, concurring.

*   *   *

The interest in uniformity, however, has a dimension that is of still greater importance for me. It is the interest in uniform treatment for the members of all religious faiths. The very strength of Captain Goldman's claim creates the danger that a similar claim on behalf of a Sikh or a Rastafarian might readily be dismissed as

"so extreme, so unusual, or so faddish an image that public confidence in his ability to perform his duties will be destroyed."

*   *   *

Justice **Brennan**, with whom Justice **Marshall** joins, dissenting.

Simcha Goldman invokes this Court's protection of his First Amendment right to fulfill one of the traditional religious obligations of a male Orthodox Jew—to cover his head before an omnipresent God. The Court's response to Goldman's request is to abdicate its role as principal expositor of the Constitution and protector of individual liberties in favor of credulous deference to unsupported assertions of military necessity. I dissent.

*   *   *

The Government maintains in its brief that discipline is jeopardized whenever exceptions to military regulations are granted. Service personnel must be trained to obey even the most arbitrary command reflexively. Non-Jewish personnel will perceive the wearing of a yarmulke by an Orthodox Jew as an unauthorized departure from the rules and will begin to question the principle of unswerving obedience. Thus shall our fighting forces slip down the treacherous slope toward unkempt appearance, anarchy, and, ultimately, defeat at the hands of our enemies.

The contention that the discipline of the Armed Forces will be subverted if Orthodox Jews are allowed to wear yarmulkes with their uniforms surpasses belief. It lacks support in the record of this case, and the Air Force offers no basis for it as a general proposition. While the perilous slope permits the services arbitrarily to refuse exceptions requested to satisfy mere personal preferences, before the Air

Force may burden free exercise rights it must advance, at the *very least,* a rational reason for doing so.

* * *

The Government also argues that the services have an important interest in uniform dress, because such dress establishes the pre-eminence of group identity, thus fostering esprit de corps and loyalty to the service that transcends individual bonds. In its brief, the Government characterizes the yarmulke as an assertion of individuality and as a badge of religious and ethnic identity, strongly suggesting that, as such, it could drive a wedge of divisiveness between members of the services.

First, the purported interests of the Air Force in complete uniformity of dress and in elimination of individuality or visible identification with any group other than itself are belied by the service's own regulations. The dress code expressly abjures the need for total uniformity:

"(1) The American public and its elected representatives draw certain conclusions on military effectiveness based on what they see; that is, the image the Air Force presents. The image must instill public confidence and leave no doubt that the service member lives by a common standard and responds to military order and discipline.
"(2) Appearance in uniform is an important part of this image. . . . Neither the Air Force nor the public expects absolute uniformity of appearance. Each member has the right, within limits, to express individuality through his or her appearance. However, the image of a disciplined service member who can be relied on to do his or her job excludes the extreme, the unusual, and the fad." AFR 35-10, ¶¶ 1-12a(1) and (2) (1978).

It cannot be seriously contended that a serviceman in a yarmulke presents so extreme, so unusual, or so faddish an image that public confidence in his ability to perform his duties will be destroyed. Under the Air Force's own standards, then, Dr. Goldman should have and could have been granted an exception to wear his yarmulke.

* * *

Implicit in Justice Stevens' concurrence, and in the Government's arguments, is what might be characterized as a fairness concern. It would be unfair to allow Orthodox Jews to wear yarmulkes, while prohibiting members of other minority faiths with visible dress and grooming requirements from wearing their saffron robes, dreadlocks, turbans, and so forth. While I appreciate and share this concern for the feelings and the free exercise rights of members of these other faiths, I am baffled by this formulation of the problem. What puzzles me is the implication that a neutral standard that could result in the disparate treatment of Orthodox Jews and, for example, Sikhs is *more* troublesome or unfair than the existing neutral standard that does result in the different treatment of Christians, on the one hand, and Orthodox Jews and Sikhs on the other. *Both* standards are constitutionally suspect; before either can be sustained, it must be shown to be a narrowly tailored means of promoting important military interests.

* * *

As I have shown, that uniformity is illusory, unless uniformity means uniformly accommodating majority religious practices and uniformly rejecting distinctive minority practices.

* * *

Justice **Blackmun**, dissenting.

*   *   *

... But Goldman's modest supplement to the Air Force uniform clearly poses by itself no threat to the Nation's military readiness. Indeed, the District Court specifically found that Goldman has worn a yarmulke on base for years without any adverse effect on his performance, any disruption of operations at the base, or any complaints from other personnel. ...

The Air Force argues that it has no way of distinguishing fairly between Goldman's request for an exemption and the potential requests of others whose religious practices may conflict with the appearance code, perhaps in more conspicuous ways. In theory, this argument makes some sense. Like any rules prescribing a uniform, the Air Force dress code is by nature arbitrary; few of its requirements could be defended on purely functional grounds. Particularly for personnel such as Goldman who serve in noncombat roles, variations from the prescribed attire frequently will interfere with no military goals other than those served by uniformity itself. There thus may be no basis on which to distinguish some variations from others, aside from the degree to which they detract from the overall image of the service, a criterion that raises special constitutional problems when applied to religious practices. To allow noncombat personnel to wear yarmulkes but not turbans or dreadlocks because the latter seem more obtrusive—or, as Justice Brennan suggests, less "polished" and "professional,"—would be to discriminate in favor of this country's more established, mainstream religions, the practices of which are more

familiar to the average observer. Not only would conventional faiths receive special treatment under such an approach; they would receive special treatment precisely *because* they are conventional. In general, I see no constitutional difficulty in distinguishing between religious practices based on how difficult it would be to accommodate them, but favoritism based on how unobtrusive a practice appears to the majority could create serious problems of equal protection and religious establishment, problems the Air Force clearly has a strong interest in avoiding by drawing an objective line at visibility.

The problem with this argument, it seems to me, is not doctrinal but empirical. The Air Force simply has not shown any reason to fear that a significant number of enlisted personnel and officers would request religious exemptions that could not be denied on neutral grounds such as safety, let alone that granting these requests would noticeably impair the overall image of the service.

In these circumstances, deference seems unwarranted. Reasoned military judgments, of course, are entitled to respect, but the military has failed to show that this particular judgment with respect to Captain Goldman is a reasoned one. If, in the future, the Air Force is besieged with requests for religious exemptions from the dress code, and those requests cannot be distinguished on functional grounds from Goldman's, the service may be able to argue credibly that circumstances warrant a flat rule against any visible religious apparel. That, however, would be a case different from the one at hand.

DISCUSSION QUESTIONS

1. What are the main rationales for administrative standardization discussed by the majority opinion, Justice Stevens's concurring opinion, and by Justice Blackmun's dissent? Are these rationales fully compatible with one another? Which, if any, are most convincing to you? What are the countervailing constitutional values raised by Justices Brennan and Blackmun? Do you think the outcome of the case was correct with regard to standardization versus free exercise of religion, or do you think the majority's opinion is better explained by its deference to the Air Force?

2. *Yarmulke* is a Yiddish word; many people prefer the Hebrew term *kipah* (pronounced key-*pah*) for the religious skullcap. An ordinary *kipah* measures about five inches in diameter, though some are as large as approximately eight inches. Although they come in a variety of designs and colors, unobtrusive black, brown, and grey ones that lie flat on the head are easily obtained. A *kipah* is not out of keeping with such public ideals as a nation "under God" or one in which "In God We Trust." Does the chain of causality by which the wearing of such an item could compromise the Air Force's effectiveness and compromise the nation's defense seem too attenuated to be believable, as Justice Brennan claims in his dissent? Do you think Justice Brennan is correct in suggesting that the application of the regulations discriminate against non-Christians by seeking to force them into conformity with the way Christians commonly wear religious symbols? There is no barrier either to wearing or not wearing a *kipah* in the Israeli Air Force (and military generally). Does this fact have any bearing on your thinking about the standardization imposed in the U.S.? Why or why not?

3. Justice Brennan's dissent included a paragraph, not reprinted, to the effect that "Guardianship of this precious liberty [of free exercise of religion] is not the exclusive domain of the federal courts. It is the responsibility as well of the States and other branches of the Federal Government." He also claimed that "Our constitutional commitment to religious freedom is one of our greatest achievements. . . ." If you were an Air Force official responsible for dealing with an issue like the one Goldman raised, what would you do? Is this the type of case in which the regulations should be read to require exceptions at various times?

4. Do you agree with Justice Blackmun that it is too facile to justify standardization on the claim that "if we make an exception for you, we'll have to make an exception for everyone"? Should the Air Force be required to wait and see how many claims like Goldman's arise and how difficult they are to resolve in a principled manner? Is there a conflict between administrative management and adjudication at work here?

5. The U.S. Navy has regulations barring alcoholic beverages at sea, but makes an exception for a chaplain who brings wine aboard for sacramental purposes. Under the Goldman ruling, do you think the Navy would be free to reverse this exception, thereby denying Catholic, Anglican, and Greek Orthodox sailors the right to celebrate Mass appropriately while on ship? How would you defend such a reversal? How would you challenge it?

CASE 6.2:
UNIFORMS VERSUS FREEDOM OF
EXPRESSION

ROBERT LEONARD, et al.,
Plaintiffs-Appellants,

v

The CITY OF COLUMBUS, et al.,
Defendants-Appellees.
No. 82-8158.
United States Court of Appeals,
Eleventh Circuit.
May 23, 1983.
705 F.2d 1299
Rehearing and Rehearing En Banc
Denied Sept. 9, 1983.

Summary

Black former policemen brought suit against city seeking damages for wrongful discharge, and reinstatement. The United States District Court for the Middle District of Georgia, J. Robert Elliott, J., dismissed their claims, and police officers appealed. The Court of Appeals, Kravitch, Circuit Judge, held that black police officers' removal of American flag from their uniforms in an effort to emphasize a widely held perception of racially discriminatory practices in city's police force constituted symbolic speech which was protected under First and Fourteenth Amendments; thus, their dismissal for removing flag from their uniforms was unconstitutional.

Opinion

KRAVITCH, Circuit Judge:
Appellants are former policemen of the City of Columbus, dismissed by the City for events occurring in May, 1971. In this action challenging their dismissal they assert numerous grounds for relief under the United States Constitution. The district court found merit in none of the grounds asserted. We conclude differently, holding appellants' dismissal violated their first amendment right of free speech; consequently, we reverse.

In early 1971 black members of the City of Columbus Police Department (the "Department") formed the Afro-American Patrolmen's League ("the League") in order to present effectively grievances of the black officers. At that time there was a growing tension among black officers, who perceived that the Department was treating blacks in a discriminatory manner. Specific complaints involved discriminatory hiring and promotion of blacks, discriminatory assignment and disciplinary practices, and alleged police brutality toward members of the black community. Although several black police officers had brought complaints before the Board of Public Safety, they believed no progress was made.

*   *   *

. . . After attempts to pursue the matter with Department officials failed, black officers began to picket the police station on May 29 and 30. At all times the demonstrations were peaceful and orderly. Department officials did not inform plaintiffs that the picketing was unlawful, or could result in their dismissal.

On May 30 black officers and various civic leaders met to discuss the increasingly tense situation. The evidence is unclear as to what, if anything, was agreed upon by those who participated in the meeting. League members testified the civic leaders and intermediaries suggested a "cooling-off" period during which the black officers would cease picketing and continue performing their duties, in return for which no charges would be brought for previous picketing. . . .

Angered by what League members perceived to be a violation of the "cooling-off" period, the League voted to resume picketing the next day. They also agreed to participate in the "flag incident," which gave rise to this suit. On the morning of May 31 seven officers, six of whom are appellants in this action, began to picket the Department. All officers were off-duty, but in uniform. Appellants carried signs with captions such as "WE DON'T WANT TO BE POLICEBOYS; WE WANT TO BE POLICEMEN" and "HAVE YOU EVER HEARD OF POLICE BEING ARRESTED FOR CONTEMPT OF COURT."

Later, after members of the press arrived, the picketing officers assisted one another in removing an American flag emblem from the sleeve of each uniform shirt. The flags were removed carefully, thread by thread, with a razor. At no time was the flag treated with disrespect; to the contrary, Officer Leonard, speaking for the others present, explained the high respect the officers had for the American flag and the ideals it represented, particu-larly liberty and equal justice for all. The officers, many of whom had served in Viet Nam, did not believe the Department had extended them just treatment consistent with these principles; accordingly, they considered it inappropriate to wear the flag on their uniform. After Deputy Chief Brown refused Leonard's attempts to present the flag emblems to him, Leonard placed the emblems in his pocket. The incident was at all times peaceful, unaccompanied by disorder, violence or boisterousness. Photographs of the incident portray the scene as peaceful.

At the time the "flag incident" was occurring an emergency conference was held at which Chief McGuffey, Joseph W. Sargis, the Director of Public Safety, and City of Columbus Mayor Allen agreed that discharge of the officers was in order. Although Chief McGuffey indicated the primary reason for the firing was the flag incident, Sargis characterized it as a "crescendo" of the activity of past days, referring specifically to prior League activities. The dismissal letter . . . refers specifically, and solely, to removal of the flag patch.

*   *   *

. . . Sargis accused appellants of making "baseless allegations of unlawful conduct, racism, and discrimination" against the Department without first bringing those complaints through "channels." His statement concluded "[t]oday they picketed the Columbus City Police Department and removed the American Flag from their uniforms. These men did not enlist in the Police Department, they do not have to wear that uniform or flag again; they are dismissed."

*   *   *

Appellants' claim under the First Amendment that they were discharged for removing the flag from their uniform, that the removal of the flag constituted symbolic speech, that the symbolic speech was protected under the First and Fourteenth Amendments, and that, consequently, dismissal on the basis of an exercise of a protected right was unconstitutional. The district judge denied appellants' First Amendment claim, concluding that removing a flag patch from the uniform, when the patch was required by City resolution, was not symbolic speech:

This was a calculated show of contempt for the City authority and a demonstration of refusal to obey its lawful ordinances, rules and commands. If this was not "conduct unbecoming an officer which might be detrimental to the service" and an "act contrary to the good order and discipline of the department," then the Court does not know how it could be categorized. If this was only "symbolic speech," then it might well be presumed that punching the Police Chief in the nose would also be so regarded. There was no denial of freedom of speech.

We disagree.

*   *   *

The law underlying whether appellants' activities were protected under the First and Fourteenth Amendments is more complex. We must weigh "the interests of the [employee] as a citizen, in commenting upon matters of public concern and the interests of the State, as an employer, in promoting the efficiency of the public services it performs through its employees." . . . The facts of each case will affect the balance uniquely; in this case we weigh the conduct of officers that goes beyond "pure speech" . . . against the interest of the City of Columbus in seeing that its police services, a function traditionally accorded special respect, remain effective. . . .

We address initially the interests of appellants, and conclude that despite the fact that the activities of appellants involved conduct as well as "pure speech" their interest in expressing themselves was substantial. Three factors lead to this conclusion. First, the conduct here at issue was symbolic speech, closely "akin to pure speech,". . . The conduct of the officers involved no violence or disorder: they peacefully removed the American flag from their uniforms. Representing as it does precepts fundamental to this nation, the American flag frequently has been the focal point of suits involving freedom of expression. . . . Significantly, the officers in no way mutilated or defaced the flag; rather in their view they expressed their deep respect for it and the principles it represented. Removal of the patch under these circumstances bears great similarity to pure speech. Second, although we do not evaluate the content, or "social worth" of ideas, . . . certain types of speech traditionally are accorded greater protection in our society by virtue of the fact that the speech goes to the heart of our democratic process. . . . Appellants sought to emphasize a widely-held perception of racially discriminatory practices in the City of Columbus Police force. These practices concerned not only internal police matters, but matters of interest to the community-at-large as well. . . . For example, appellants publicized a perception of discriminatory hiring of police officers, and a concern that beat assignments were being made along racial lines, i.e. black officers in black communities. For a police force to be effective it must have the respect and support of the community as well as its officers; our system of government demands that support be garnered through informed evaluation of circumstance, and not through the suppression of dissent. Third, and finally, courts repeatedly have held that a police officer does not receive a "watered-down version" of constitutionally protected rights by virtue of his public employment on the police force. . . . In this context, appellants' interest in peaceful, effective expression of their views was great, and we accord it commensurate weight.

Balanced against the interest of appellants is the interest of the City and Police Department in promoting "the effectiveness of the force." We must go beyond asserting the need for "discipline" in "paramilitary" or "quasi-military" organizations, . . . and identify the true interest the Department has in suppressing the speech and conduct that resulted in appellants' dismissal. That interest must derive from the reason appellants were dismissed.

Appellees' brief states "[n]one of the plaintiffs in this case were dismissed for speaking, nor were they dismissed for flag abuse; all of them were dismissed for [d]efying properly constituted authority," . . . Brief of Appellee at 38 (emphasis supplied). The district court elaborated upon the "properly constituted authority." "[Removing the flag] was a calculated show of contempt for the City authority and a demonstration of refusal to obey its lawful ordinances, rules and commands."

Simply stated, the officers were dismissed for failing to obey a resolution of the City of Columbus requiring the flag patch on police uniform. That the speech/conduct that led to dismissal is proscribed by statute is irrelevant to First Amendment analysis, however, if that statute suppresses constitutionally protected activity. . . . In other words, there must be an interest apart from compliance with a statute; a statute which inhibits constitutional rights without sufficient governmental interest is invalid.

Although the district court restrained appellants from eliciting testimony concerning the purpose of the flag requirement itself, it was the obligation of appellees to develop that interest, and they did not seek to do so. Given the nature of the ordinance violated, however, we can deduce what the interest would be. The resolution required a flag patch on the sleeve of a police uniform, it did nothing more and nothing less. Testimony confirms the presence of the patch had no relation to the efficient performance of police duties. What the flag patch did accomplish is an integration of the police into the community, the flag patch representing a devotion to, and concern for, American ideals. Although this sort of goal is most admirable, it is specifically because of what the flag stands for that the interest in having the patch worn must bow to the greater interest of the dismissed officers' free speech.

We can discern yet another interest here, one intimately tied to appellants' status as police officers. Although the City fails to advance this argument itself, we recognize an intrinsic interest in having police officers comply with ordinances of a properly constituted governing body. This interest is a valid and important one. It is not determinative in every instance, however, and certainly is insufficient here. Uncontroverted evidence at trial indicated that a number of police officers invariably were without the flag patch. Whether this was because "old" uniform shirts did not have the patch, and whether the officers wilfully or negligently failed to sew them on, is irrelevant: if the City's interest in police compliance with City ordinances was compelling, discipline should have followed every violation. It is likewise undisputed that appellants were the first officers ever disciplined for failing to wear the patch. It was not until after appellants were dismissed that a white officer was disciplined for failing to wear the flag; in contrast to the dismissals here, that officer was suspended for five days.

Witnesses for the City acknowledged the above facts, but sought to distinguish this case on the basis that appellants stood up in front of the media and removed the flag patch, announcing they could not wear it because of injustice on the force. Such testimony only serves to emphasize that appellants were not punished for fail-ing or refusing to wear the flag, they were punished for speaking. That the City may not do. . . . Weighing the strong interest of appellants in speaking on a matter of pub-lic importance against the interest of the City in having the flag worn on the uni-form, an interest no City official showed concern for until these black officers took the patch off, we can only conclude the speech was protected.

DISCUSSION QUESTIONS

1. What are the critical distinctions between the Goldman and Leonard cases? Do they seem substantial enough to justify the different outcomes?
2. Does the Leonard case suggest that cultural factors may impinge on admin-istrative standardization? For instance, the Black police officers alleged that there was police brutality toward Blacks in the community? Does this suggest that they may have seen themselves as representatives, in some sense, of the interests of African-Americans generally? If so, what would such pluralism and representation in administration portend for standardization? For public administration in the U.S. generally?
3. Do you agree with the court that in removing their flags from their uniforms, the police officers were engaging in "speech" that should be protected by the First Amendment? What if they had burned their flag patches or superim-posed a symbol of Black power or pride on them?

CASE 6.3:
STANDARDIZATION, INDIVIDUATION, AND EQUAL PROTECTION

ZOBEL et ux

v.

WILLIAMS, Commissioner of Revenue of Alaska, et al.
Appeal from the Supreme Court of Alaska
No. 80-1146.
Argued October 7, 1981—Decided June 14, 1982   457 U.S. 55 (1982)

Summary

After Alaska amended its Constitu-tion to establish a Permanent Fund into which the State must deposit at least 25% of its mineral income each year, the state legislature in 1980 enacted a dividend pro-gram to distribute annually a portion of the Fund's earnings directly to the State's adult residents. Under the plan, each adult resident receives one dividend unit for each year of residency subsequent to 1959, the first year of Alaska's statehood. Appellants, residents of Alaska since 1978, brought an action in an Alaska state court challenging the statutory dividend distribution plan as violative of, *inter alia,* their right to equal protection guarantees. The trial court granted summary judgment in appellants' favor, but the Alaska Supreme Court reversed and upheld the statute.

Held: The Alaska dividend distribution plan violates the guarantees of the Equal Protection Clause of the Fourteenth Amendment.

(a) Rather than imposing any threshold waiting period for entitlement to dividend benefits or establishing a test of bona fides of state residence, the dividend statute creates fixed, permanent distinctions between an ever-increasing number of classes of concededly bona fide residents based on how long they have lived in the State. . . .

When a state distributes benefits unequally, the distinctions it makes are subject to scrutiny under the Equal Protection Clause, and generally a law will survive that scrutiny if the distinctions rationally further a legitimate state purpose. . . .

(b) Alaska has shown no valid state interests that are rationally served by the distinctions it makes between citizens who established residence before 1959 and those who have become residents since then. Neither the State's claimed interest in creating a financial incentive for individuals to establish and maintain residence in Alaska nor its claimed interest in assuring prudent management of the Permanent Fund is rationally related to such distinctions. And the State's interest in rewarding citizens for past contributions is

not a legitimate state purpose. Alaska's reasoning could open the door to state apportionment of other rights, benefits, and services according to length of residency, and would permit the states to divide citizens into expanding numbers of permanent classes. Such a result would be clearly impermissible.

Opinion

CHIEF JUSTICE BURGER delivered the opinion of the Court.

The question presented on this appeal is whether a statutory scheme by which a State distributes income derived from its natural resources to the adult citizens of the State in varying amounts, based on the length of each citizen's residence, violates the equal protection rights of newer state citizens. . . .

* * *

I

The 1967 discovery of large oil reserves on state-owned land in the Prudhoe Bay area of Alaska resulted in a windfall to the State. The State, which had a total budget of $124 million in 1969, before the oil revenues began to flow into the state coffers, received $3.7 billion in petroleum revenues during the 1981 fiscal year. This income will continue, and most likely grow for some years in the future. Recognizing that its mineral reserves, although large, are finite and that the resulting income will not continue in perpetuity, the State took steps to assure that its current good fortune will bring long-range benefits. To accomplish this, Alaska in 1976 adopted a constitutional amendment establishing the Permanent Fund into which the State must deposit at least 25% of its mineral income each year. Alaska Const., Art. IX, § 15. The amendment prohibits the legislature from appropriating any of the principal of the Fund but permits use of the Fund's earnings for general governmental purposes.

In 1980, the legislature enacted a dividend program to distribute annually a portion of the Fund's earnings directly to the State's adult residents. Under the plan, each citizen 18 years of age or older receives one dividend unit for each year of residency subsequent to 1959, the first year of statehood. The statute fixed the value of each dividend unit at $50 for the 1979 fiscal year; a one-year resident thus would receive one unit, or $50, while a resident of Alaska since it became a State in 1959 would receive 21 units, or $1,050. The value of a dividend unit will vary each year depending on the income of the Permanent Fund and the amount of that income the State allocates for other purposes. The State now estimates that the 1985 fiscal year dividend will be nearly four times as large as that for 1979.

Appellants, residents of Alaska since 1978, brought this suit in 1980 challenging the dividend distribution plan as violative of their right to equal protection guarantees and their constitutional right to migrate to Alaska, to establish residency there and thereafter to enjoy the full rights of Alaska citizenship on the same terms as all other citizens of the State. The Superior Court for Alaska's Third Judicial District granted summary judgment in appellants' favor, holding that the plan violated the rights of interstate travel and equal protection. A divided Alaska Supreme Court reversed and upheld the statute.

[II]

A

The State advanced and the Alaska Supreme Court accepted three purposes justifying the distinctions made by the dividend program: (a) creation of a financial incentive for individuals to establish and maintain residence in Alaska; (b) encouragement of prudent management of the Permanent Fund; and (c) apportionment of benefits in recognition of undefined "contributions of various kinds, both tangible and intangible, which residents have made during their years of residency." . . .

As the Alaska Supreme Court apparently realized, the first two state objectives—creating a financial incentive for individuals to establish and maintain Alaska residence, and assuring prudent management of the Permanent Fund and the State's natural and mineral resources—are not rationally related to the distinctions Alaska seeks to make between newer residents and those who have been in the State since 1959.

Assuming, *arguendo,* that granting increased dividend benefits for each year of continued Alaska residence might give some residents an incentive to stay in the State in order to reap increased dividend benefits in the future, the State's interest is not in any way served by granting greater dividends to persons for their residency during the 21 years prior to the enactment.

Nor does the State's purpose of furthering the prudent management of the Permanent Fund and the State's resources support retrospective application of its plan to the date of statehood.

*   *   *

The last of the State's objectives—to reward citizens for past contributions— alone was relied upon by the Alaska Supreme Court to support the retrospective application of the law to 1959. However, that objective is not a legitimate state purpose.

* * *

If the states can make the amount of a cash dividend depend on length of residence, what would preclude varying university tuition on a sliding scale based on years of residence—or even limiting access to finite public facilities, eligibility for student loans, for civil service jobs, or for government contracts by length of domicile? Could states impose different taxes based on length of residence? Alaska's reasoning could open the door to state apportionment of other rights, benefits, and services according to length of residency. It would permit the states to divide citizens into expanding numbers of permanent classes. Such a result would be clearly impermissible.

III

The only apparent justification for the retrospective aspect of the program, "favoring established residents over new residents," is constitutionally unacceptable. . . . In our view Alaska has shown no valid state interests which are rationally served by the distinction it makes between citizens who established residence before 1959 and who have become residents since then.

We hold that the Alaska dividend distribution plan violates the guarantees of the Equal Protection Clause of the Fourteenth Amendment.

* * *

Justice Brennan, with whom Justice Marshall, Justice Blackmun, and Justice Powell join concurring.

I join the opinion of the Court, and agree with its conclusion that the retrospective aspects of Alaska's dividend-distribution law are not rationally related to a legitimate state purpose. I write sepa-rately only to emphasize that the pervasive discrimination embodied in the Alaska distribution scheme gives rise to constitutional concerns of somewhat larger proportions than may be evident on a cursory reading of the Court's opinion.

* * *

It is, of course, elementary that the Constitution does not bar the States from making reasoned distinctions between citizens: Insofar as those distinctions are rationally related to the legitimate ends of the State they present no constitutional difficulty, as our equal protection jurisprudence attests. But we have never suggested that duration of residence *vel non* provides a valid justification for discrimination.

* * *

Permissible discriminations between persons must bear a rational relationship to their *relevant* characteristics. While some imprecision is unavoidable in the process of legislative classification, the ideal of equal protection requires attention to individual merit, to individual need. In almost all instances, the business of the State is not with the past, but with the present: to remedy continuing injustices, to fill current needs, to build on the present in order to better the future. The past actions of individuals may be relevant in assessing their present needs; past actions may also be relevant in predicting current ability and future performance. In addition, to a limited extent, recognition and reward of past public service have independent utility for the State, for such recognition may encourage other people to engage in comparably meritorious service. But even the idea of rewarding past public service offers scarce support for the "past contribution" justification for durational-residence classifications since length of residence has only the most tenuous relation to the *actual* service of individuals to the State.

Thus, the past-contribution rationale proves much too little to provide a rational predicate for discrimination on the basis of length of residence. But it also proves far too much, for "it would permit the State to apportion all benefits and services according to the past . . . contributions of its citizens.". . . In effect, then, the past-contribution rationale is so far-reaching in its potential application, and the relationship between residence and contribution to the State so vague and insupportable, that it amounts to little more than a restatement of the criterion for discrimination that it purports to justify. But while dura-

tion of residence has minimal utility as a measure of things that are, in fact, constitutionally relevant, resort to duration of residence as the basis for a distribution of state largesse does closely track the constitutionally untenable position that the longer one's residence, the worthier one is of the State's favor. In my view, it is difficult to escape from the recognition that underlying any scheme of classification on the basis of duration of residence, we shall almost invariably find the unstated premise that "some citizens are more equal than others." We rejected that premise and, I believe, implicitly rejected most forms of discrimination based upon length of residence, when we adopted the Equal Protection Clause.

DISCUSSION QUESTIONS

1. Seeking to reward individuals for "contributions of various kinds, both tangible and intangible, which residents have made during their years of residency" by treating all individuals with equal length of residency identically is obviously irrational. For instance, someone who had spent twenty years in jail for a horrible crime could receive the same benefits as a public school teacher with twenty years seniority. Why do you suppose the State wanted to use years of residence as a surrogate measure for actual contributions to Alaska? Is the individuation that Justice Brennan calls for in his concurring opinion administratively practicable? How could actual contributions be evaluated? If the state had sought to make past tax payments by individuals or families the basis for assessing contributions, what problems might have developed?

2. In *Zobel*, how is the Equal Protection Clause used to protect *pluralism* against governmental efforts to favor some groups? Consider how equal protection serves to promote both standardized treatment (procedural regularity and equality) and diversity (pluralism). Does the constitutional commitment to both procedural equality and pluralism draw acute attention to the way public policy and administration classifies individuals? For instance, what would be the problem if Alaska had made the benefit available to women only? What if only military veterans were eligible? What if everyone who had reached the age of majority were given an equal benefit, but minors received none? What if only indigenous peoples, such as Eskimos and Aleuts, were eligible or ineligible for benefits? What are some of the differences in these classifications?

7

ECONOMY

The constitutionally competent public administrator must be interested in economy from a variety of perspectives. Regard for economic values—private ownership, production, distribution and regulation of property and services—has been central to public administration from the origins of the Constitution. Economic concerns in the realm of public administration have several forms, including the potential power of one group or class to dominate others; tensions between legal equality and economic inequality; the role of government in establishing economic policy and regulating markets; the sources and amounts of revenue needed to fund governmental activities; conduct of public business in an "economical" manner; and allocation of limited resources through budgetary and other systems. As the cases in this chapter demonstrate, pursuit of economic values can lead public administration into conflict with constitutional values, such as equal protection and due process of law. For example, *Sherbert* v. *Verner* (Case 7.2) indicates how conflicts can arise between such seemingly unrelated values as freedom of religion and the economics of employment policies and practices.

DIVERSITY OF PROPERTY

As mentioned in Chapter 6, the Framers of the Constitution were deeply concerned with the potential power of one economic or other faction to dominate other groups or society as a whole. In *Federalist* Number 10, James Madison observed that "a factious spirit has tainted our public administration."[1] In Madison's view, factions held interests which were adverse to the rights of other citizens and/or the interests of the nation generally. He reasoned that minority factions could be checked by the principle of majority rule. Safeguarding against majority factions, on the other hand, was best accomplished by protecting individuals' different and unequal interests and abilities in acquiring property, which would ensure a division of society into diverse and often competing parties and interests.[2]

Competing parties and interests confront government with the dual problem of protecting legitimate differences while preventing one group from dominating others. The constitutional system of representative government, as distinguished from direct democracy, is designed to cure the "mischief of factions" through election of representatives of different constituencies to the Congress, and through the broad geographical scope of the federal government. While one economic or other group may be able to dominate a relatively small unit of government, such as county or even a state, it will have great difficulty in dominating a government representing diverse geographical, economic, and other interests from across the entire nation. Representation of diverse interests ensures bargaining, reconciliation, and balance among interests in seeking the common good.

The constitutional solution of the problem of factions is a primary source of the obligation of public administration to avoid the "factious spirit" that Madison asserted had tainted public administration before adoption of the Constitution—the tendency of individuals holding public office to favor one group or region or class over others in interpreting and carrying out public laws and powers. Public administration is charged with faithfully executing the laws adopted through constitutionally established processes. The realities of interest group politics and the passions of private groups to define their own visions of the public good create strong tendencies for public administration to side with and become captive of private interests. Consequently, public administrators may be induced to substitute private policies for those publicly agreed on through legal processes. This tendency is particularly strong when the constituencies or clients of public agencies are organized economic and ideologically based groups. However, the Constitution firmly establishes the obligation of public administration to adhere to policies and values established through representative processes, and not to substitute privately or administratively determined policies and practices for those arrived at through representative government.[3]

---

[1] Alexander Hamilton, James Madison, and John Jay, *The Federalist Papers,* ed. by Clinton Rossiter (New York: The New American Library, 1961), p. 78.

[2] Ibid., p. 80.

[3] The Iran–Contra affair is a dramatic case of the use of public office for purposes arrived at through processes of private decision-making. See William S. Cohen and George Mitchell, *Men of Zeal* (New York: Viking Press, 1988).

LEGAL EQUALITY AND ECONOMIC INEQUALITY

The constitutional system also creates fundamental tensions for public administration between the values of legal equality and economic inequality. In the perspective of the Constitution, each individual is entitled to justice, equal protection, and due process of law. At the same time, each individual is free to pursue his or her economic self-interest in the marketplace. The constitutional-capitalist system promotes a double standard—legal equality and economic inequality.[4] The Constitution protects both, and in doing so places public administration in a position of tension in mediating between such values as life, shelter and food, and the need of society to promote socially and economically productive activity. Basic rights such as liberty cannot be bought and sold in the marketplace, but the exercise and protection of such rights often requires resources which must be produced through work and investment. Because each citizen does not have to pay directly for exercising his or her rights, the citizen may have little incentive to limit such exercise. At some point, exercise of rights may impose heavy costs which other citizens are reluctant to pay.

To a considerable extent, rights remove certain transactions from the domination of the marketplace, on the grounds that a person is more than an economic being. At the same time, such matters as infant malnutrition and mortality raise profound questions of what transactions should be treated as rights, and what transactions should be left to individual discretion, judgment, and the marketplace.

The constitutional-marketplace system is replete with questions of the appropriate boundary between rights and transactions in the market. Under what circumstances can the operators of a private club refuse admission on the basis of sex? What makes a club "private"? Can the owners of a "public" shopping center limit exercise of freedom of speech on the premises of the center? Can a state or city condition receipt of welfare benefits on residency requirements? Case 7.1, *Shapiro* v. *Thompson* (1969), raises this question and discusses the relevant countervailing values. What rights to goods and services do individuals under the institutional control of government have? As *Wyatt* v. *Stickney* (1971), Case 7.3, shows, in terms of some features, such as room temperature and sanitary facilities, individuals who are involuntarily confined to public mental health facilities may have rights to conditions that much of the citizenry cannot afford in their own residences.

COST REDUCTION

Administrative economy is often viewed as the reduction of costs per unit of output. Its value is self-evident in a federal government that currently spends, on average, over $34,000 per second, every second of the year. Lack of

---

[4]Arthur M. Okun, *Equality and Efficiency: The Big Tradeoff* (Washington, D.C.: The Brookings Institution, 1975).

administrative economy unnecessarily burdens the nation with debt and taxes. But can cost reduction or budgetary limits enable a public agency such as a juvenile home, mental institution, or prison to restrict the goods and services it provides to those in its custody? As *Wyatt* v. *Stickney* illustrates, administrative economizing and budgetary limitations do not justify policies and practices that are found to deprive individuals of rights guaranteed under the Constitution and laws of the United States. The tension between basic rights and the economic capacity of public organizations to protect and satisfy those rights pervades the operations of many human service and correctional institutions. These tensions have resulted in extensive judicial supervision of many public institutions, under the equity powers of courts to order remedial action after a systematic deprivation of rights is found.[5] Public administrators almost always are at the center of such controversies, and are often sued as individuals, for money damages, by residents of public institutions claiming they have been deprived of civil rights.

PUBLIC ADMINISTRATION AND THE ECONOMY

Public administration also faces continuing tensions over the question of the roles and responsibilities of public organizations in the American constitutional system for regulating and promoting economic development, productivity, and growth in the domestic and international economies. This tension appeared at the origins of the constitutional systems in the differences in the administrative theories of Alexander Hamilton and Thomas Jefferson.[6] In Thomas Jefferson's view, the primary role of government and public administration is to protect personal freedom and to advance human development through education. In this view, public administration does not have a substantial role in altering the operations of the marketplace, or in actively participating in the marketplace through subsidizing industry and capital formation. In Hamilton's view, government should provide leadership in planning and directing the nation's economic and social development. Hamilton envisioned a major role for government in the development of national and international commerce, in the development of manufacturing, in capital formation, and in promotion of economic growth. These conflicting views have been modified and refined by two centuries of experience. At the same time, they continue to pose a central value question to public administration: To what extent should the leaders of public organizations rely on the marketplace as presently constituted to produce goods and services, and to what extent should the leaders of public organizations advocate and adopt policies and practices that significantly alter market operations?

[5]See Donald L. Horowitz, *The Courts and Social Policy* (Washington, D.C.: The Brookings Institution, 1977).
[6]See Lynton K. Caldwell, *The Administrative Theories of Hamilton and Jefferson* (New York: Holmes and Meier, 1988).

In the twentieth century, students of public finance have identified a number of market failures that may justify governmental intervention in the economy.[7] These include concerns with equity, particularly for the disabled and the poor; public goods or goods that the private market economy cannot provide, such as defense; externalities, or costs or benefits imposed by one economic activity on others, such as pollution of a river by an upstream firm; economies of scope and scale, such as the initial development of space technologies; instabilities in business cycles, requiring policies by government to stabilize the economy; and inadequate growth in capital formation, which may require governmental action to spur the rate of growth through saving, investment, and productivity improvements.

Governmental activity directed to these concerns can be classified into three parts. The first is allocation, involving the provision of governmental services and the allocation of resources to meet social needs. The second is distribution, involving redistribution of income from one segment of society to another. The third is stabilization and growth, through such policies as regulation of the money supply. The extent of contemporary government's involvement with the economy constantly poses value choices to public administration as to whether public administrative organizations should further modify market activities and, if so, how. Some of these choices are delegated to public administrative organizations by legislation, while others are inherent in setting organizational policies in international and domestic matters. The choices often reflect in contemporary form the differences between the views of public administration originally expressed by Alexander Hamilton and Thomas Jefferson.[8]

Perhaps the most fundamental economic tension confronted by public administration is between the obligation of public administrative organizations to accomplish the missions defined for them by political bodies, in an economical manner within budgetary and other constraints imposed by law. As Case 5.1, *Cleveland Board of Education* v. *Loudermill*, and Case 5.2, *Cleveland Board of Education* v. *LaFleur* illustrate, satisfying the requirements of due process in granting or denying public employment under various statutory schemes can impose heavy costs on public organizations. *Wyatt* v. *Stickney* shows that humane policies consistent with constitutional requirements can strain the resources of a public mental institution or other public organization. In a period of high federal budget deficits and extensive concerns over the productivity of the economy, such tensions will persist and may become acute. Managing these tensions will increasingly challenge the creativity of public administrators to pursue the rights established by the Constitution (and laws) and to conduct the public's business in an economical manner. Public administrators are accountable to a Constitution that protects individual rights, diversity of property, and

---

[7]The classic work on public finance is Richard Musgrave, *The Theory of Public Finance* (New York: McGraw-Hill, 1959). See also Okun, *Equality and Efficiency*.
[8]Herbert Stein, *Presidential Economics: The Making of Economic Policy from Roosevelt to Reagan and Beyond* (New York: Simon and Schuster, 1984), is an excellent review of the dilemmas of formulating economic policies for the federal government

economic freedom in the marketplace. Reconciling these different and sometimes conflicting sets of values continues to be one of the major challenges of public administration.[9]

The following cases speak to the broad mix of economic concerns with which the constitutionally competent public administrator must deal. *Shapiro* and *Sherbert* evidence not just a strong interest in reducing administrative costs, but also an effort to ensure that individuals will actively participate in the work force. In both these cases, the Supreme Court finds that governments have placed intolerable burdens on the rights of citizens who are dependent on administrative organizations for their economic welfare. These cases are part of the "new property" discussed in Chapter 1. The *Wyatt* case explicitly demonstrates how administrative cost-cutting can ignore constitutional and other values, including the value of fundamental decency. Together, these cases indicate that the constitutionally competent public administrator must be wary in passing administrative costs on to private individuals.

ADDITIONAL READING

CALDWELL, LYNTON K. *The Administrative Theories of Hamilton and Jefferson.* New York: Holmes and Meier, 1988.

DAHRENDORF, RALF. *The Modern Social Conflict.* New York: Weidenfeld and Nicolson, 1988.

HOROWITZ, DONALD L. *The Courts and Social Policy.* Washington, D.C.: The Brookings Institution, 1977.

KUPERBERG, MARK, AND CHARLES BEITZ, EDS. *Law, Economics, and Philosophy.* Totowa, N.J.: Rowan and Allanheld, 1983.

OKUN, ARTHUR M. *Equality and Efficiency: The Big Tradeoff.* Washington, D.C.: The Brookings Institution, 1975.

[9]See Isabel V. Sawhill, ed., *Challenge to Leadership* (Washington, D.C.: The Urban Institute, 1988).

CASE 7.1:
ADMINISTRATIVE COSTS VERSUS EQUAL PROTECTION AND THE RIGHT TO TRAVEL

SHAPIRO, Commissioner of
Welfare of Connecticut

v

THOMPSON
[No. 9]
394 v.s. 618
Argued May 1, 1968—Reargued
October 23–24, 1968—Decided
April 21, 1969.

Summary

This case involved the following three appeals from decisions of three-judge United States District Courts holding unconstitutional a state or District of Columbia statutory provision which denies welfare assistance to residents of the state or District who have not resided within their jurisdictions for at least one year immediately preceding their applications for such assistance: (1) an appeal (No. 9) from such a decision of the District Court for the District of Connecticut with respect to such a provision in the Connecticut General Statutes . . . ; (2) an appeal (No. 33) from such a decision of the District Court for the District of Columbia with respect to such a provision adopted by Congress in the District of Columbia Code . . . ; and (3) an appeal (No. 34) from such a decision of the District Court for the Eastern District of Pennsylvania with respect to such a provision in the Pennsylvania Welfare Code. . . .

The United States Supreme Court affirmed the judgments of the District Courts in all three cases. In an opinion by BRENNAN, J., expressing the view of six members of the court, it was held that (1) absent a compelling state interest, the Connecticut and Pennsylvania statutory provisions violated the equal protection clause of the Fourteenth Amendment by imposing a classification of welfare applicants which impinged upon their constitutional right to travel freely from state to state; (2) absent a compelling governmental interest, the District of Columbia statutory provision violated the due process clause of the Fifth Amendment by imposing a discrimination which impinged upon the constitutional right to travel; and (3) § 402(b) of the Social Security Act of 1935 did not, and constitutionally could not, authorize the states to impose such one-year waiting period requirement.

Opinion

Mr. Justice **Brennan** delivered the opinion of the Court.

These three appeals were restored to the calendar for reargument. . . . Each is an appeal from a decision of a three-judge District Court holding unconstitutional a State or District of Columbia statutory provision which denies welfare assistance to residents of the State or District who have not resided within their jurisdictions for at least one year immediately preceding their applications for such assistance. We affirm the judgments of the District Courts in the three cases.

I.

In No. 9, the Connecticut Welfare Department invoked § 17–2d of the Connecticut General Statutes to deny the application of appellee Vivian Marie Thompson for assistance under the program for Aid to Families with Dependent Children (AFDC). She was a 19-year-old unwed mother of one child and pregnant with her second child when she changed her residence in June 1966 from Dorchester, Massachusetts, to Hartford, Connecticut, to live with her mother, a Hartford resident. She moved to her own apartment in Hartford in August 1966, when her mother was no longer able to support her and her infant son. Because of her pregnancy, she was unable to work or enter a work training program. Her application for AFDC assistance, filed in August, was denied in November solely on the ground that, as required by § 17–2d, she had not lived in the State for a year before her application was filed. She brought this action in the District Court for the District of Connecticut where a three-judge court, one judge dissenting, declared § 17–2d unconstitutional. . . . The majority held that the waiting-period requirement is unconstitutional because it "has a chilling effect on the right to travel." . . . The majority also held that the provision was a violation of the Equal Protection Clause of the Fourteenth Amendment because the denial of relief to those resident in the State for less than a year is not based on any permissible purpose but is solely designed, as "Connecticut states quite frankly," "to protect its fisc by discouraging entry of those who come needing relief." . . .

In No. 33, there are four appellees. Three of them—appellees Harrell, Brown, and Legrant—applied for and were denied AFDC aid. The fourth, appellee Barley, applied for and was denied benefits under the program for Aid to the Permanently and Totally Disabled. The denial in each case was on the ground that the applicant had not resided in the District of Columbia for one year immediately preceding the filing of her application, as required by § 3–203 of the District of Columbia Code.

Appellee Minnie Harrell, now deceased, had moved with her three children from New York to Washington in September 1966. She suffered from cancer and moved to be near members of her family who lived in Washington.

Appellee Barley, a former resident of the District of Columbia, returned to the District in March 1941 and was committed a month later to St. Elizabeth's Hospital as mentally ill. She has remained in that hospital ever since. She was deemed eligible for release in 1965, and a plan was made to transfer her from the hospital to a foster home. The plan depended, however, upon Mrs. Barley's obtaining welfare assistance for her support. Her application for assistance under the program for Aid to the Permanently and Totally Disabled was denied because her time spent in the hospital did not count in determining compliance with the one-year requirement.

Appellee Brown lived with her mother and two of her three children in Fort Smith, Arkansas. Her third child was living with appellee Brown's father in the District of Columbia. When her mother moved from Fort Smith to Oklahoma, appellee Brown, in February 1966, returned to the District of Columbia where she had lived as a child. Her application for AFDC assistance was approved insofar as it sought assistance for the child who had lived in the District with her father but was denied to the extent it sought assistance for the two other children.

Appellee Legrant moved with her two children from South Carolina to the District of Columbia in March 1967 after the death of her mother. She planned to live with a sister and brother in Washington. She was pregnant and in ill health when she applied for and was denied AFDC assistance in July 1967.

The several cases were consolidated for trial, and a three-judge District Court was convened. The court, one judge dissenting, held § 3–203 unconstitutional. . . . The majority rested its decision on the ground that the one-year requirement was unconstitutional as a denial of the right to equal protection secured by the Due Process Clause of the Fifth Amendment. We noted probable jurisdiction. . . .

In No. 34, there are two appellees, Smith and Foster, who were denied AFDC aid on the sole ground that they had not been residents of Pennsylvania for a year prior to their applications as required by § 432(6) of the Pennsylvania Welfare Code. Appellee Smith and her five minor children moved in December 1966 from Delaware to Philadelphia, Pennsylvania, where her father lived. Her father supported her and her children for several months until he lost his job. Appellee then applied for AFDC assistance and had received two checks when the aid was terminated. Appellee Foster, after living in Pennsylvania from 1953 to 1965, had moved with her four children to South Carolina to care for her grandfather and invalid grandmother and had returned to Pennsylvania in 1967. A three-judge District Court for the Eastern District of Pennsylvania, one judge dissenting, declared § 432(6) unconstitutional. . . . The majority held that the classification established by the waiting-period requirement is "without rational basis and without legitimate purpose or function" and therefore a violation of the Equal Protection Clause. . . . The majority noted further that if the purpose of the statute was "to erect a barrier against the movement of indigent persons into the State or to effect their prompt departure after they have gotten there," it would be "patently improper and its implementation plainly impermissible." . . . We noted probable jurisdiction. . . .

II.

There is no dispute that the effect of the waiting-period requirement in each case is to create two classes of needy resident families indistinguishable from each other except that one is composed of residents who have resided a year or more, and the second of residents who have resided less than a year, in the jurisdiction. On the basis of this sole difference the first class is granted and the second class is denied welfare aid upon which may depend the ability of the families to obtain the very means to subsist—food, shelter, and other necessities of life. In each case, the District Court found that appellees met the test for residence in their jurisdictions, as well as all other eligibility requirements except the requirement of residence for a full year prior to their applications. On reargument, appellees' central contention is that the statutory prohibition of benefits to residents of less than a year creates a

classification which constitutes an invidious discrimination denying them equal protection of the laws. We agree. The interests which appellants assert are promoted by the classification either may not constitutionally be promoted by government or are not compelling governmental interests.

III.

Primarily, appellants justify the waiting-period requirement as a protective device to preserve the fiscal integrity of state public assistance programs. It is asserted that people who require welfare assistance during their first year of residence in a State are likely to become continuing burdens on state welfare programs. Therefore, the argument runs, if such people can be deterred from entering the jurisdiction by denying them welfare benefits during the first year, state programs to assist long-time residents will not be impaired by a substantial influx of indigent newcomers.

There is weighty evidence that exclusion from the jurisdiction of the poor who need or may need relief was the specific objective of these provisions. In the Congress, sponsors of federal legislation to eliminate all residence requirements have been consistently opposed by representatives of state and local welfare agencies who have stressed the fears of the States that elimination of the requirements would result in a heavy influx of individuals into States providing the most generous benefits. . . .

We do not doubt that the one-year waiting-period device is well suited to discourage the influx of poor families in need of assistance. An indigent who desires to migrate, resettle, find a new job, and start a new life will doubtless hesitate if he knows that he must risk making the move without the possibility of falling back on state welfare assistance during his first year of residence when his need may be most acute. But the purpose of inhibiting migration by needy persons into the State is constitutionally impermissible.

This Court long ago recognized that the nature of our Federal Union and our constitutional concepts of personal liberty unite to require that all citizens be free to travel throughout the length and breadth of our land uninhibited by statutes, rules, or regulations which unreasonably burden or restrict this movement. That proposition was early stated by Chief Justice Taney in the Passenger Cases . . . (1849):

"For all the great purposes for which the Federal government was formed, we are one people, with one common country. We are all citizens of the United States; and, as members of the same community, must have the right to pass and repass through every part of it without interruption, as freely as in our own States."

We have no occasion to ascribe the source of this right to travel interstate to a particular constitutional provision. It suffices that, as Mr. Justice Stewart said for the Court in United States v Guest . . . (1966):

"The constitutional right to travel from one State to another . . . occupies a position fundamental to the concept of our Federal Union. It is a right that has been firmly established and repeatedly recognized.

". . . [The] right finds no explicit mention in the Constitution. The reason, it has been suggested, is that a right so elementary was conceived from the beginning to be a necessary concomitant of the stronger Union the Constitution created. In any event, freedom to travel throughout the United States has long been recognized as a basic right under the Constitution."

Thus, the purpose of deterring the in-migration of indigents cannot serve as justification for the classification created by the one-year waiting period, since that purpose is constitutionally impermissible. If a law has "no other purpose . . . than to chill the assertion of constitutional rights by penalizing those who choose to exercise them, then it [is] patently unconstitutional." . . . Alternatively, appellants argue that even if it is impermissible for a State to attempt to deter the entry of all indigents, the challenged classification may be justified as a permissible state attempt to discourage those indigents who would enter the State solely to obtain larger benefits. We observe first that none of the statutes before us is tailored to serve that objective. Rather, the class of barred newcomers is all-inclusive, lumping the great majority who come to the State for other purposes with those who come for the sole purpose of collecting higher benefits. In actual operation, therefore, the three statutes enact what in effect are nonrebuttable presumptions that every applicant for assistance in his first year of residence came to the jurisdiction soley to obtain higher benefits. Nothing whatever in any of these records supplies any basis in fact for such a presumption.

More fundamentally, a State may no more try to fence out those indigents who seek higher welfare benefits than it may try to fence out indigents generally. Implicit in any such distinction is the notion that indigents who enter a State with the hope of securing higher welfare benefits are somehow less deserving than indigents who do not take this consideration into account. But we do not perceive why a mother who is seeking to make a new life for herself and her children should be regarded as less deserving because she considers, among other factors, the level of a State's public assistance. Surely such a mother is no less deserving than a mother who moves into a particular State in order to take advantage of its better educational facilities.

Appellants argue further that the challenged classification may be sustained as an attempt to distinguish between new and old residents on the basis of the contribution they have made to the community through the payment of taxes. . . . Appellants' reasoning would logically permit the State to bar new residents from schools, parks, and libraries or deprive them of police and fire protection. Indeed it would permit the State to apportion all benefits and services according to the past tax contributions of its citizens. The Equal Protection Clause prohibits such an apportionment of state services.

We recognize that a State has a valid interest in preserving the fiscal integrity of its programs. It may legitimately attempt to limit its expenditures, whether for public assistance, public education, or any other program. But a State may not accomplish such a purpose by invidious distinctions between classes of its citizens. It could not, for example, reduce expenditures for education by barring indigent children from its schools. Similarly, in the cases before us, appellants must do more than show that denying welfare benefits to new residents saves money. The saving of welfare costs cannot justify an otherwise invidious classification.

In sum, neither deterrence of indigents from migrating to the State nor limitation of welfare benefits to those regarded as contributing to the State is a constitutionally permissible state objective.

IV.

Appellants next advance as justification certain administrative and related governmental objectives allegedly served by the waiting-period requirement. They argue that the requirement (1) facilitates the planning of the welfare budget; (2) provides an objective test of residency; (3) minimizes the opportunity for recipients fraudulently to receive payments from more than one jurisdiction; and (4) encourges early entry of new residents into the labor force.

At the outset, we reject appellants' argument that a mere showing of a rational relationship between the waiting period and these four admittedly permissible state objectives will suffice to justify the classification. . . . The waiting-period provision denies welfare benefits to otherwise eligible applicants solely because they have recently moved into the jurisdiction. But in moving from State to State or to the District of Columbia appellees were exercising a constitutional right, and any classification which serves to penalize the exercise of that right, unless shown to be necessary to promote a *compelling* governmental interest, is unconstitutional. . . .

The argument that the waiting-period requirement facilitates budget predictability is wholly unfounded. The records in all three cases are utterly devoid of evidence that either State or the District of Columbia in fact uses the one-year requirement as a means to predict the number of people who will require assistance in the budget year. . . .

The argument that the waiting period serves as an administratively efficient rule of thumb for determining residency similarly will not withstand scrutiny. The residence requirement and the one-year waiting-period requirement are distinct and independent prerequisites for assistance under these three statutes, and the facts relevant to the determination of each are directly examined by the welfare authorities. Before granting an application, the welfare authorities investigate the applicant's employment, housing, and family situation and in the course of the inquiry necessarily learn the facts upon which to determine whether the applicant is a resident.

Similarly, there is no need for a State to use the one-year waiting period as a safeguard against fraudulent receipt of benefits; for less drastic means are available, and are employed, to minimize that hazard. Of course, a State has a valid interest in preventing fraud by any applicant, whether a newcomer or a long-time resident. It is not denied, however, that the investigations now conducted entail inquiries into facts relevant to that subject. In addition, cooperation among state welfare departments is common. . . . Since double payments can be prevented by a letter or a telephone call, it is unreasonable to accomplish this objective by the blunderbuss method of denying assistance to all indigent newcomers for an entire year.

Pennsylvania suggests that the one-year waiting period is justified as a means of encouraging new residents to join the labor force promptly. But this logic would also require a similar waiting period for long-term residents of the State. A state purpose to encourage employment provides no rational basis for imposing a one-year waiting-period restriction on new residents only.

We conclude therefore that appellants in these cases do not use and have no need to use the one-year requirement for the governmental purposes suggested. Thus, even under traditional equal protection tests a classification of welfare applicants according to whether they have lived in the State for one year would seem irrational and unconstitutional. But, of course, the traditional criteria do not apply in these cases. Since the classification here touches on the fundamental right of interstate movement, its constitutionality must be judged by the stricter standard of whether it promotes a *compelling* state interest. Under this standard, the waiting-period requirement clearly violates the Equal Protection Clause.

DISCUSSION QUESTIONS

1. The Court notes that the Constitution does not specifically provide for a "right to travel interstate," but that such a right is fundamental. What criteria does the Court use in *Shapiro* to determine that the right to travel interstate is fundamental? Can you think of other fundamental individual rights that are not explicitly mentioned in the Constitution? Would marriage and procreation be such rights? What criteria would you use to support the conclusion that whatever such rights you identify are constitutionally protected?

2. Under what circumstances, if any, do you believe that residency requirements might be justified to preserve the fiscal integrity of state programs? Would you draw a distinction between the circumstances in *Shapiro* and those presented by state universities that charge less tuition for "in-staters" than for "out-of-staters"?

3. Do you believe that a federal court should have the power to order a state legislature to raise taxes to pay for a state program when, due to the number of clients, claims under that program exceed the available funds? Suppose the program is mandated by the federal government and jointly financed by it and the states. Would that affect your answer? Do you see any important

difference between the Supreme Court declaring the District of Columbia's residency requirement in *Shapiro* to be unconstitutional and its holdings with regard to the states involved?

CASE 7.2:
COST REDUCTION VERSUS FREE EXERCISE OF RELIGION

SHERBERT

v.

VERNER et al., MEMBERS OF
SOUTH CAROLINA
EMPLOYMENT SECURITY
COMMISSION, et al.
374 US 398
[No. 526]
Argued April 24, 1963—Decided
June 17, 1963.

Summary

A Seventh-Day Adventist was discharged by her employer for her refusal to work on Saturday, the Sabbath Day of her faith, and was refused unemployment compensation by the South Carolina Employment Security Commission on the ground that her refusal to work Saturdays, causing other employers to refuse to hire her, disqualified her for failure to accept suitable work. The commission's finding was sustained by the Court of Common Pleas for Spartanburg County. The South Carolina Supreme Court affirmed on the ground that disqualifying the Seventh-Day Adventist from unemployment compensation did not restrict her religious freedom. . . .

On appeal, the Supreme Court of the United States reversed. In an opinion by BRENNAN, J., expressing the views of five members of the Court, it was held that (1) the denial of unemployment compensation benefits to the Seventh-Day Adventist restricted the free exercise of her religion, (2) the state's interest in preserving the unemployment compensation fund from dilution by false claims, and in not hindering employers from scheduling necessary Saturday work, did not justify the state's restriction of the Seventh-Day Adventist's religious freedom, and (3) the extension of unemployment compensation benefits to Sabbatarians in common with Sunday worshippers does not foster the establishment of the Seventh-Day Adventist religion in South Carolina.

Opinion

Mr. Justice **Brennan** delivered the opinion of the Court.

Appellant, a member of the Seventh-Day Adventist Church, was discharged by her South Carolina employer because she would not work on Saturday, the Sabbath Day of her faith. When she was unable to obtain other employment because from conscientious scruples she would not take Saturday work, she filed a claim for unemployment compensation benefits under the South Carolina Unemployment Compensation Act. That law provides that, to be eligible for benefits, a claimant must be "able to work and . . . available for work"; and, further, that a claimant is ineligible for benefits "[i]f . . . he has failed, without good cause . . . to accept available suitable work when offered him by the employment office or the employer. . . ." The appellee Employment Security Commission, in administrative proceedings under the statute, found that appellant's restriction upon her availability for Saturday work brought her within the provision disqualifying for benefits insured workers who fail, without good cause, to accept "suitable work when offered . . . by the employment office or the employer. . . ." The Commission's finding was sustained by the Court of Common Pleas for Spartanburg County. That court's judgment was in turn affirmed by the South Carolina Supreme Court, which rejected appellant's contention that, as applied to her, the disqualifying provisions of the South Carolina statute abridged her right to the free exercise of her religon secured under the Free Exercise Clause of the First Amendment through the Fourteenth Amendment. The State Supreme Court held specifically that appellant's ineligibility infringed no constitutional liberties because such a construction of the statute "places no restriction upon the appellant's freedom of religion nor does it in any way prevent her in the exercise of her right and freedom to observe her religious beliefs in accordance with the dictates of her conscience."

. . . We reverse the judgment of the South Carolina Supreme Court and remand for further proceedings not inconsistent with this opinion.

I.

The door of the Free Exercise Clause stands tightly closed against any govern-

mental regulation of religious *beliefs* as such. . . . Government may neither compel affirmation of a repugnant belief . . . nor penalize or discriminate against individuals or groups because they hold religious views abhorrent to the authorities . . . nor employ the taxing power to inhibit the dissemination of particular religious views. . . . On the other hand, the Court has rejected challenges under the Free Exercise Clause to governmental regulation of certain overt acts prompted by religious beliefs or principles, for "even when the action is in accord with one's religious convictions, [it] is not totally free from legislative restrictions." . . . The conduct or actions so regulated have invariably posed some substantial threat to public safety, peace or order.

Plainly enough, appellant's conscientious objection to Saturday work constitutes no conduct prompted by religious principles of a kind within the reach of state legislation. If, therefore, the decision of the South Carolina Supreme Court is to withstand appellant's constitutional challenge, it must be either because her disqualification as a beneficiary represents no infringement by the State of her constitutional rights of free exercise, or because any incidental burden on the free exercise of appellant's religon may be justified by a "compelling state interest in the regulation of a subject within the State's constitutional power to regulate. . . ." . . .

We turn first to the question whether the disqualification for benefits imposes any burden on the free exercise of appellant's religion. We think it is clear that it does. In a sense the consequences of such a disqualification to religious principles and practices may be only an indirect result of welfare legislation within the State's general competence to enact: it is true that no criminal sanctions directly compel appellant to work a six-day week. But this is only the beginning, not the end, of our inquiry. For "[i]f the purpose or effect of a law is to impede the observance of one or all religions or is to discriminate invidiously between religions, that law is constitutionally invalid even though the burden may be characterized as being only indirect." . . . Here not only is it apparent that appellant's declared ineligibility for benefits derives solely from the practice of her religion, but the pressure upon her to forego that practice is unmistakable. The ruling forces her to choose between following the precepts of her religion and forfeiting benefits, on the one hand, and abandoning one of the precepts of her religion in order to accept work, on the other hand. Governmental imposition of such a choice puts the same kind of burden upon the free exercise of religion as would a fine imposed against appellant for her Saturday worship.

Nor may the South Carolina court's construction of the statute be saved from constitutional infirmity on the ground that unemployment compensation benefits are not appellant's "right" but merely a "privilege." It is too late in the day to doubt that the liberties of religion and expression may be infringed by the denial of or placing of conditions upon a benefit or privilege. . . . [T]he Court recognized with respect to Federal Social Security benefits that "[t]he interest of a covered employee under the Act is of sufficient substance to fall within the protection from arbitrary governmental action afforded by the Due Process Clause." In Speiser v Randall . . . we emphasized that conditions upon public benefits cannot be sustained if they so operate, whatever their purpose, as to inhibit or deter the exercise of First Amendment freedoms. We there struck down a condition which limited the availability of a

tax exemption to those members of the exempted class who affirmed their loyalty to the state government granting the exemption. While the State was surely under no obligation to afford such an exemption, we held that the imposition of such a condition upon even a gratuitous benefit inevitably deterred or discouraged the exercise of First Amendment rights of expression and thereby threatened to "produce a result which the State could not command directly." . . . "To deny an exemption to claimants who engage in certain forms of speech is in effect to penalize them for such speech." . . . Likewise, to condition the availability of benefits upon this appellant's willingness to violate a cardinal principle of her religious faith effectively penalizes the free exercise of her constitutional liberties.

Significantly South Carolina expressly saves the Sunday worshipper from having to make the kind of choice which we here hold infringes the Sabbatarian's religious liberty. When in times of "national emergency" the textile plants are authorized by the State Commissioner of Labor to operate on Sunday, "no employee shall be required to work on Sunday . . . who is conscientiously opposed to Sunday work; and if any employee should refuse to work on Sunday on account of conscientious . . . objections he or she shall not jeopardize his or her seniority by such refusal or be discriminated against in any other manner." . . . No question of the disqualification of a Sunday worshipper for benefits is likely to arise, since we cannot suppose that an employer will discharge him in violation of this statute. The unconstitutionality of the disqualification of the Sabbatarian is thus compounded by the religious discrimination which South Carolina's general statutory scheme necessarily effects.

III.

We must next consider whether some compelling state interest enforced in the eligibility provisions of the South Carolina statute justifies the substantial infringement of appellant's First Amendment right. It is basic that no showing merely of a rational relationship to some colorable state interest would suffice; in this highly sensitive constitutional area, "[o]nly the gravest abuses, endangering paramount interests, give occasion for permissible limitation." . . . No such abuse or danger has been advanced in the present case. The appellees suggest no more than a possibility that the filing of fraudulent claims by unscrupulous claimants feigning religious objections to Saturday work might not only dilute the unemployment compensation fund but also hinder the scheduling by employers of necessary Saturday work. But that possibility is not apposite here because no such objection appears to have been made before the South Carolina Supreme Court, and we are unwilling to assess the importance of an asserted state interest without the views of the state court. Nor, if the contention had been made below, would the record appear to sustain it; there is no proof whatever to warrant such fears of malingering or deceit as those which the respondents now advance. Even if consideration of such evidence is not foreclosed by the prohibition against judicial inquiry into the truth or falsity of religious beliefs, . . .—a question as to which we intimate no view since it is not before us—it is highly doubtful whether such evidence would be sufficient to warrant a substantial infringement of religious liberties. For even if the possibility of spurious claims did threaten to dilute the fund and disrupt the scheduling of work, it would plainly be incumbent upon the appellees to demonstrate that no alternative forms of regulation would combat such abuses without infringing First Amendment rights. . . .

*   *   *

IV.

In holding as we do, plainly we are not fostering the "establishment" of the Seventh-Day Adventist religion in South Carolina, for the extension of unemployment benefits to Sabbatarians in common with Sunday worshippers reflects nothing more than the governmental obligation of neutrality in the face of religious differences, and does not represent that involvement of religious with secular institutions which it is the object of the Establishment Clause to forestall. . . . Nor does the recognition of the appellant's right to unemployment benefits under the state statute serve to abridge any other person's religious liberties. Nor do we, by our decision today, declare the existence of a constitutional right to unemployment benefits on the part of all persons whose religious convictions are the cause of their unemployment. This is not a case in which an employee's religious convictions serve to make him a nonproductive member of society. . . . Finally, nothing we say today constrains the States to adopt any particular form or scheme of unemployment compensation. Our holding today is only that South Carolina may not constitutionally apply the eligibility provisions so as to constrain a worker to abandon his religious convictions respecting the day of rest. This holding but reaffirms a principle that we announced a decade and a half ago, namely that no State may "exclude individual Catholics, Lutherans, Mohammedans, Baptists, Jews, Methodists, Nonbelievers, Presbyterians, or the members of any other faith, *because of their faith, or* *lack of it,* from receiving the benefits of public welfare legislation." . . .

DISCUSSION QUESTIONS

1. *Sherbert* was one of the first Supreme Court decisions to reject the historic "doctrine of privilege." Under that doctrine, governments were permitted to place conditions on individuals' receipt of benefits, such as public employment and welfare, that interfered with the exercise of their ordinary constitutional rights. The doctrine did not require governments to demonstrate a compelling state interest for such conditions or that they were the least restrictive alternatives. For instance, as the South Carolina State Supreme Court reasoned, under this doctrine the government did not abridge Sherbert's constitutional right to free exercise of religion because it left her free to observe the Sabbath as she saw fit; the government merely denied her a benefit to which she had no right (and which, therefore, was considered a "privilege"). The demise of the doctrine of privilege during the 1960s and early 1970s dramatically changed the relationship between the Constitution and public administration; but in *Sherbert,* the U.S. Supreme Court took only a few terse sentences to reject it.

    Think back over the cases presented earlier in this book. Identify those that implicitly or explicitly reject the logic of the doctrine of privilege and consider how public administration has been changed by its demise.

2. In dissent, Justice Harlan, joined by Justice White, argued that under the majority's decision, "The State . . . must *single out* for financial assistance those whose behavior is religiously motivated, even though it denies such assistance to others whose identical behavior . . . is not religiously motivated." Thus, Sherbert can receive assistance if her reason for not working on Saturdays is based on her religion, but not if it is because she likes to watch Saturday morning TV. To what extent does there appear to be a tension between the two prongs of the Constitution's guarantee of freedom of religion in this case; that is, between the rights of individuals to free exercise of religion and the prohibition on governmental establishment of religion? What criteria would you use to determine the extent to which government should be required to accommodate individuals' religious practices? Suppose, for example, Sherbert's religion required so many hours of daily prayer that she could be available for work only for six hours, rather than eight. Under the Court's ruling, would she be eligible for unemployment compensation benefits?

3. Consider the extent to which *Goldman* v. *Weinberger* (Case 6.1) is consistent with *Sherbert.*

CASE 7.3:
CONSTITUTIONAL RIGHTS AND BUDGET CONSTRAINTS

Ricky WYATT, by and through his Aunt and legal guardian Mrs. W. C. Rawlins, Jr., et al, Plaintiffs,

v.

Dr. Stonewall B. STICKNEY, as Commissioner of Mental Health and the State of Alabama Mental Health Officer, et al., Defendants
Civ. A. No. 3195–N.
United States District Court, M. D. Alabama, N.D. March 12, 1971
325 F. Supp. 781

Summary

Class action was initiated by guardians of patients confined at state mental hospital and by certain employees assigned to such hospital. The District Court, Johnson, Chief Judge, determined that programs of treatment in use at state mental hospital were scientifically and medically inadequate and deprived patients of their constitutional rights, but court reserved ruling to afford state officials opportunity to promulgate and implement proper standards but failure on part of defendants to implement fully within six months an adequate treatment program would require court's appointment of panel of experts to determine what standards will be required.

Ordered accordingly.

Opinion

JOHNSON, Chief Judge.

This is a class action that was initiated by guardians of patients confined at Bryce Hospital, Tuscaloosa, Alabama, and by certain employees of the Alabama Mental Health Board who are assigned to Bryce Hospital. The plaintiffs sue on behalf of themselves and on behalf of other members of their respective classes.

The defendants are the commissioner and the deputy commissioner of the Department of Mental Health of the State of Alabama, the members of the Alabama Mental Health Board, the Governor of the State of Alabama, and the probate judge of Montgomery County, Alabama, as representative of the other judges of probate in the State of Alabama.

* * *

The Alabama Mental Health Board is a public corporation created by the State of Alabama. . . . This board is responsible for the administration of all State mental health facilities and treatment centers, including Bryce Hospital, Tuscaloosa, Alabama. When not in session, the Alabama Mental Health Board acts through its chief administrative officer whose title is State Mental Health Officer. This position is presently held by Dr. Stonewall B. Stickney.

Bryce Hospital is located in Tuscaloosa, Alabama, and is a part of the mental health service delivery system for the State of Alabama. Bryce Hospital has approximately 5,000 patients, the majority of whom are involuntarily committed through civil proceedings by the various probate judges in Alabama. Approximately 1,600 employees were assigned to various duties at the Bryce Hospital facility when this case was heard on plaintiffs' motion for a preliminary injunction.

During October 1970, the Alabama Mental Health Board and the administration of the Department of Mental Health terminated 99 of these employees. These terminations were made due to budgetary considerations and, according to the evidence, were necessary to bring the expenditures at Bryce Hospital within the framework of available resources. This budget cut at Bryce Hospital was allegedly necessary because of a reduction in the tax revenues available to the Department of Mental Health of the State of Alabama, and also because an adjustment in the pay periods for personnel which had been directed by the Alabama legislature would require additional expenditures. The employees who were terminated included 41 persons who were assigned to duties such as food service, maintenance, typing, and other functional duties not involving direct patient care in the hospital therapeutic programs. Twenty-six persons were discharged who were involved in patient activity and recreational programs. These workers were involved in planning social and other types of recreational programs for the patient population. The remaining 32 employees who were discharged included 9 in the department of psychology, 11 in the social service department, with varying degrees of educational background and experience, three registered nurses, two physicians, one dentist, and six dental aides. After the termination of these employees, there remained at Bryce Hospital 17 physicians, approximately 850 psychiatric aides, 21 registered nurses, 12 patient activity workers, and 12 psychologists with varying academic qualifications and experience, together with 13 social service workers. Of the employees remaining whose duties involved direct patient care in the hospital therapeutic programs, there are only one Ph.D. clinical psychologist, three medical doctors with some psychiatric training (including one board eligible but no board-certified psychiatrist) and two M.S.W. social workers.

*   *   *

Included in the Bryce Hospital patient population are between 1,500 and 1,600 geriatric patients who are provided custodial care but no treatment. The evidence is without dispute that these patients are not properly confined at Bryce Hospital since these geriatric patients cannot benefit from any psychiatric treatment or are not mentally ill. Also included in the Bryce patient population are approximately 1,000 mental retardates, most of whom receive only custodial care without any psychiatric treatment. Thus, the evidence reflects that there is considerable confusion regarding the primary mission and function of Bryce Hospital since certain nonpsychotic geriatric patients and the mental retardates, and perhaps other nonmentally ill persons, have been and remain committed there for a variety of reasons.

The evidence further reflects that Alabama ranks fiftieth among all the states in the Union in per-patient expenditures per day. This Court must, and does, find from the evidence that the programs of treatment in use at Bryce Hospital ... were scientifically and medically inadequate. These programs of treatment failed to conform to any known minimums established for providing treatment for the mentally ill.

The patients at Bryce Hospital, for the most part, were involuntarily committed through noncriminal procedures and without the constitutional protections that are afforded defendants in criminal proceedings. When patients are so committed for treatment purposes they unquestionably have a constitutional right to receive such individual treatment as will give each of them a realistic opportunity to be cured or to improve his or her mental condition. . . . Adequate and effective treatment is constitutionally required because, absent treatment, the hospital is transformed "into a penitentiary where one could be held indefinitely for no convicted offense." . . . The purpose of involuntary hospitalization for treatment purposes is *treatment* and not mere custodial care or punishment. This is the only justification, from a constitutional standpoint, that allows civil commitments to mental institutions such as Bryce. According to the evidence in this case, the failure of Bryce Hospital to supply adequate treatment is due to a lack of operating funds. The failure to provide suitable and adequate treatment to the mentally ill cannot be justified by lack of staff or facilities. . . .

There can be no legal (or moral) justification for the State of Alabama's failing to afford treatment—and adequate treatment from a medical standpoint—to the several thousand patients who have been civilly committed to Bryce's for treatment purposes. To deprive any citizen of his or her liberty upon the altruistic theory that the confinement is for humane therapeutic reasons and then fail to provide adequate treatment violates the very fundamentals of due process.

*   *   *

. . . The evidence reflects that the defendant Dr. Stonewall B. Stickney is, if he is afforded adequate funds for staffing and facilities, qualified to study, to evaluate, to institute, and to implement fully appropriate mental health treatment programs. A failure on the part of the defendants to implement fully, within six months from the date of this order, a treatment program so as to give each of the treatable patients committed to Bryce facility a realistic opportunity to be cured or to improve his or her mental condition, will necessitate this Court's appointing a panel of experts in the area of mental health to determine what objective and subjective hospital standards will be required to furnish adequate treatment to the treatable mentally ill in the Bryce facility. This will include an order requiring a full inspection of the existing facilities, a study of the operational and treatment practices and programs, and recommendations that will enable this Court to determine what will be necessary in order to render the Bryce facilities a mental health unit providing adequate and effective treatment, in a constitutional sense, for the patients who have been involuntarily committed and are confined there.*

---

*Editor's note: Subsequently, the court held

". . . that defendants had failed to promulgate and implement a treatment program satisfying minimum medical and constitutional requisites. Generally, the Court found that defendants' treatment program was deficient in three fundamental areas. It failed to provide: (1) a humane psychological and physical environment, (2) qualified staff in numbers sufficient to administer adequate treatment and (3) individualized treatment plans."

As a result, in *Wyatt* v. *Stickney*, 344 F. Supp. 373 (1972), the court mandated massive reforms that would achieve these three conditions. Among the reforms were specific treatment rules, such as a right to be free of unnecessary or excessive medication; staffing ratios; and physical improvements, including a temperature range of between 68 and 83 degrees F and one tub or shower for each fifteen patients.

DISCUSSION QUESTIONS

1. In *Wyatt,* the court held that "the failure to provide suitable and adequate treatment to the mentally ill cannot be justified by the lack of staff or facilities." Consider the relationship between constitutional rights and budgetary costs. There are rights, as in *Wyatt* and under the Eighth Amendment's ban on cruel and unusual punishment, that can entail substantial administrative costs. Compare how judges and legislators think about such rights and budgetary costs generally. For instance, does the judge in *Wyatt* appear to be concerned with the source of the revenues necessary to accomplish the reforms he finds constitutionally required? Identify some plausible sources from which such revenues might be drawn. What might be the legislative reaction to drawing on each of these? How do the "constituencies" of courts and legislatures differ? Should the principles of U.S. constitutional democracy support majority sentiment as reflected by legislatures even when it is mean-spirited, though not in violation of *specific* constitutional rights, such as freedom of speech?

2. If you were in Dr. Stonewall B. Stickney's place, how would you respond to the Court's ruling? How can public administrators respond effectively when they are caught in the crossfire between state legislatures' cost-cutting and federal courts' "rights-funding"?

3. Technically speaking, after the court's ruling in *Wyatt,* 344 F. Supp. 373 (1972), patients at Bryce Hospital had a *constitutional* right to a temperature range of between 68 and 83 degrees F, as well as to certain amounts of square footage in the various rooms. Restate and explore the logic through which these rights were established. What might be some of the administrative ramifications of such detailed judicial involement in the management of public institutions? For instance, what might be some of the consequences of making state health administrators "subordinates" of federal judges?

8

INTEGRATING PUBLIC ADMINISTRATION AND THE CONSTITUTION

By now you should be thoroughly convinced that contemporary public administrators in the United States need constitutional competence. Over the past three decades or so, the federal judiciary has brought the Constitution to bear directly on a broad range of routine public administrative activities—from street-level administration to personnel management to welfare administration and the running of public institutions for the purposes of education, mental health care, and incarceration. The long-standing debate over whether the judiciary has become *too* involved in public administration remains interesting (and predictably inconclusive).[1] But from the immediate perspectives of the public administrator, who has to understand the constitutional rights of those individuals on whom he or she acts in an official capacity, it is beside the point. As the foregoing chapters and cases make obvious, contemporary public administration has become infused with constitutional values and requirements. Contemporary civil servants must still be administratively effective, efficient, and economical; they are not expected to be constitutional lawyers. However, they cannot be considered competent if they lack reasonable knowledge of the

[1]See, among many others, John Dickson, *Administrative Justice and the Supremacy of Law* (Cambridge: Harvard Univesrity Press, 1927); Marshall Dimock, *Law and Dynamic Administration* (New York: Praeger, 1980); James O. Freedman, *Crisis and Legitimacy* (New York: Cambridge University Press, 1978); Donald Horowitz, *The Courts and Social Policy* (Washington, D.C.: Brookings Institution, 1977); Horowitz, "Decreeing Organizational Change: Judicial Supervision of Public Institutions," *Duke Law Journal*, 1983 (1983), 1265–1307; and Richard Stewart, "The Reformation of American Administrative Law," *Harvard Law Review*, 88 (1975), 1609–1813.

constitutional law that governs their official responsibilities. They need the elements of constitutional competence posited in the first chapter: (a) a broad familiarity with constitutional values; (b) knowledge of the scope and structure of individuals' substantive, procedural, and equal protection rights; and (c) a concern with integrating constitutional values and rights into administrative practice. In reality, public administration has moved well beyond the issue of whether or not administrators are "always happy about judges meddling in their affairs" or judges are "always happy with administrative responses to their meddling."[2] The task ahead is, as Woodrow Wilson wrote in his seminal essay "The Study of Administation" in 1887, to develop a public administration for the United States on "principles which have democratic policy very much at heart."[3]

The older public administrative theory held that "good" public administration is simply effective, efficient, and economical and that it can be achieved through the organization of a civil service based solely on technical competence and political neutrality. This theory is no longer deemed adequate by the judiciary, as even the few cases in this text indicate. Nor has it been in vogue among public administration scholars since the late 1940s.[4] Whether the traditional theory was benign is a moot point. Its quest for efficiency, economy, and effectiveness certainly contributed to abominable conditions in prisons and public mental health facilities, as well as to serious infringements on the constitutional rights of public employees and welfare recipients. It also failed to check some outrageous administrative practices, including an "experiment" by the United States Public Health Service, running from 1932 to 1972, to determine what would happen to a sample 399 African-American men if their syphilis was left untreated.[5] But there were also other factors at work for which classical public administration was not responsible. Whatever one's stance on the old public administration, however, it should be evident that the proceess of bringing constitutional competence to contemporary administration offers an opportunity for considerable improvements.

Constitutionally competent public administrators can do much to "retrofit" the contemporary administrative state into the constitutional order. By integrating constitutional values more fully into public administrative practice, they can create a public administration that is in greater harmony with American democratic constitutionalism. As was evident at the Founding, public administration can do much to achieve the Constitution's objectives. Above all, constitutionally competent public administrators will help to further "promote the general Welfare, and secure the Blessings of Liberty." They will take seriously

[2]David Bazelon, "Impact of the Courts on Public Administration," *Indiana Law Journal,* 52 (1976), 101–10, at pp. 104–5.

[3]Woodrow Wilson, "The Study of Administration," *Political Science Quarterly,* 56 (December 1941), 481–506, at p. 504.

[4]See Howard McCurdy, *Public Administration: A Bibliographic Guide to the Literature* (New York: Marcel Dekker, 1986).

[5]See James H. Jones, *Bad Blood: The Tuskegee Syphilis Experiment* (New York: Free Press, 1981). The Public Health Service maintained that "there was nothing in the experiment that was unethical or unscientific."

the constitutional requirement that they "shall be bound by Oath or Affirmation, to support this Constitution" (Article VI). The judiciary has called for constitutionally competent public administrators. Its doctrine of qualified immunity provides civil servants with a direct, personal incentive to exercise such competence. But constitutional competence cannot really be decreed or created from above. It requires public administrative education that views First and Fourteenth Amendment analysis, for instance, as central as statistical regression techniques in the preparation of students for the public service. It also depends on the active efforts of individual public administrators to embrace it and act on it. The next steps in developing the century-old ideal of a public administration that has "democratic policy very much at heart" will depend on what teachers, students, today's public administrators, and the next generation of public servants do.

LIST OF CASES

Baker v. City of St. Petersburg, 400 F.2d 294 (1968)

Browsher v. Synar, 478 U.S. 714 (1986)

Cleveland Board of Education v. LaFleur, 414 U.S. 632 (1974)

Cleveland Board of Education v. Loudermill, 470 U.S. 532 (1985)

Craig v. Boren, 429 U.S. 190 (1976)

Delaware v. Prouse, 440 U.S. 648 (1979)

Elrod v. Burns, 427 U.S. 347 (1976)

Goldman v. Weinberger, 475 U.S. 503 (1986)

Harley v. Schuylkill County, 476 F. Supp. 191 (1979)

Harlow v. Fitzgerald, 457 U.S. 800 (1982)

Hawkins v. Town of Shaw, 437 F.2d 1286 (1971)

Immigration and Naturalization Service v. Chadha, 462 U.S. 919 (1983)

Kolender v. Lawson, 461 U.S. 352 (1983)

Leonard v. City of Columbus, 705 F.2d 1299 (1983)

Local 2677, the American Federation of Government Employees
    v. Phillips, 358 F. Supp. 60 (1973)